Christianity

Putting the Christ Back in Christianity

Kristopher David Grepke

Christianity: Putting the Christ Back in Christianity
Kristopher David Grepke

Woodsong Publishing
Seymour, IN

ISBN: 978-1-961482-20-3

Acknowledgements

Before diving into this topic, I feel it is of the utmost importance to take a moment and acknowledge those in my life that have had a profound impact on me and my walk with Jesus. In the introduction I give honor to those in my family that birthed our Apostolic heritage; here, I want to give honor to those outside my immediate family who have gone above and beyond to pour into my life. It is an unfortunate truth that I cannot name them all, if I tried I would, inevitably, overlook a few. Therefore, I will take time to just mention a few that have truly impacted my life in life-changing ways.

First, I give honor to my first youth pastor, Dallas Cole, from Abundant Life Church in Fort Wayne, Indiana. He likely is completely unaware of the profound impact he had on my life. That is often how it is in genuine discipleship. However, I can say with all sincerity that I would not be where I am today without his influence during my younger years.

I give honor to my pastor, Pastor Brian Lane, and my assistant pastor, Pastor Brent Fisher. My family moved to Liberty Tabernacle in Whiteland, Indiana toward the end of my teenage years. It was a very rocky time in my life. I was at a point where I was not sure what life I wanted to live. Truly, the wisdom and influence of these two mighty men aided me in establishing my walk. Not only that, they have continued to pour into me and mentor me as I have continued my journey of Christ-likeness and ministry. Pastor Lane has been a mentor to me, helping me to greater understand what God has called me to, and Pastor Fisher has become, in all honesty, one of my absolute closest friends as well as a treasured mentor. Jesus knew exactly who I needed as spiritual authorities in my life.

I likewise give honor to elders in my life that have mentored me and poured into me. Namely, Brother and Sister Larkin, words cannot express the level of gratitude I have for them both. They have endeavored to spend genuine time with my wife and me, instructing, correcting, encouraging, and edifying us.

I would be remiss if I did not mention and give honor to my parents, Heath and Michelle Grepke. No parent is perfect, but I am extremely grateful for the ones God gave me. They have always modeled faithfulness and consistency to Jesus and His house. This set the precedent for me and now, because of their example, I seek to operate at the same level of faithfulness and consistency.

Last, but most certainly not least, I could never compile a list of acknowledgments without the addition of my beautiful wife, Audrey. God knew exactly the type of person I needed to be married to, and she is exactly it. The areas wherein I lack, she excels in, and vice versa. We complement one another. Further, our conversations are consistently Christ-centered, sharing with one another what we felt in prayer, what we read in the Bible, or something we have been thinking about pertaining to Him. We learn together, grow together, pray together, and seek Him above all together. I would not be the man I am today without her in my life.

I love you, Audrey Lynn Grepke.

Table of Contents

Foreword

What does it mean to be a Christian? Is it only placing faith in Christ for salvation? "Putting the Christ back in Christianity" examines the teachings of Christ and challenges us to reevaluate our understanding of what it means to be Christ-Like. It will provoke you, challenge you and stir your soul and spirit to allow the LORD to be both the author and finisher of your faith. You will be blessed in the time given to prayerfully consider and meditate on the scriptural truths within.

Dennis Larkin,
Former Youth Leader, Assistant to the Pastor,
Teacher and Elder at Liberty Tabernacle, New Whiteland, IN

As we all endeavor to live our lives in total commitment to God, it is imperative that we have all the ingredients necessary to fulfill such an order. I have always enjoyed diving into the deeper callings of God. We are not just called to be His, called to be "saved," called to be evangelize. We are also called to be separate, called to live above sin, called to love, called to forgive. It refreshes my soul to dwell on such topics because I believe it is in these details of living for Christ that we purposefully find ourselves living "in" Christ.

Kristopher Grepke has become a great student of the Word, and through his submission and love towards God, he has allowed God to help transform knowledge into script once again. I have enjoyed seeing his heart poured into not only informative words, but divine inspiration on each page.

As the reader, I pray that you do not read through this book to check it off a list. However, it is time we dig deeper into the things that make us Christians. What makes us different? What keeps us separate? Apply the divine daily principles and disciplines to your life that God would be glorified in your life. Enjoy this uniquely brought together guide to living a life in Christ as every chapter reminds us of what the world should see as they behold our reflection of Him.

Kristopher, I am deeply and godly proud of you for your accomplishments. Continue to brave the winds of the temporal and never cease to discover the depths of God's eternal purpose for your life.

Pastor Brent Fisher
Assistant Pastor at Liberty Tabernacle, New Whiteland, IN

Introduction

There are many individuals in the world today that can boast of a strong, Apostolic heritage. Such can trace their Apostolic lineage back generation upon generation. Such individuals abide in a great blessing, and I pray that they recognize the blessing they abide in. While I am not able to number myself among such individuals, I also cannot say that I have no Apostolic lineage but am somewhere in between. From what I have been able to piece together from my relatives, as far as their understanding is concerned, my family's Apostolic heritage on my mother's side began with my great-great grandpa, Stanley Purvis, but I never knew him and know little about him. My connection to my Apostolic heritage on my mother's side is with my great grandpa, Papaw Purvis. On my father's side, my Apostolic heritage began with my grandma, Grandma Mary. Though they have both gone onto glory, I want to give them great honor here and recognize the lives they lived for Christ.

For many, life is all about accumulation. Their focus is on getting and storing up as much as they can. The thing which they seek after and store up is unique to the individual, but, unfortunately, most times it is something temporal, something that will soon fade and be forgotten. In the Gospel of Luke, Jesus tells us the parable of the rich fool:

> Someone in the crowd said to him, "Teacher, tell my brother to divide the inheritance with me." But he said to him, "Man, who made me a judge or arbitrator over you?" And he said to them, "Take care, and be on your guard against all covetousness, for one's life does not consist in the abundance of his possessions." And he told them a parable, saying, "The land of a rich man produced plentifully, and he thought to himself, What shall I do, for I have nowhere to store my crops?' And he said, 'I will do this: I will tear down my barns and build larger ones, and there I will store all my grain and my goods. And I will say to my soul, "Soul, you have ample goods laid up for many

years; relax, eat, drink, be merry.'" But God said to him, Fool! This night your soul is required of you, and the things you have prepared, whose will they be?' So is the one who lays up treasure for himself and is not rich toward God."
-Luke 12:13-21

Because we are temporal in our flesh, our focus is often on that which is temporal. Temporal things may hold value at the moment for which they are needed, but their value is not eternal. It is often said by many various individuals that the only true thing of value that will live on after we have died is our legacy. Oxford Languages defines "legacy" as, "the long-lasting impact of particular events, actions, etc. that took place in the past, or of a person's life." While oftentimes we approach the terminology of one's legacy positively, one can also leave a negative legacy. We don't have to think too hard to picture individuals from history that left a negative legacy.

Paul wrote to Timothy, his son in the Gospel, regarding his Apostolic legacy that he had been made a partaker of in II Timothy 1:5-6: "I am reminded of your sincere faith, a faith that dwelt first in your grandmother Lois and your mother Eunice and now, I am sure, dwells in you as well. For this reason, I remind you to fan into flame the gift of God, which is in you through the laying on of my hands." Timothy inherited something that first began in his grandmother, but his mother did not allow that legacy to die with her but fanned the flame in her own life. The torch then was passed to Timothy. He had inherited a great legacy, but if he failed to fan the flame as his mother did, the legacy would die with him. Thus each generation bears the responsibility of maintaining that flame of faith.

In this regard, my mind shifts to the legacy left by my papaw and Grandma Mary, the pioneers of my family's Apostolic voyage. My papaw was by no means a perfect man, he had his faults and shortcomings. He had areas of weakness and aspects of his life that were less than praiseworthy, but that's because he was human. Despite these shortcomings, my papaw left a strong Apostolic legacy, at least he did so in my life.

I can easily recall many stories that I have been told

throughout my life regarding my papaw's relationship with Jesus. I can recall stories of how you could be having a conversation with him regarding something about Jesus, and amid the conversation, tears would begin to flow down his cheeks, and he would begin to pray in the Spirit. I can recall stories of times when there would be a family member who was sick or injured, and he would lay hands on them and pray with authority and healing would manifest. Finally, I can recall stories (and memories of times witnessed) where he would be asked to testify at church, and he would speak the Word of God with such power and authority.

I have been abundantly blessed to have been given one of his (and from appearances, one of his most used) Bibles. I cherish this gift. I carry it with me in my backpack everywhere that I go, I hold it in my hands during service, and I have even slept with it on my chest before. Why? Not because I am worshipping the man, but honoring the relationship he had, and the One with whom he had it. If I could be blessed with but a touch of the anointing that was on his life, my life would be forever changed. This was the legacy that he left.

I would be remiss if I did not speak on the legacy of my Grandma Mary. My grandma was not born into the Apostolic faith, but at a young age, she was invited by a classmate to her church. The church she was invited to was an Apostolic Church. At a young age, my grandma was filled with His Spirit and baptized in His Name, alas, her parents did not approve of this church and their "radical" beliefs. Thus, they forbade her from going back. However, even at a young age, my grandma knew that she had found something real. So, she prayed very simply about her situation and promised Jesus that when the time came and she could move out and make her own decisions, she would find that church again. True to her word, when the day came that she was able to make such a decision, she went back to that Apostolic Church.

My Grandma Mary lived a life of sincere devotion to Jesus. I will not get into the details of things, but even when married to a man who loathed this faith of hers and did all he could to stop her from going to church and taking their kids with her (even going so far as to dismantle their only car), she still would make her way with children in hand to that old Apostolic Church.

She lived a life of discipline and faithfulness. She maintained a servant's heart in all that she did. Even my existence I must, in part, attribute to her. My parents had my older sister and were not sure they wanted another. However, all of her grandchildren were girls, and all she wanted was a grandson. So, she took to prayer and asked Jesus to bless her with a grandson. Not long after, even though my parents were taking precautions, I was conceived. I was her only grandson.

I can recall countless memories of how she would specifically spend time with me, and pour into me. One might say that I was her beloved, as Joseph was Jacob's. The times spent with me, and the wisdom poured into me, continue with me even until this day. This was the legacy she left.

At the time of writing this, my wife (Audrey) and I just recently had our first daughter, Eden Anastasia. When I think of her future and my influence on her life, my mind gravitates toward the legacy I will leave in her life and the lives of our future children. I do not want to simply be known as a "good dad." I want to be known as a loving father who displayed the character of Christ in all that he did. I want it to be said of me that I was a man after God's own heart. I want it to be said of me that I was a lover of truth. Finally, I want to be said of me that I was strong in the Spirit. I want the legacy of my life to impact generations to come. Not so that my name is praised, but so that His power is glorified through the life that I lived so that when people would think of me, they would think of Him.

The premise of the writing that follows pertains to just this. I fear that we have lost sight of Him, and the importance of Him being the legacy that we leave. This is the great weight that Jesus has placed on my heart as of late, and I pray that He grants me the grace and wisdom to properly pen what He has placed on my heart.

May the God of Love order your every step,
Kristopher David Grepke

1
Redefining Christianity

In our present day and age here in the 21st century, the term "Christian" has come to carry a certain idea that is, unfortunately, far from its original intent. I understand that with the passing of time and the arrival of new generations, things change. Ideas change, motives change, verbiage changes, and even how words are defined and used in sentences changes. It is truly incredible yet can also be truly terrible. Not all change is indeed bad, but that does not classify all change as good either. We must approach the possibility of change with careful discernment. However, trusting in our ability to discern properly is futile, for our understanding and wisdom are limited and often flawed. The only true way to obtain proper discernment is by the Spirit of Jesus.

Jesus, speaking on His Spirit abiding in humanity, said, "When the Spirit of truth comes, he will guide you into all the truth, for he will not speak on his own authority, but whatever he hears he will speak, and he will declare to you the things that are to come" (John 16:13). Further, one of the Gifts that His Spirit gives is the Gift of Discernment (see I Corinthians 12:10). In essence, we are blind and unable to see the path ahead clearly apart from His Spirit. Jesus put it this way: "If the blind lead the blind, both will fall into a pit" (Matthew 15:14).

I say all of this to say, when we approach the topic of change, no matter what the subject of that change is, we ought to be carefully led by the Spirit. Paul said, "For all who are led by the Spirit of God are sons of God" (Romans 8:14). Whether the change in question pertains to our relationship with Jesus or not, He ought to be the final say in the matter. Does not the Word say that He is the Author and Finisher, or Founder and Perfecter, of our faith (see Hebrews 12:2)? Further, does not the Word declare that He is our Lord? The word for "lord" in Greek is "kurios" and it refers to one who has been given or one who exercises supreme authority over another. No matter how "big" of a decision is set before us, or how important we think it is, as our Lord His divine will regarding that situation ought to be sought after. Some say that there are certain situations we encounter in life that Jesus has a definitive will regarding, and others where He lets us choose our way. I am not truly sure where they are getting this philosophy from, but I do not find it in the Bible. Rather, what I do find over and over again is that He is a very loving, caring, and mindful God who is intricately a part of every facet of our being. He is not some far-off distant being who has no care for the affairs of His people. Psalms 46:1 states that He is a "very present help in trouble." The word for "trouble" here (tsârâh) does not merely refer to bad situations, but to any situation wherein there is uncertainty. Truly, where there is a decision to be made in any capacity, there is uncertainty to some degree.

Circling back to change; change is not always a bad thing, but as I said that does not make it always a good thing. Times may change but we must be very careful regarding what we allow to change with those times. A new generation may come in and change virtually everything from the previous generation, and that may be okay for the most part, but some things must never change no matter the generation that is presently coming up.

When speaking on the change that has been made involving Christianity and the Church, we must be very cautious. For we read in the Word such Scriptures as Psalms 119:89, "Forever, O LORD, your word is firmly fixed in the heavens." Additionally, we read Malachi 3:6 which says, "For I the LORD do not change; therefore you, O children of Jacob, are not consumed." Finally, we read that "Jesus Christ is the same yesterday and today and forever" (Hebrews 13:8). Therefore keeping Scriptures such as these in the forefront of our minds should be the way we define "change" in Christianity. I feel strongly that I have the backing of the Scripture regarding this matter, so I will declare authoritatively that it should never change, and it never should have changed. Who Jesus calls us to be today is exactly who He called the patriarchs of our faith to be.

I keep referencing the change that has transpired within Christianity, but what exactly am I referring to? According to the Pew Research Center in 2015 there were 2.3 billion (not a million) people in the world who professed to be Christian of some sort. That is a staggering number. In truth, that number is truly incredible and entices a song of praise and worship within my soul. However, what pains me is the sad truth that only a small percentage of those 2.3 billion people are truly Christians according to the biblical definition thereof. Some may detest me for making such a statement, thinking that I am not taking seriously the faith of all those who don't align with biblical Christianity. Such people would be wrong. I rejoice over anyone who claims to be a follower of Christ, for that tells me to some degree you have begun to walk a life of devotion with Him. I thank Jesus for all who believe. But at the same time, I am not content with you merely confessing that you "believe in Him as your personal Lord and Savior." There is so much more, and I desire all to live in that dimension of more.

In our present day and age, the term Christian refers to a multiplicity of things. First, many who profess to be Christians simply use it to mean they attend (regardless of how faithfully) a Christian church of some sort. Others use the word simply to point to being a "good person" (how exactly they define what is "good" is a whole other ordeal). Some understand that to be called a Christian is to be a follower of Christ, but their understanding of what it means to follow Him falls short of the true scope. What is sad is that the persona of those who profess to be Christian is often that of a haughty spirit, full of judgment and self-righteousness. How far have we strayed from our Master's example. It is truly heartbreaking.

In truth, we don't need to look hard to witness all the examples around us as to what Christianity is not. Even those who have little to no experience with Scripture can discern that some who profess to be Christian are anything but. However, I do not write with the intent of "going after" those who fall short of what it means to be Christian. Rather, I write with the intent of bringing to the forefront of our realization that what we claim to be Christian is anything but. This not only applies to those who are not but also to those who may appear to be but are in truth not.

In I Samuel we read a particular story regarding the genesis of David's story arc. In such we read how Saul had strayed from a relationship with God, ceasing to serve Him, he had begun to serve himself. He traded obedience for rebellion, submission for stubbornness, and humility for a proud spirit. He no longer thought of God and His desires, but only of what pleased him. Due to these multiplying factors, God declared that His anointing would no longer rest with Saul or his house, but that He would anoint another to be king. The story goes that God sends Samuel to the house of Jesse, for one of his sons would be the next king. Jesse had several sons, and almost all of them were stereotypical "king" material. Tall, strong, and handsome, Samuel thought this was going to be easy! Yet, as each son stepped up to the prophet, God said no to each one. Naturally, Samuel was greatly confused. That is when He said, "Do not look on his appearance or on the height of his stature, because I have rejected him. For the LORD sees not as man sees: man looks on the outward appearance, but the LORD looks on the heart" (I Samuel 16:7).

As most of us know, the story goes on and Jesse sends for David (he thought so little of David that he did not even think to have him come to stand before Samuel). Upon his arrival, Samuel immediately knew that this little lad who outwardly was nothing significant was to be the next king. Earlier in the story we read that in His search for a new king, God sought a man after His own heart (see I Samuel 13:14). Therefore, since David was the one He found, it is said of him that he is a man after God's own heart (see Acts 13:22).

Outward appearances mean very little to God. Do not misunderstand, outward appearance does matter, but only when it is preceded by proper inward being. It is to this effect that Jesus said, "You hypocrites! Well did Isaiah prophesy of you, when he said: 'This people honors me with their lips, but their heart is far from me; in vain do they worship me, teaching as doctrines the commandments of men'" (Matthew 15:7-9).

There are many professing Christians who know how to properly respond in worship, who can recite beautiful prayers, and who can quote a various number of Scriptures. Outwardly, many would look at them and judge them to be great and passionate Christians. But when the crowds are gone, when the door is shut, and the lights are off, who are they then? When it is just them and their Creator, who are they? When there is no one to commend them for their devotion and passion, do they still exhibit the same? Are they the same around their "non-church" friends as they are with their "church" friends? If the two groups met, would they think the other is talking about a different person? If their coworkers were told of how they responded in church, how would the coworker respond? In shock and awe (in the sense of never imagining them like that)? Or in recognition due to their consistent character?

For too long we have allowed the term "Christian" to be a melting pot for numerous ideologies, philosophies, and behaviors. In doing so we break one of the fundamental decrees of Jesus given in the Ten Commandments: "You shall not take the name of the LORD your God in vain, for the LORD will not hold him guiltless who takes his name in vain" (Exodus 20:7). Many regard this commandment as merely refraining from speaking His Name in vain. However, the word for "take" in Hebrew is "nâsâ'" and it means "to bear up; to carry." You shall not bear or carry the Name of the LORD your God in vain, for the LORD will not hold him guiltless who bears or carries His Name in vain.

If only we truly understood the magnitude of this truth! It is our indifferent neglect of this vital commandment that has caused our hearts to be waxed cold. Jesus said "Because lawlessness will be increased, the love of many will grow cold" (Matthew 24:12). The longer we abide in that place of bearing His Name in vain, defining who He is according to the way we want to live, the more our hearts will begin to harden as cold wax. Often the Bible uses the verbiage of a "hard heart" to refer to one who has rejected God and is living in defiance of Him. I pray that our eyes would be open to see, and hearts open to truly receive that the love of Jesus would abound within us and lead us into true Christianity.

Speaking on these very things, Paul wrote to Timothy:

> But understand this, that in the last days there will come times of difficulty. For people will be lovers of self, lovers of money, proud, arrogant, abusive, disobedient to their parents, ungrateful, unholy, heartless, unappeasable, slanderous, without self-control, brutal, not loving good, treacherous, reckless, swollen with conceit, lovers of pleasure

rather than lovers of God, having the appearance of godliness, but denying its power. Avoid such people. For among them are those who creep into households and capture weak women, burdened with sins and led astray by various passions, always learning and never able to arrive at a knowledge of the truth. Just as Jannes and Jambres opposed Moses, so these men also oppose the truth, men corrupted in mind and disqualified regarding the faith. But they will not get very far, for their folly will be plain to all, as was that of those two men.

-II Timothy 3:1-9

It is easy to read this description by Paul and attribute it to those living outside of a relationship with Jesus. However, there are a few key points that are important to examine that convey the opposite.

First, regarding these of which he spoke, Paul warned us to "avoid such people." If Paul were referring to those who were lost, this statement would stand in contradiction to all that Jesus has taught us. One, in the ever-popular Great Commission (see Matthew 28:19-20) Jesus admonished us to "Go therefore and make disciples of all nations, baptizing them in the name of the Father and of the Son and of the Holy Spirit, teaching them to observe all that I have commanded you. And behold, I am with you always, to the end of the age." A similar statement by Him is recorded in Mark 16:15-16: "And he said to them, "Go into all the world and proclaim the gospel to the whole creation. Whoever believes and is baptized will be saved, but whoever does not believe will be condemned.""

Further, we can examine the life and ministry of Jesus Himself and His example would contradict Paul if Paul were admonishing us to avoid those who were lost. Matthew, in his Gospel account, records the circumstances surrounding Jesus' call to him:

And as Jesus reclined at the table in the house, behold, many tax collectors and sinners came and were reclining with Jesus and his disciples. And

when the Pharisees saw this, they said to his disciples, "Why does your teacher eat with tax collectors and sinners?" But when he heard it, he said, "Those who are well have no need of a physician, but those who are sick. Go and learn what this means: I desire mercy, and not sacrifice.' For I came not to call the righteous, but sinners."
-Matthew 9:10-13

Finally, Jesus speaking of Himself and His ministry says: "For the Son of Man came to seek and to save the lost" (Luke 19:10). Many dubbed as sinners and lost would align with many of the characteristics mentioned by Paul in II Timothy 3. However, their sin is a sin of ignorance. Therefore, grace is offered unto them to give them the opportunity to repent and turn away from their sin. Once grace has been offered, their sin is no longer out of ignorance, but defiance. But until that point wherein they have defiantly rejected grace and continued in sin, how could we "avoid such people?" For if we (who have been saved and sanctified) avoid them, who would preach to them the only hope in life? They would forever be consumed in their sinful ignorance. We must follow the example of our Lord and "seek and save the lost."

Finally, regarding those to whom he was referring, Paul explicitly said that they have "the appearance of godliness." Meaning, he is directly referring to those who outwardly walk the walk and talk the talk of the Christian life, yet inwardly they are living the same life of sin and iniquity that they were before they were "saved." Further, Paul is not simply referring to new believers who have recently been saved and are still struggling to overcome the things of the past. No, he is referring to those who refuse to let go of those past things. This is a very conscious defiance that he is referring to. These are the people that Paul admonishes us to avoid, for they are cancer within the body of Christ.

It is of these same kinds of people that Jesus spoke about through John in the Book of Revelation:

"I know your works: you are neither cold nor hot.

Would that you were either cold or hot! So, because you are lukewarm, and neither hot nor cold, I will spit you out of my mouth. For you say, I am rich, I have prospered, and I need nothing, not realizing that you are wretched, pitiable, poor, blind, and naked. I counsel you to buy from me gold refined by fire, so that you may be rich, and white garments so that you may clothe yourself and the shame of your nakedness may not be seen, and salve to anoint your eyes, so that you may see. Those whom I love, I reprove and discipline, so be zealous and repent. Behold, I stand at the door and knock. If anyone hears my voice and opens the door, I will come in to him and eat with him, and he with me."
-Revelation 3:15-20

Those who profess to be Christians yet do not abide in the Spirit of Christ are like the people of Laodicea. They thought of themselves as so rich, they needed nothing more than what they had. They were satisfied with their present state of "spirituality." Yet to them, Jesus says, "You are wretched, pitiable, poor, blind, and naked." However, His words to such people do not cease with merely a rebuke, but a call to repentance. For He says, "I counsel you to buy from Me gold refined by fire, so that you may be rich, and white garments so that you may clothe yourself and the shame of your nakedness may not be seen, and salve to anoint your eyes, so that you may see." He is saying that if we would only turn away from our comfortable "Christianity" and turn toward the right relationship with Him that He would turn our situations completely around. No longer would we be in spiritual poverty, but we would abound in His glory!

The Apostle Peter echoes these sentiments in his second epistle:

But do not overlook this one fact, beloved, that with the Lord one day is as a thousand years, and a thousand years as one day. The Lord is not slow

to fulfill his promise as some count slowness, but is patient toward you, not wishing that any should perish, but that all should reach repentance. But the day of the Lord will come like a thief, and then the heavens will pass away with a roar, and the heavenly bodies will be burned up and dissolved, and the earth and the works that are done on it will be exposed.
-II Peter 3:8-10

We often misunderstand the timing of God as "slow" or "late" but in truth, He is perfect in His timing. We are limited in our perspective because we are confined purely to time and its restraints, yet He is not bound by any such restraint. He sees all and knows all. His "delayed" response to those who are unrepented is due to His mercy toward them. He does not desire that any should perish, but that all would turn from their sin. Yet, His mercy and grace are not something to be abused, for despite such there will still come a day wherein His judgment is released. Those who did not seize the opportunity of repentance while it was afforded to them will lose the said opportunity. This opportunity for repentance is afforded to both those who have never known grace and those who have abused grace.

This "abuse of grace" is an adequate way to describe many professing Christians today. Paul said, "What shall we say then? Are we to continue in sin that grace may abound" (Romans 6:1)? He follows that statement with, "By no means! How can we who died to sin still live in it" (Romans 6:2)? If we have truly received His gospel and partaken of His death, burial, and resurrection then we will not continue in the life of sin we lived before His grace. Thereby, for those who continue in their sin, it means they have not truly partaken of His grace. Or, if they have, it means they have abandoned His grace and have invited His judgment upon their lives.

All this which has been said thus far has been to emphatically demonstrate how far "Christianity" has strayed from its source, that is Christ. We have allowed time and season to change our definition of an unchanging subject. Therefore, by changing the definition of that which does not change, it ceases to be connected to the original subject. I do not say anything which has been said to condemn but with the hope of enticing a desire within our hearts to return to that original definition. To rediscover what it means to be a Christian in its original form. He is the God of Love and mercy. He hears the cries of a truly broken heart (see Psalms 51:17), and He is faithful to forgive if we truly repent (see I John 1:9). But our "repentance" cannot merely be an "I'm sorry," but a truly contrite heart. A heart that weeps over mistakes and failures and that truly desires change. If a hunger for redirection is not at the heart of our repentance, then it is not repentance, and He will not honor it. We cannot repent out of religious duty and expect everything to be okay. Such an approach will keep us bound in the same place we have been.

Hear the word of the Lord spoken to Israel:

> If my people who are called by my name humble themselves, and pray and seek my face and turn from their wicked ways, then I will hear from heaven and will forgive their sin and heal their land. Now my eyes will be open and my ears attentive to the prayer that is made in this place.
> -II Chronicles 7:14-15

We must return to the source of our faith, that is, Christ Jesus. We are warned in the New Testament that entrance into the eternal Kingdom of God is not granted through good works, but by relationship. This is not to say that good works are of no effect, for such a statement would likewise stand in contradiction to Scripture. However, we must understand and follow the proper flow of these things. Relationship first, then good works. For as Paul said: For by grace you have been saved through faith. And this is not your own doing; it is the gift of God, not a result of works, so that no one may boast. For we are his workmanship, created in Christ Jesus for good works, which God prepared beforehand, that we should walk in them (Ephesians 2:8-10). Many negate the last verse quoted, focusing primarily on the first two to stress salvation by grace through faith. But we cannot forsake the truth that we are still called to good works, but we can only truly do them once we have been filled with His grace. Paul confirms this elsewhere when he said, "for it is God who works in you, both to will and to work for his good pleasure" (Philippians 2:13). It is impossible for anyone to do or be good apart from the Spirit of Jesus working in them and through them. As Jesus Himself said, there is no one good but One (see Matthew 19:17; Mark 10:18; Luke 18:19). Paul comes into unity with this when he said that no good thing dwells in his flesh (see Romans 7:18). We are dependent upon Him and His grace working in us to bring us into goodness.

We have thereby arrived at the place where, since much of what we deem "Christianity" today is not so, we must ask, "What does it mean and look like to be Christian?" A seemingly simple question with a very complex answer. Many say that to be "Christian" is simply to be Christ-like, but what does it mean to be "Christ-like"? Again, this is a seemingly simple question with a very complex answer.

The remainder of this book will attempt to adequately answer that question and I pray bring greater understanding and revelation. Such will only come to pass with the help of His Spirit working through my hands to write what needs to be written. He is the only One who can unveil the truth, as His Word says, it is His Spirit of Truth that will lead and guide into all truth (see John 16:13).

Before we close this chapter and dive into the proceeding chapters wherein we will seek to answer the question posed above, we will first lay a foundation here that will act as a springboard as we endeavor to become more like Him.

The term "Christian" only appears once throughout the entire Bible and that one reference is found in Acts 11:26: "...For a whole year they met with the church and taught a great many people. And in Antioch the disciples were first called Christians." The word for "Christians" in Greek is "Christianos" and it very simply means, "a follower of Christ." There has been some debate surrounding the motivation behind this new term attributed to the Church. Notice that the disciples of Christ did not dub themselves as Christians (followers of Christ), but were so dubbed by the local population in Antioch. The debate then is as follows: some argue the term is sincere, that the people of Antioch truly recognized the character of Christ in the lives of His disciples and thus readily classified them as being connected to Him. We see another similar occurrence to this vein of thought earlier in Acts.

> Now when they saw the boldness of Peter and John, and perceived that they were uneducated, common men, they were astonished. And they recognized that they had been with Jesus.
> -Acts 4:13

The context of this Scripture is that Peter and John healed a lame man in the street. The Council then took them aside to strictly charge them to not preach in His Name, nor to work miracles in the same. Peter responded with a strong rebuttal, testifying to the power of Jesus and His Name. The quoted verse above directly follows Peter and John's strong response to the Council. They saw Jesus in the lives of His disciples.

The second argument then is that some say the term "Christians" attributed to the Church of Antioch was not a recognition of their relationship with Jesus, but a jest, mocking His disciples for trying to be like Jesus. Essentially, they were calling them "try-hards" (using today's vernacular).

Whether the term's origins are that the locals recognized Jesus in the lives of the disciples, or that they were making fun of them for trying to be like Jesus does not truly matter, either way, the important point is that the people recognized Jesus in their lives and dubbed them "followers of Christ." The question we must ask ourselves is, would those around us (strangers and neighbors alike) truly be able to see Christ in our lives? Would they look at us and without prompt acknowledge His character in us? Anyone who truly desires to be a Christian would like to think so, but such a testament only comes through intentionality. One cannot be a "passive Christian" and be a true representation of Jesus Himself. To be like Him we must (in the truest sense of the word) lay aside ourselves and pursue Him.

Jesus said, "If anyone would come after me, let him deny

himself and take up his cross daily and follow me. For whoever would save his life will lose it, but whoever loses his life for my sake will save it. For what does it profit a man if he gains the whole world and loses or forfeits himself? For whoever is ashamed of me and of my words, of him will the Son of Man be ashamed when he comes in his glory and the glory of the Father and of the holy angels" (Luke 9:23-26). Paul said in like fashion, "I have been crucified with Christ. It is no longer I who live, but Christ who lives in me. And the life I now live in the flesh I live by faith in the Son of God, who loved me and gave himself for me" (Galatians 2:20). Finally, he said once more, "For to me to live is Christ, and to die is gain" (Philippians 1:21).

I will share here at the conclusion an experience I had with Jesus in a time of corporate prayer that I feel puts a fitting end to this chapter. Some time ago, at the time of writing this, Jesus began to transition me into a season wherein all my focus and attention were set firmly on Him. This sounds obvious, our focus should always be on Him. This, however, was a call to a greater degree than the norm. This fine-tuned focus went on for some time. I then attended a conference hosted by the organization I am a part of, the UPCI, and on the final day of this conference, we had a time of focused prayer for the young ministers, of which I was a part. During this time of prayer, Jesus began speaking to me about some of the specifics of what He was calling me to do. I will not share those here, for they are not necessary for the message to be presented. But at the end of this time of impartation, illumination, and affirmation, He ended by saying, "Why do you think I have had you so focused on Me, and becoming more like Me? In this next season I have for you in ministry, I do not want you to look like anyone else but Me."

I pray that in the pages that follow I adequately, by His grace, convey the necessity of becoming more Christlike and what exactly that looks like.

Focused Reflection

C.S. Lewis in his book, Mere Christianity, made a correlation between the words "gentleman" and "Christian." Lewis writes how "gentleman" as we define it today is far from its original meaning. How, in fact, the word had nothing to do with character, but status. Quite literally, all the word meant was that one owned land and possessed the title of "lord." However, through consistent misuse of the word over time, the definition of the word has completely changed from its original meaning. So much so that it is no longer even associated with its original meaning.

In Lewis' assessment, the word "Christian" is not far from the same fate. He asserts that "Christian" is becoming just another complimentary word to indicate that someone performed a nice, kind, or good thing, regardless of the true character and state of that person. Lewis argues that if the present course is continued, "Christian" will no longer be an indicator of spiritual stature, but merely be another in a long list of complimentary words.

1. How would you define what it means to be a "Christian"?

2. Is Christianity something you merely profess, or something you demonstrate? If demonstrated, how so?

3. Does your demonstration of Christianity align with Christ? If not, be honest with yourself, what are some areas in your life that don't align?

And the disciples were first called Christians in Antioch.
-Acts 11:26

2
Christians Are Monotheistic

> And one of the scribes came up and heard them disputing with one another, and seeing that he answered them well, asked him, "Which commandment is the most important of all?" Jesus answered, "The most important is, Hear, O Israel: The Lord our God, the Lord is one."
> ~Mark 12:28-29

To properly define what Christianity is, it is imperative that we begin with the very foundation and then build upon it. A building without a firm foundation has no chance of standing, but will eventually crumble due to lack of support. Keeping the chapter title in view, our focus pertains to how exactly monotheism acts as the foundation for Christianity.

First, it is essential to understand that monotheism is the bedrock of the Jewish faith. In our passage of focus, we quoted the interaction between Jesus and a scribe who sought to trip Him up. The scribe asked Him, "Which commandment is the most important of all?" The word "important" is "prōtos" in Greek meaning, "first in order; chief; most important." Jesus promptly answered with, "Hear, O Israel: The Lord our God, the Lord is one." Jesus here is quoting Deuteronomy 6:4, which reads, "Hear, O Israel: The LORD our God, the LORD is one." Several key aspects of this Scripture bear examination.

First, the word "hear" is "shâma'" in Hebrew which not only means "to hear," but also encompasses the desired response of those who hear, that is, "to obey." In essence, in Hebrew culture one was not considered to have heard until they responded in obedience to what was said. Therefore, by employing the word "shâma'" at the start of this doctrinal statement, Moses (who was being used as the mouth of God) was setting a strict standard that God wanted all of Israel to adhere to. Or in other words, the statement to follow was foundational to all else.

Second, the word "LORD" is not merely referring to "Lord" as we typically understand it in English. Whenever the Bible has "LORD" spelled out like this in all capitals it means that the Hebrew word there is the sacred name of God revealed in the Old Testament. This sacred name is YAHWEH or JEHOVAH depending on who you ask, both point to the same thing. I prefer YAHWEH, so I will be employing it instead of JEHOVAH. Understanding that God's sacred name was originally employed here is crucial, for the text is not referring to some generic god, but the God of Israel, YAHWEH. Therefore, this text more accurately reads, "YAHWEH our God, YAHWEH is one." We must understand that YAHWEH is not just another title for God, but the sacred name of God revealed in the Old Testament.

Throughout Genesis we read of the name YAHWEH being used; however, this was not because the people already knew the name, rather it was Moses (the author of Genesis) implementing the revelatory name wherein it fit. The name YAHWEH was first revealed to Moses as God was calling him to deliver Israel from Egyptian bondage.

The text reads:

> Then Moses said to God, "If I come to the people of Israel and say to them, 'The God of your fathers has sent me to you,' and they ask me, 'What is his name?' what shall I say to them?" God said to Moses, "I AM WHO I AM." And he said, "Say this to the people of Israel: 'I AM has sent me to you.'"
> -Exodus 3:13-14

The name given to Moses, "I AM WHO (or THAT) I AM" is "hâyâh 'ăsher hâyâh" in Hebrew. "I am who (or that) I am" is an accurate translation of this phrase, however, a concise meaning was attributed to it as well, that is, "the Self-Existent One." In essence, this phrase demonstrates that He has no equal and that He is completely by Himself. He alone is God, and there is no other. One may wonder how this phrase has anything to do with the name YAHWEH. It in fact has everything to do with YAHWEH, for it is directly connected to the sacred name. Essentially, the name YAHWEH is a shortened, condensed version of the phrase spoken to Moses. Therefore, YAHWEH holds the same meaning as "I AM WHO I AM," that is, "the Self-Existent One." There is another translation of this name as well, which we will come back to later.

Returning to our focus Scripture, Deuteronomy 6:4, there is one final word that bears examination. We are told that YAHWEH is "one." The Hebrew here is "'echâd" which some have taken to refer to unity, however, the word more accurately refers to absolute oneness. Some translations of this word are, "one (in number); only; first." There is another translation of this word that is very interesting. If we look to ancient Hebrew pictographs, the two pictographs that make up this word are a wall and a door. The understanding of this pictograph is that there is a wall that can only be passed utilizing this one door. How does this correlate at all to our discussion? Significantly so actually. Using this word in its most ancient meaning, keeping it in context with the rest of Deuteronomy 6:4, it demonstrates to us that the only way to understand who God is (the wall) is to understand that YAHWEH is God (the only door on the wall). Implying that He is the only true understanding of who God is.

If you talked to a Jew, even today, and asked them what their belief was pertaining to God (in terms of how many there are) they would answer that He is absolutely One. If you followed that question by asking if there is any variation or division within Him (three in one for example), they would emphatically answer, "No."

I own a Key Word ESV Study Bible that contains commentary, and regarding Deuteronomy 6:4 it states (paraphrasing) that the truth of the Trinity was not yet understood by Israel, that they did not possess the full revelation of who He was. Words cannot express how wrong of a statement this is. While the author of the commentary may have thought he was revealing the ignorance of an age-old people, what he was doing was actually saying that God was wrong about Himself and that we know God better than He knows Himself. While it is true, YAHWEH did come and reveal Himself more perfectly (which we will come to), this revelation did not unveil two additional members that operated under the title of

"God," but merely more perfectly revealed who YAHWEH was and is.

We can examine several passages throughout the Old Testament and easily find that they all correlate to this understanding of YAHWEH being the only understanding of who God is. The Book of Isaiah is full of examples of such passages:

> O LORD of hosts, God of Israel, enthroned above the cherubim, you are the God, you alone, of all the kingdoms of the earth; you have made heaven and earth.
> -Isaiah 37:16

> Thus says the LORD, the King of Israel and his Redeemer, the LORD of hosts: "I am the first and I am the last; besides me there is no god. Who is like me? Let him proclaim it. Let him declare and set it before me, since I appointed an ancient people. Let them declare what is to come, and what will happen. Fear not, nor be afraid; have I not told you from of old and declared it? And you are my witnesses! Is there a God besides me? There is no Rock; I know not any."
> -Isaiah 44:6-8

> Remember this and stand firm, recall it to mind, you transgressors, remember the former things of old; for I am God, and there is no other; I am God, and there is none like me.
> -Isaiah 46:8-9

Another interesting verse to take into consideration is found in Isaiah 42:8: "I am the LORD; that is my name; my glory I give to no other, nor my praise to carved idols." As to why exactly this Scripture is interesting we will examine later.

The monotheism of the Jewish faith is truly quite incredible, for Israel was constantly surrounded by other nations and cultures that were polytheistic. Being so greatly surrounded by so many polytheistic faiths, there were times wherein Israel failed and allowed these various false gods and idols to creep into their culture. Notice though, whenever Israel allowed any false god or idol into their faith, YAHWEH always promptly responded with correction. YAHWEH was emphatic in conveying the truth that He was and is absolutely One, with no division in His power or authority.

The very idea of "God" refers to a being who is sovereign and supreme. Therefore, if there are multiple "gods" then they are not rightfully classified as a god, for if there are multiple required to make up that sovereignty and supremacy, then the "gods" themselves are not sovereign or supreme. In various polytheistic beliefs the gods do not overlap, but each operates in their sphere of influence. Thus, they are not rightly identified as "gods" but (in keeping with the same language) are likely more closely related to "demi-gods." Therefore, to approach YAHWEH with the theology of Him being divided in any sense is to declare Him to be less than God. For if He is divided then He is not supreme or sovereign. The Jews understood this and emphatically declared that He is absolutely One who has no division, therefore He is sovereign and supreme.

Earlier we drew attention to the Ten Commandments, specifically relating to not taking His name in vain. Well, the very first command of the Ten Commandments falls in line with the first and great commandment given by Jesus, that is, "You shall have no other gods before me" (Exodus 20:3). He then follows that with the second commandment: "You shall not make for yourself a carved image, or any likeness of anything that is in heaven above, or that is in the earth beneath, or that is in the water under the earth. You shall not bow down to them or serve them, for I the LORD your God am a jealous God, visiting the iniquity of the fathers on the children to the third and the fourth generation of those who hate me, but showing steadfast love to thousands of those who love me and keep my commandments" (Exodus 20:4-6). The word "jealous" here is "qannâ'" which is a very telling word. In one usage of the word it does refer to being jealous, but in this context it is only ever used concerning God, never human jealousy. However, the word can also refer to something being in the possession of another. Therefore, the reason why He is a jealous God is because He was declaring that Israel was strictly His people and He would not share them with any other false god or idol.

Some may read all this and say that it is all well and good, but what does it have to do with Christianity? In many people's eyes, Judaism and Christianity are two separate beliefs. To a degree such people would be right because they are not identical, but they are also wrong because they are, in fact, eternally connected. Or, we could put it another way and say that Christianity is the fulfillment of the Jewish faith. It was out of Judaism that Christianity was born.

In Matthew 5:17-19, Jesus says, "Do not think that I have come to abolish the Law or the Prophets; I have not come to abolish them but to fulfill them. For truly, I say to you, until heaven and earth pass away, not an iota, not a dot, will pass from the Law until all is accomplished. Therefore whoever relaxes one of the least of these commandments and teaches others to do the same will be called least in the kingdom of heaven, but whoever does them and teaches them will be called great in the kingdom of heaven."

The word "abolish" is "katalyō" and it means "to destroy; to dissolve; to nullify." Further, the word "fulfill" is "plēroō" which means "to perform fully; to be fully arrived." The Old Testament was all about salvation through works, which we could not faithfully perform because of our sinful nature. Therefore, salvation was always just out of reach. However, YAHWEH knew that we could not save ourselves through works, so He performed those works on our behalf. He fulfilled the requirements of the Old Testament so we would not have to. Some may wonder, "Does not His fulfilling them, therefore, nullify them?" No, for as He said, "Until heaven and earth pass away, not an iota, not a dot, will pass from the Law until all is accomplished." He fulfilled it on our behalf, now we must walk in it according to His grace.

Paul said it like this:

> Therefore, if anyone is in Christ, he is a new creation. The old has passed away; behold, the new has come. All this is from God, who through Christ reconciled us to himself and gave us the ministry of

reconciliation; that is, in Christ God was reconciling the world to himself, not counting their trespasses against them, and entrusting to us the message of reconciliation...For our sake he made him to be sin who knew no sin, so that in him we might become the righteousness of God.
-II Corinthians 5:17-19, 21

Elsewhere he says, "For by grace you have been saved through faith. And this is not your own doing; it is the gift of God, not a result of works, so that no one may boast. For we are his workmanship, created in Christ Jesus for good works, which God prepared beforehand, that we should walk in them" (Ephesians 2:8-10).

By faith (which encompasses obedience [we will discuss this later]) we walk in His grace. Walking in His grace enables us to walk righteously, fulfilling the requirements of the Law and the Prophets. He did what we could not do and then gave us the ability to do it according to His power working in us.

This act of fulfilling the requirements of the Law on our behalf was not some random decision that was made when He realized after some time that we could not fulfill them ourselves. Rather, this plan of action was in the mind and heart of YAHWEH from the beginning. Immediately after the fall of man in the Garden of Eden, we read of God speaking to Adam, Eve, and the serpent. To the serpent, He says, "I will put enmity between you and the woman, and between your offspring and her offspring; he shall bruise your head, and you shall bruise his heel" (Genesis 3:15). The bruising of the head refers to a crushing of the power or authority of the serpent, or in other words, the power of sin which brings forth death. The bruising of the heel refers to how He would crush the authority of sin, that was His death, burial, and resurrection. The reason why it merely bruised His heel is that His death was not permanent but only for three days. Death could not hold due to Him never having sinned.

We see this further demonstrated in the more ancient translation of the name YAHWEH that we mentioned earlier. The name YAHWEH in the original Hebrew is "yod hey vav hey," YHWH in English. Translated literally, this name means, "Behold the Hand, Behold the Nail." Even from the first utterance of who He was, He was prophetically declaring what He planned to do.

Finally, looking to the New Testament, we see this same truth echoed. We read in Revelation 13:8 that He is the "Lamb slain from the foundation of the world" (KJV). The word "foundation" is "katabolē" which can be translated as, "conception in the womb." Therefore, as soon as the world was first brought forth, even in the most minute sense, He had the plan in mind.

Some may say, "What does His atonement have to do with monotheism?" It is imperative we understand who Jesus was and is. Earlier we quoted II Corinthians 5:17-19, 21 and in that passage, it very clearly states that God was in Christ reconciling the world unto Himself. He was not simply a good man or merely a prophet, but truly God manifest in the flesh. However, the term "God" can be a little ambiguous. Truly, "God" is not a name, but merely a title. Therefore, merely leaving it at "God was in Christ" leaves it open to misinterpretation and misunderstanding. For those who hold the belief that there are multiple "gods" who make up the true title of "God," this passage merely attests to them that Jesus was God, but that does not mean He is the only God. Therefore, to leave no room for misunderstanding, we will examine who exactly Jesus was and is.

We will examine a few passages, but we will begin with a close look at John 8. In this chapter, we read of an interaction between Jesus and the religious leaders of the day. In this interaction, Jesus makes several crucial comments about who He is.

First, we read, "They said to him therefore, 'Where is your Father?' Jesus answered, 'You know neither me nor my Father. If you knew me, you would know my Father also'" (John 8:19). We won't examine this passage just yet, but we will come back to it shortly.

Second, we read, "He said to them, 'You are from below; I am from above. You are of this world; I am not of this world. I told you that you would die in your sins, for unless you believe that I am he you will die in your sins'" (John 8:23-24). Here we receive key insights into the nature of Jesus. The word "below" is "katō" which can specifically refer to that which is earthly. Jesus made a clear distinction between Himself and humanity. "Above" is a reference to heaven, which would immediately make this statement a declaration of His Godhood. But again, we cannot merely stop at defining Him as God, for it leaves too much room for misunderstanding. We receive insight into His nature with the statement, "Unless you believe that I am he you will die in your sins." The key to understanding this Scripture comes from examining the original Greek. In the Greek translation, the word "he" is not present. Therefore, it says, "Unless you believe that I AM." Recall our look at Exodus 3:13-14, how the name I AM given to Moses was a direct reference to His sacred name, YAHWEH.

The religious leaders were not ignorant of His statements, so they asked Him, "Who are you?" Wanting Him to speak these things more clearly to accuse Him of blasphemy. Instead, He says, "Just what I have been telling you from the beginning" (John 8:25). The word "beginning" is "archē" which is not merely the beginning of an event, such as the beginning of Jesus' ministry. Rather, it means "origins." Therefore, who Jesus was declaring to be He had been declaring from the beginning of creation.

Many other passages from this chapter speak on this topic, but many simply repeat what we've already demonstrated. Therefore, for the sake of not being repetitious, we will not examine them here. There is, however, one final passage to examine. At the close of chapter eight, we read, "'Your father Abraham rejoiced that he would see my day. He saw it and was glad.' So the Jews said to him, 'You are not yet fifty years old, and have you seen Abraham?' Jesus said to them, 'Truly, truly, I say to you, before Abraham was, I am.' So they picked up stones to throw at him, but Jesus hid himself and went out of the temple" (John 8:56-59). Again we see the I AM statement by Jesus, declaring Himself to be YAHWEH. This statement is of extreme interest though, for Abraham was the father of the Jewish people. He was considered to be the patriarch of all Jewish patriarchs. Therefore, for Jesus to say He is before Abraham ("Before Abraham was, I AM"), He was placing Himself at the forefront of the Jewish people. In essence, He was saying, "I

AM YAHWEH, who is the Father of Abraham, whom you claim to be your father." The Jews perfectly understood what He was saying which is why they responded so violently.

Let's return to this "Father" language seen in John 8:19. Later in John 10:30, He says, "I and the Father are one." And again we read, "Philip said to him, 'Lord, show us the Father, and it is enough for us.' Jesus said to him, 'Have I been with you so long, and you still do not know me, Philip? Whoever has seen me has seen the Father. How can you say, 'Show us the Father'''" (John 14:8-9)? It is evident from these referenced passages (John 8:18; 10:30; 14:8-9) that Jesus is declaring there to be no distinction between Him and the Father. First, He says, "If you knew me, you would know my Father also." Then, "I and the Father are one." Lastly, "Have I been with you so long, and you still do not know me, Philip? Whoever has seen me has seen the Father." So who exactly is this Father?

It is important to understand that while the "Father" language is prevalent in the New Testament, it is not unique to the New Testament. We see the same language in a few Old Testament passages. Below are a few examples:

> For to us a child is born, to us a son is given; and the government shall be upon his shoulder, and his name shall be called Wonderful Counselor, Mighty God, Everlasting Father, Prince of Peace.
> -Isaiah 9:6

> For you are our Father, though Abraham does not know us, and Israel does not acknowledge us; you, O LORD, are our Father, our Redeemer from of old is your name.
> -Isaiah 63:16

> But now, O LORD, you are our Father; we are the clay, and you are our potter; we are all the work of your hand.
> -Isaiah 64:8

Have we not all one Father? Has not one God
created us? Why then are we faithless to one another,
profaning the covenant of our fathers?
-Malachi 2:10

In Isaiah 9:6 we read of a prophecy regarding the birth of
Jesus, in this prophecy, we see that He would be the Mighty God,
the Everlasting Father. Further, we learn just who this Father is in
Isaiah 63:16 and 64:8, it is declared that YAHWEH (''LORD'') is
the Father. Finally, Malachi 2:10 echoes this truth by saying that the
One God of Israel (YAHWEH) was their One Father. Therefore, the
Jews understood the language of the "Father" to be in reference to
YAHWEH. Thereby, Jesus proclaims Himself to be YAHWEH in
two different ways; first, in using the I AM identifier, and second, in
declaring Himself to be the Father made manifest.

Keeping with this present flow, we will discuss the Holy Spirit
in relation to monotheism. We've already examined the language of
"the Father," a title for YAHWEH pointing to His creative work, and
how Jesus was and is the incarnation of YAHWEH. How, then, does
the Holy Spirit relate to YAHWEH and, thereby, Jesus?

Similar to what was said concerning the language of "the
Father," the specific term "Holy Spirit" or "Holy Ghost" is much
more prevalent in the New Testament, however, the Spirit is not
unique to the New Testament. We see the Spirit being referenced
almost immediately as Scripture begins. We read in Genesis 1:1-
2, "In the beginning, God created the heavens and the earth. The
earth was without form and void, and darkness was over the face of
the deep. And the Spirit of God was hovering over the face of the
waters."

In the Trinitarian mindset, the Holy Spirit is the third member
of the divine council that makes up the title of "God." However,
we run into some issues when we attempt to isolate the Spirit as a
separate entity, apart from the Father and the Son. In Ephesians 4:4
Paul specifically states that there is only One Spirit. Therefore, if
we attempt to isolate the Holy Spirit as a separate entity, what then
is YAHWEH, and thereby Jesus, identified as? If there is only One
Spirit then clearly YAHWEH cannot be a Spirit. However, we again

run into Scriptural resistance with this frame of mind. In several places throughout the Old Testament we read where the "Spirit of the LORD (YAHWEH)" is referenced (some examples are II Samuel 23:2; Isaiah 11:2; 40:3; 61:1; Zechariah 4:6). Our troubles do not end here if we attempt to isolate the Holy Spirit. Since Jesus is YAHWEH made manifest, there are also a plethora of New Testament examples wherein the "Spirit of Christ" or the "Spirit of Jesus" or the "Spirit of the Lord" are mentioned (some examples are Romans 8:9; II Corinthians 3:17; Galatians 4:6; I Peter 1:11).

Jesus gives further insight into the Holy Spirit in His final teaching to His disciples. He begins His discourse regarding the Spirit with, "If you love me, you will keep my commandments. And I will ask the Father, and he will give you another Helper, to be with you forever, even the Spirit of truth, whom the world cannot receive, because it neither sees him nor knows him. You know him, for he dwells with you and will be in you" (John 14:15-17). We've already demonstrated how there is no distinction between the Father and Jesus, so don't let this language used by Jesus cause confusion. Jesus refers to the Holy Spirit in two different ways here: first, as the "Helper," and second, as "the Spirit of truth." Trinitarians take passages such as these to preach their doctrine. Yet they arrive at a misunderstanding due to merely skimming the text and not gleaning from it what was intended. For after Jesus speaks of the giving of the Spirit, He says, "You know him, for he dwells with you and will be in you." In His teachings, Jesus often made side comments that, on the surface, were nothing significant, but in truth were key to complete understanding. This statement is just that. Jesus, speaking of the Spirit, says, "You know him, for he dwells with you." The word "know" is "ginōskō" which specifically refers to knowledge gained through relationship. Who did they have a relationship with? Jesus. Further, the word "dwells" is "menō" which means, "to continue to be present." Who was present with them? Jesus.

Jesus follows this with an emphatic declaration as to the nature of the Spirit. He says, "I will not leave you as orphans; I will come to you" (John 14:18). Such clear statements such as this were rare in Jesus' teachings. He mainly spoke in various figures of speech to separate those who simply wanted to go with the crowd from those who were serious and intentional. Jesus' clear speech was likely due to the fact that He was only with His disciples, who He more often spoke plainly to. Jesus did not want His disciples to be confused regarding what was to come. Therefore, He made a statement that could not be misunderstood or misinterpreted.

Examining one final passage from John 14: we read Jesus continue later on and say, "But the Helper, the Holy Spirit, whom the Father will send in my name, he will teach you all things and bring to your remembrance all that I have said to you. Peace I leave with you; my peace I give to you. Not as the world gives do I give to you. Let not your hearts be troubled, neither let them be afraid" (John 14:26-27). First, we see that the Holy Spirit would come in the name of Christ. This is very telling, for this reveals to us that He would be identified as Jesus. But again, Jesus makes a clear statement afterward. He switches from this third-person language to the first-person. Still speaking concerning the Holy Spirit, He says, "Peace I leave with you; my peace I give to you." Some may try and argue that Jesus changed topics and was no longer speaking concerning the Spirit, but the Scripture gives us no indication of a subject change. Therefore, keeping Scripture in context with Scripture, it is apparent that Jesus was informing us that we would have peace when we receive Him as the Spirit.

It is evident, through our study here, that Jesus embodies the three supposed members of the Trinity, that is, the Father, the Son, and the Holy Spirit. All three exist in Him, for He is the Father, the Son, and the Holy Spirit. Scripture confirms this truth to us. Looking to the Book of Colossians, Paul intricately outlines and defines the divinity of Jesus.

First, he says of Him, "He is the image of the invisible God, the firstborn of all creation" (Colossians 1:15). That is, He is God made manifest, and it was in the mind of God to manifest Himself from the very beginning.

Second, he says of Him, "For by him all things were created, in heaven and on earth, visible and invisible, whether thrones or dominions or rulers or authorities—all things were created through him and for him. And he is before all things, and in him all things hold together" (Colossians 1:16-17). Paul is, therefore, declaring that Jesus is the Creator of all things, and the Sustainer of all things. Further, saying that he is "before all things" declares that He has preeminence and power over all things.

Next, he says, "For in him all the fullness of God was pleased to dwell, and through him to reconcile to himself all things, whether on earth or in heaven, making peace by the blood of his cross" (Colossians 1:19-20). The word "fullness" is "plērōma" which means, "full measure; entire content; full extent." Therefore, the full extent of who God is was pleased ("eudokeō," which is "take delight or please; be willing") to dwell bodily in Jesus for the sake of reconciliation and peace. In essence, the text is saying that even though God knew He would have to die a horrendous death on the cross, He willingly took delight (eudokeō) in it because He longed for us to be reconciled to Him.

He continues in chapter two with, "That their hearts may be encouraged, being knit together in love, to reach all the riches of full assurance of understanding and the knowledge of God's mystery, which is Christ, in whom are hidden all the treasures of wisdom and knowledge" (Colossians 2:2-3). Paul is saying that Jesus is the revelation (the revealing) of the mystery of who God is. Further, that in Him abides all wisdom and knowledge. The word "all" is "pas" which always refers to the sum total of a thing. It is Jesus who possesses the sum total of wisdom and knowledge. Or in other words, omniscient.

The last passage we will examine from Colossians is found in Colossians 2:9-10, which reads, "For in him the whole fullness of deity dwells bodily, and you have been filled in him, who is the head of all rule and authority." The NKJV reads, "For in Him dwells all the fullness of the Godhead bodily; and you are complete in Him, who is the head of all principality and power." The ESV more accurately translates verse 9, the word translated "deity" in the ESV and "Godhead" in the NKJV is "theotēs" which refers to the full nature of deity. Many have grossly misinterpreted this passage to indicate that there is some sort of divine council referred to as the "Godhead" that is comprised of the members of the Trinity. Several things are wrong with this viewpoint. One, the Greek word does not point to "Godhead" in that understanding at all, but, as I said, refers to the full nature of deity. Second, this Scripture is not saying that Jesus is in the Godhead, but that the Godhead is in Him. Therefore, to assert that He is merely a part of it is to completely ignore the wording of the Scripture. It is interesting when you study the Greek words behind Paul's declaration in verse 9. He says that the whole ("pas," which refers to the sum total) fullness ("plērōma," which is "the full extent") of deity ("theotēs," the full

nature of deity) are in Him. In essence, Paul did not want to leave any room for any sort of misconception or misunderstanding as to who Jesus was and is.

I do, however, prefer the NKJV translation of verse 10. I feel it brings greater clarity as to what the text is conveying. The word "complete" is "plēroō" which means, "to render full; complete." It is Christ alone who fills us to the point of completion.

Earlier we quoted Isaiah 42:8 wherein YAHWEH declares that He will not give His glory to another. That is interesting when you take into account the words of Jesus when He said, "Father, I desire that they also, whom you have given me, may be with me where I am, to see my glory that you have given me because you loved me before the foundation of the world" (John 17:24). There are several conclusions that must be drawn when this Scripture is read in correlation to John 17:24. One, the Father has to be in reference to YAHWEH, for the glory came from the Father, but Isaiah 42:8 says that the glory belongs to YAHWEH. Therefore, YAHWEH is the Father. Second, if Jesus were to be understood as a separate entity apart from the Father (who is YAHWEH), then YAHWEH would have contradicted Himself. For He declared that He would not give His glory to another. In essence, He would have just lied. But He cannot lie. Therefore, we are forced to conclude that the only way Jesus could have the glory is if He was YAHWEH, i.e. the Father, made manifest.

Now that we have thoroughly examined who exactly Jesus is, we arrive at a commonly asked question: If Jesus is YAHWEH made manifest, why did He often talk in the third person about the Father, or the Holy Spirit; further, why did He pray?

To answer the first part of this question, we look to the words of Jesus found in Matthew 13:10-15:

Then the disciples came and said to him, "Why do you speak to them in parables?" And he answered them, "To you it has been given to know the secrets of the kingdom of heaven, but to them it has not been given. For to the one who has, more will be given, and he will have an abundance, but from the one who has not, even what he has will be taken away. This is why I speak to them in parables, because seeing they do not see, and hearing they do not hear, nor do they understand. Indeed, in their case the prophecy of Isaiah is fulfilled that says: "'You will indeed hear but never understand, and you will indeed see but never perceive." For this people's heart has grown dull, and with their ears they can barely hear, and their eyes they have closed, lest they should see with their eyes and hear with their ears and understand with their heart and turn, and I would heal them.'"

It may not be immediately obvious just what exactly Jesus was saying here. We will attempt to provide some clarity and insight regarding what Jesus was referring to.

One can scour through all the various teachings of Jesus and easily find a common thread that connected them all. That is, He rarely ever spoke plainly, and when He did speak plainly, it was only in the presence of His disciples. Why? We must understand that God's invitation to eternal life in Him is given to all people. The Apostle Peter said, "The Lord is not slow to fulfill his promise as some count slowness, but is patient toward you, not wishing that any should perish, but that all should reach repentance" (II Peter 3:9).

However, Jesus Himself said, "For many are called, but few are chosen" (Matthew 22:14). This statement by Jesus was issued in context with a parable regarding eternal life with Him. The word "many" here is "polys" which means, "great in number and magnitude." Therefore, Jesus was not saying that some are called to salvation and others aren't, but that the number of those called (which is all people) is too great to quantify. He follows that with "few are chosen." Again, this does not point to some form of predestination, for He shows no partiality (see Deuteronomy 10:17; Acts 10:34; Romans 2:11). What this word "chosen," "eklektos," refers to in this context is the individual who does what is needed in order to become the elect of God. Thus indicating that there are those not willing to live the life needed to be lived in order to see Him.

While Jesus is the God of love (see I John 4:8,16) and desires all to be saved, He also wants a people that love Him. He doesn't want a people who are there for the show, or who merely follow the crowd. Additionally, He doesn't want a people who can perform religious duties well but have no heart for Him. No, He desires to be loved just as He loves. We read, "Has the LORD as great delight in burnt offerings and sacrifices, as in obeying the voice of the LORD? Behold, to obey is better than sacrifice, and to listen than the fat of rams" (I Samuel 15:22).

Therefore, the reason He spoke in parables, metaphors, and the third person was to separate those who truly wanted the truth from those who were just there for the show. For those whose desire is true, His Words are not out of reach of understanding. With intentional desire and diligent pursuit, all can be understood. However, for those who were not sincere, the parabolic language with which He spoke only brought confusion and, thereby, frustration.

We see this perfectly demonstrated in a session recorded in John 6. Jesus is speaking on being the Bread of Life and makes several metaphoric statements that, to the casual listener, were outrageous. For example, He says in verse 56, "Whoever feeds on my flesh and drinks my blood abides in me, and I in him." It was statements such as these that made many of those in attendance say, "This is a hard saying; who can listen to it" (v.60)? Later in verse 66 it is recorded, "After this many of his disciples turned back and no longer walked with him."

The second question we come to is along the lines of, "If Jesus was and is indeed God, why did He do such things as pray?" We must understand that Jesus was God fully made manifest (as we demonstrated earlier). However, it is also of great importance that we understand that Jesus was God fully manifested in the flesh. Jesus was not a theophany (a temporal appearance of God, but not a true, physical manifestation), but truly human. Further, He was not half God, half human. Rather, He was fully God and fully man. His Godhood did not diminish His humanity, and His humanity did not diminish His Godhood. The reason for such was due to the reason for His manifestation. As John the Baptizer proclaims, "Behold, the Lamb of God, who takes away the sin of the world" (John 1:29)! The entire purpose for His coming was to pay the price for sin that we could not pay ourselves, thus reconciling the world unto Himself. He would have never been able to pay the price for sin, which is death (see Romans 6:23), as a mere theophany. The only way He could die in our place was if He robed Himself in flesh and became genuinely human.

Therefore, even though He was YAHWEH, being birthed in the flesh He had to submit that flesh to the Spirit. Just as we must engage in spiritual disciplines for the sake of denying the flesh, so did He. As a man, He consistently engaged in spiritual disciplines, such as prayer, for the express purpose of bringing the flesh in closer alignment with the Spirit. His prayer in the Garden of Gethsemane reflects this truth. For on the final night of His life, when He knew everything was coming to a point, there was never a more crucial time to bring the flesh into submission. For knowing what was to come, the survival instinct of the flesh, even the flesh of Jesus, was to do anything other than what needed to be done, that was, to die. Therefore, He brought Himself to that place of crushing (the Garden of Gethsemane was located on the Mount of Olives which was an olive press [see Luke 22:39]) and prayed the same prayer three times. What was that prayer? "Not as I will, but as you will." It was a prayer of surrender and submission.

It would be impossible to touch on and explain everything in Scripture pointing to Oneness and the monotheistic foundation of Judaism and, thereby, Christianity. Entire books are written on the subject and yet they still don't cover it all. What we have attempted to do here is not present an exhaustive commentary on Christian monotheism, but relay a concise, yet thorough examination of the Oneness in a way that brings clarity and insight to the subject. I pray that what has been written here has accomplished just that.

Focused Reflection

Monotheism is simply defined as belief in only one God. Strict monotheism abides at the core of the Jewish faith. I say "strict" because some have attempted to morph the definition of monotheism to be more inclusive in its reach. However, for the Jews, God is One and there is no variation or division within Him. This belief is central to Judaism, they remind themselves of it day and night through the utterance of the Shema.

A binitarian or trinitarian view of God was not present within the understanding of the first apostles. In fact, such views were not prevalent until 200-300 A.D. when Roman and Greek philosophers began professing to be "Christian." However, rather than abandon their previous beliefs in favor of engrafting themselves into the Christian doctrine, these philosophers sought to integrate their philosophy into the DNA of Christianity. One of the biggest effects this had was on the view of God and the understanding of monotheism.

1. In your own understanding, why is it essential we understand the Oneness of God?

2. If someone were to ask you, how would you explain the incarnation of Jesus in correlation to the Oneness?

3. In what ways does an Oneness view of Jesus impact your relationship with Him?

Christianity: Putting the Christ Back in Christianity

Hear, O Israel: The LORD our God, the LORD is one!

-Deuteronomy 6:4

3

Christians Abide with Christ

Abide in me, and I in you. As the branch cannot bear fruit by itself, unless it abides in the vine, neither can you, unless you abide in me. I am the vine; you are the branches. Whoever abides in me and I in him, he it is that bears much fruit, for apart from me you can do nothing. If anyone does not abide in me he is thrown away like a branch and withers; and the branches are gathered, thrown into the fire, and burned. If you abide in me, and my words abide in you, ask whatever you wish, and it will be done for you. By this my Father is glorified, that you bear much fruit and so prove to be my disciples. As the Father has loved me, so have I loved you. Abide in my love. If you keep my commandments, you will abide in my love, just as I have kept my Father's commandments and abide in his love.
~John 15:4-10

We continue our discussion with the topic of abiding in Christ. Truly, if abiding in Him is not present at the cornerstone of what we claim to be a relationship with Him, then the relationship we claim to have is not what He desires it to be. Therefore, for the next little bit, we are going to examine these words of Jesus and seek to develop a proper understanding of what He is saying here.

Let's begin by defining the word, "abide." "Abide" here in Greek is "menō" which carries several different possible definitions that all align in a similar vein of thought. It can mean to stay, to continue, to settle, to continue unchanged, to be permanent, to be constant, and to be in unity. Each definition is slightly different in its own right and carries a slightly different idea, but the overall idea each definition carries is the same. To define it cohesively, "abide" here in Greek refers to remaining in one place without variation. It carries with it the idea of faithfulness and consistency.

Jesus follows this admonition to abide with further instructions on the state we are to abide in. First, He says to "Abide in me," followed by, "and I in you." What we see played out here, in a very straightforward manner, is that there is meant to be a two-way relationship. We are to abide in Him, and we are to allow Him to abide in us. One without the other falls short of what it truly means to abide. One way we could word it would be, abiding in Him and Him in us creates the proper relationship wherein we abide with Him. The question then becomes, what does it mean to abide in Him and Him in us? Jesus answered the first part of this question for us in the remaining portion of the quoted passage. We will endeavor to properly examine His teaching to more perfectly understand this first crucial state. For the second half of the question, we will again endeavor to bring clarity to it once we have properly examined abiding in Him.

Before continuing though, I feel it pertinent to examine the remainder of Jesus' words on this relationship of abiding in Him and Him in us. After making the statement that we examined above, He continues with, "As the branch cannot bear fruit by itself, unless it abides in the vine, neither can you, unless you abide in me. I am the vine; you are the branches. Whoever abides in me and I in him, he it is that bears much fruit, for apart from me you can do nothing. If anyone does not abide in me he is thrown away like a branch and withers; and the branches are gathered, thrown into the fire, and burned."

In further explaining the relationship of abiding with Him, He gives us the illustration of the vine and the branches of the vine. He is the vine. The vine is the base of the plant. It is from the vine that the rest of the plant finds its source. It is from the vine that the branches receive the necessary nutrients to be able to bear healthy fruit. We are the branches. We are directly connected to Him. We are not sustained apart from Him. Jesus goes so far as to say, "Apart from me, you can do nothing." The word "nothing" is "oudeis" which is an absolute negative, not pertaining to one specific thing but an over-arching negative. Meaning, if we are not properly connected to Him and abiding with Him, we lose the ability to properly do anything at all. We are not speaking only religiously here, but generally. When we abide properly with Him we bear healthy fruit.

Throughout His ministry, Jesus often used illustrations surrounding fruit and plants to convey spiritual constructs and ideas. In Matthew 7:15-20, Jesus gives us specific teaching on discerning the genuineness of one's ministry. He says, "Beware of false prophets, who come to you in sheep's clothing but inwardly are ravenous wolves. You will recognize them by their fruits. Are grapes gathered from thornbushes, or figs from thistles? So, every healthy tree bears good fruit, but the diseased tree bears bad fruit. A healthy tree cannot bear bad fruit, nor can a diseased tree bear good fruit. Every tree that does not bear good fruit is cut down and thrown into the fire. Thus you will recognize them by their fruits."

Fruit is the natural by-product of a seed-bearing organism. This can be interpreted literally, or figuratively. For example, the natural by-product (fruit) of an apple tree (planted by a seed) is apples. However, we could take a more figurative approach to it and say, the natural by-product (fruit of the womb) of a sexual relationship between a man and woman (seed being planted) is babies. It is important to understand that the state of the fruit (what is produced) is directly dependent upon the state of the original seed-bearing organism. If that which bore the fruit is healthy, then the fruit itself will be healthy. On the flip side, if the seed-bearing organism is unhealthy, the fruit itself will be unhealthy. The reason for such is, the fruit is a direct product of what it receives from that which is born from. Jesus makes it plain: "Every healthy tree bears good fruit, but the diseased tree bears bad fruit. A healthy tree cannot bear bad fruit, nor can a diseased tree bear good fruit."

It is only when the branches are properly connected to the source (the vine which is Christ) that they can bear good fruit. It is important to understand that the branches must be properly connected. Some may think that it is merely a matter of being generally connected, and the rest will sort itself out. But if a branch is not properly connected to the vine it will bear only bad fruit, even if it is connected in part. The reason is, the branch is not able to fully supply the necessary nutrients to the fruit for it to grow properly. Thereby, whether a branch is improperly connected or not connected at all, the result is the same: bad fruit.

At the close of both referenced passages, John 15 and Matthew 7, we see Jesus give the same warning to those who are improperly connected and bearing bad fruit. In John 15:6 He says, "If anyone does not abide in me he is thrown away like a branch and withers; and the branches are gathered, thrown into the fire, and burned." Then in Matthew 7:19, He says, "Every tree that does not bear good fruit is cut down and thrown into the fire." The question we must ask ourselves is, "What constitutes good fruit? What does this pertain to?"

There are two different ways that we could interpret the meaning of fruit. The first is more obvious seeing as we have a direct reference to this being fruit in our lives, that is, the Fruit of the Spirit (which we will examine momentarily). The second is less obvious but just as vital. Jesus said, "Not everyone who says to me, 'Lord, Lord,' will enter the kingdom of heaven, but the one who does the will of my Father who is in heaven. On that day many will say to me, 'Lord, Lord, did we not prophesy in your name, and cast out demons in your name, and do many mighty works in your name?' And then will I declare to them, 'I never knew you; depart from me, you workers of lawlessness'" (Matthew 7:21-23). What is the will of God that Jesus is referring to? In theory, this could be far-reaching. However, I believe this refers to a specific admonishment. My reasoning for believing it refers to a specific admonishment is due to Jesus' accompanying parabolic conversation. The context is ministry. Those not abiding according to His will were doing "mighty" things, but the "mighty" things were not what Jesus was concerned about. In Jesus' eyes, they were not truly doing the work of ministry. What, then, is the work of ministry? This is where I place my belief that this passage is about something specific. That specific thing that I believe He is referring to is found in Matthew 28:19-20, "Go therefore and make disciples of all nations, baptizing them in the name of the Father and of the Son and of the Holy Spirit, teaching them to observe all that I have commanded you. And behold, I am with you always, to the end of the age;" Mark 16:15-18, "Go into all the world and proclaim the gospel to the whole creation. Whoever believes and is baptized will be saved, but whoever does not believe will be condemned. And these signs will accompany those who believe: in my name they will cast out demons; they will speak in new tongues; they will pick up serpents with their hands; and if they drink any deadly poison, it will not hurt them; they will lay their hands on the sick, and they will recover;" and Luke 24:46-47, "Thus it is written, that the Christ should suffer and on the third day rise from the dead, and that repentance for the forgiveness of sins should be proclaimed in his name to all nations, beginning from Jerusalem." The will of God for the ministry He has called us to is for us to bear the good fruit of discipleship.

The three passages quoted above are all worded differently, speaking to their uniqueness of authorship, yet they all present the same idea. The will of God is for us to take what He has given us and then pour that out into the lives of others. Jesus says, "Everyone to whom much was given, of him much will be required, and from him to whom they entrusted much, they will demand the more" (Luke 12:48). He does not give us an abundance of revelation simply for us to hoard it for ourselves. Rather, what He gives to us He expects us to in turn give to ourselves. As we give to others He will then give more to us. Additionally, in Matthew 25:14-30 Jesus gives us the Parable of the Talents. In the parable, the Lord gives "talents" (which could be interpreted in a plethora of ways) to use in and for his kingdom. Upon his return, he speaks with his servants, beginning with the two who were given five talents and two talents. Learning of how they used what had been given to them in a way that glorified him, he then says, "Well done, good and faithful servant. You have been faithful over a little; I will set you over much. Enter into the joy of your master" (Matthew 25:21, 23). He then comes to the servant who was afforded one talent, and upon learning how he did nothing with what he was given, the master then says, "So take the talent from him and give it to him who has the ten talents. For to everyone who has will more be given, and he will have an abundance. But from the one who has not, even what he has will be taken away. And cast the worthless servant into the outer darkness. In that place there will be weeping and gnashing of teeth" (Matthew 25:28-30).

As we use what He has given us for His glory, we will be given more in abundance. As we give, we get. This nature of His Kingdom trips up many, for it stands in contradiction to the natural order. Remember, we serve a God who created the natural order and can transcend it as He pleases. The natural says, "Give and you will have less." But God says, "Give and you will never be in lack." If we hoard what He has given us (whether that be wealth or revelation of the truth), what was given will be taken away and given to one who proved they will glorify Him with it.

Seeing as discipleship is so vital, what, then, is discipleship? This is a seemingly simple question, but the answer is not so simple. Discipleship is multifaceted; it is comprised of several various integral parts. Bro. Stan Gleason and Bro. Brandon Cremeans do a wonderful job explaining what discipleship is and its cruciality in their books "Follow to Lead" and "Discipled Together." In my previous book, "Kingdom Progression: Insights into Kingdom Operation," I also endeavor to adequately explain what discipleship is and its essentiality in the final chapter, "The Call to All." However, how might we define discipleship without taking an entire book or even a whole chapter to do so?

Discipleship is comprised of a two-fold relationship. The first aspect of it is us following Him. Looking to the twelve disciples as our example, we read of four specific examples throughout the four Gospels that revolve around His call to His disciples (see Matthew 4:18-22; Mark 1:16-20; Luke 5:2-12; John 1:40-43). Using John 1:43 as a reference, we read Jesus simply saying, "Follow Me." "Follow" is "akoloutheō" which means, "to follow as a disciple; imitate." It is important to understand that the first-century terminology of "disciple" did not merely refer to a student, this is a much too short-sighted understanding of this crucial subject. In the first-century Jewish culture, there were rabbis and these rabbis would extend an invitation to individuals who showed promise. The purpose of this invitation was for the disciple to follow at the heels of the rabbi. To walk where they walked, watch what they did, listen to how they spoke, and absorb all they could from them while being at their side at all times. Once the rabbi felt the disciple had gleaned adequately, he was then tasked with demonstrating what he had learned during the time of following. We are called to be disciples of Christ. As demonstrated above, this does not merely refer to being a casual "student," but to walking on the figurative heels of Jesus and being at His side at all times. Gleaning from Him all we possibly can. Walking how He walks, listening to how He speaks, watching how He acts, and then demonstrating the same in our own lives. This is the first vital aspect of discipleship.

Discipleship does not stop there, however. As we discussed above, Jesus expects us to take what He has given us and pour it into the lives of others. Therefore, discipleship cannot merely be vertical (between us and Him), but must also be horizontal (between us and others). Those who are true disciples will, in turn, make disciples. Paul said, "Be imitators of me, as I am of Christ" (I Corinthians 11:1). Paul was admonishing the Church of Corinth to become his disciples and follow his example as he did the same with Christ.

This point demonstrates an important truth regarding discipleship. Many think that making disciples is merely about being a good example or being a light in the world. However, it is important to note that being a light to others is not the same thing as them becoming your disciple. We are called to be the light of the world (see Matthew 5:14-16). However, Jesus was the Light (see John 1:4-5), yet not all became His disciples. To be a light simply means you are allowing the character of Christ to be made manifest in your life. It may be that through His light in your life that some may eventually become your disciples, but it does not mean that all who see your light automatically are. Earlier we looked at what exactly a disciple is and explained it to mean an intimate follower. Therefore, if one is not carefully, attentively, and purposefully following you in your walk with God, then they are not yet your disciple.

The spiritual principle of multiplication is intricately tied to discipleship. What do I mean by that? Let's take Jesus as our example. Jesus, as YAHWEH incarnate, was one man. However, Jesus called to the twelve, "Follow me," and instantly one man, Jesus, multiplied Himself into twelve people. Let's say eleven of those twelve (not counting Judas for obvious reasons) then discipled three people as well. Eleven just became thirty-three. We could continue this pattern further, but I believe the point is clear. One man became, in total, forty-six through discipleship. If we operate in discipleship according to the biblical pattern thereof, we will multiply ourselves (which will hopefully be multiplying Jesus) exponentially. This is why Jesus gave His disciples the pattern of discipleship as the means to reach the world, because of the spiritual principle of multiplication.

The second interpretation of the fruit mentioned by Jesus is a bit more obvious, that is, the Fruit of the Spirit. The Fruit of the Spirit is very well-known by those who profess to be Christian and those who do not. It has become a familiar subject in our culture which can be a very good thing, but incorrect familiarity can breed misunderstanding and deception. Therefore, before we address what the Fruit of the Spirit is, we are going to examine some key points regarding it.

The common reference for the Fruit of the Spirit is Galatians 5:22-23 wherein Paul says, "But the fruit of the Spirit is love, joy, peace, patience, kindness, goodness, faithfulness, gentleness, self-control; against such things there is no law." This is where many stop. However, the verses that follow the passage referenced above are crucial to proper understanding. Paul continues with, "And those who belong to Christ Jesus have crucified the flesh with its passions and desires. If we live by the Spirit, let us also keep in step with the Spirit" (Galatians 5:24-25).

In mentioning "the flesh with its passions and desires," Paul is referencing back to the first list he gave before the Fruit of the Spirit. That is, "Now the works of the flesh are evident: sexual immorality, impurity, sensuality, idolatry, sorcery, enmity, strife, jealousy, fits of anger, rivalries, dissensions, divisions, envy, drunkenness, orgies, and things like these. I warn you, as I warned you before, that those who do such things will not inherit the kingdom of God" (Galatians 5:19-21). Notice at the end of this list Paul says, "and things like these." By adding that qualifier he is drawing attention to the truth that what he has listed as the works (or fruit) of the flesh are not the totality of them, but merely act as our reference for what they look like. However, looking at the Fruit of the Spirit, no such qualifier is added at the end of this list. Thereby, we come to understand what Paul has listed as the Fruit of the Spirit is the totality of such. Therefore, we can readily discern that if one is not operating in the Fruit of the Spirit listed, then they are operating in the fruit of the flesh.

Additionally, there is debate surrounding the true makeup of the Fruit of the Spirit. What do I mean by that? In I John 4:8 and 16, the Apostle John specifically states that "God is love." John is saying here that the very makeup of who God is is love. If you stripped away every layer that made up Jesus, when you reached the very foundation of His Being you would see love. Further, he is also saying that He defines what love is. By being the true embodiment of love, all other "love" that is separated from Him is not what love truly is. No aspect of His character is so distinctly engrafted into His Being the way that love is. Further, it is love that has been the driving force behind all that He has done for His creation. It was love and the desire to be loved that drove Him to creation; it was love that caused Him to show mercy to Adam and Eve in the Garden while also giving the prophetic promise of redemption; it was only through love that Israel was not consumed, but kept in His protective covering; it was love that drove Him to the cross for our sake; and it is love for His people and His Church that will spur Him to come back at the End of the Age. Because of this truth that love is the very center of who He is, many believe there are not nine Fruit of the Spirit, but one. Bringing such an understanding to the text, we could translate it as "But the Fruit of the Spirit is Love. Love is joy, peace, patience, kindness, goodness, faithfulness, gentleness, and self-control."

We can readily see how this interpretation could be true. Understanding that He is love and love is Him, it would make sense that love would be the ultimate Fruit of the Spirit with all other characteristics then flowing from it. However, whether this interpretation is accurate or the traditional understanding of there being nine individual Fruit of the Spirit matters little. The important thing to understand is that love is the catalyst from which all else flows.

Paul said, "If I speak in the tongues of men and of angels, but have not love, I am a noisy gong or a clanging cymbal. And if I have prophetic powers, and understand all mysteries and all knowledge, and if I have all faith, so as to remove mountains, but have not love, I am nothing. If I give away all I have, and if I deliver up my body to be burned, but have not love, I gain nothing" (I Corinthians

13:1-3). We could in-depth break down this passage, but to put it simply, without love at the center of all that we do, all that we do is done in vain. Love is the driving force behind anything meaningful. Therefore, to reiterate, whether love is the Fruit of the Spirit, or if all nine comprise the Fruit of the Spirit matters little. What is vital to understand is that all the other characteristics of Jesus flow from love.

Finally, referencing back to Galatians 5:24-25, Paul gives us further insight into the presence of the Fruit of the Spirit. He specifically tells us that the Fruit of the Spirit is present in the lives of "those who belong to Christ Jesus" and "have crucified the flesh with its passions and desires." He continues by stating the Fruit of the Spirit is present "if we live by the Spirit" and "keep in step with the Spirit." It is of vital importance we take verses 24-25 in context with 22-23, lest we think that Paul is speaking on something else. Context is key to proper interpretation. Therefore, the Fruit of the Spirit is not something that can be accidentally operated in by just anybody. The Fruit of the Spirit is only present in those who abide with Christ.

In his breakdown of proper operation, Paul points to two crucial aspects that must be present. First, he speaks on belonging to Jesus and dying to our flesh. By using this language of belonging to Jesus, he is drawing attention to belonging to His heavenly family. We are only His and belong to Him when we take on His family name. How do we take on His name? We take on the name of Christ as it is pronounced over us at water baptism. Paul said, "For as many of you as were baptized into Christ have put on Christ. There is neither Jew nor Greek, there is neither slave nor free, there is no male and female, for you are all one in Christ Jesus. And if you are Christ's, then you are Abraham's offspring, heirs according to promise" (Galatians 3:27-29). In baptism, we are buried with Him. However, before Jesus was buried He first had to die. This is why Paul also points to dying to our flesh. Before we can truly be buried with Him in baptism, we must first die to our "flesh with its passions and desires" through repentance. John the Baptizer was the one who prepared the way for Jesus and His ministry (see Matthew 3:3). When the angel appeared to Zechariah, he said of John, "And he will turn many of the children of Israel to the Lord their God, and he will go before him in the spirit and power of Elijah, to turn the hearts of the fathers to the children, and the disobedient to the wisdom of the just, to make ready for the Lord a people prepared" (Luke 1:16-17). He did this by proclaiming, "Repent, for the kingdom of heaven is at hand" (Matthew 3:2). Repentance is the first step into entrance into His Kingdom, and it cannot be overlooked or bypassed. That is why on the Day of Pentecost when the people asked Peter what they should do, he first said, "Repent," and then he said, "Be baptized" (Acts 2:38).

Paul continues by pointing to living by the Spirit and following the Spirit. In John 6:63 Jesus is speaking and says, "It is the Spirit who gives life; the flesh is no help at all." The wages of sin is death (see Romans 6:23), and all have sinned (see Romans 3:23). Apart from His Spirit, we have no life in us. He is life and in Him is no death at all, for death is only present where there is sin and He cannot sin. Therefore, to abide with Him forever we must have partaken of His life through His Spirit. It is important to understand that the Spirit does not automatically fill someone when they are baptized as some believe, there is no Scripture for such an idea. Additionally, the Spirit does not fill someone after they have merely said, "I confess Jesus as my personal Lord and Savior." Those who believe such base their belief on the passages that say, "All who call upon the name of the Lord shall be saved." Such a doctrine takes these passages out of context completely. What we do find throughout the Book of Acts (the biblical blueprint for how the Church is meant to operate) is that the infilling of the Spirit was a separate and distinct event from baptism that was obvious to those nearby. In each event where someone is filled with the Spirit it either specifically says they spoke in tongues or alludes to it (see Acts 2:1-4; 8:14-18; 10:44-48; 19:1-7). It was through dividing tongues that God brought disunity to a unified people whose hearts were only on evil (see Genesis 11:4-9). Thereby, it is through unifying tongues that He brings those whose hearts are pure into unity with Him and each other (see Acts 2:1-4). Each time a new covenant was implemented in the Old Testament, it was inaugurated with a sign. God keeps in line with His Old Testament pattern in the New

Testament by inaugurating the new and perfect covenant with the sign of speaking in tongues.

After Paul mentions living by the Spirit, he points to following after the Spirit. Paul says elsewhere, "For all who are led by the Spirit of God are sons of God" (Romans 8:14). Salvation is not a one-time event. The doctrine of "once saved always saved" stands in contradiction to Scripture. A careful study of Scripture will present three different stages (if that is the correct terminology) of salvation. That is, initial salvation, pursuing salvation daily, and final salvation (when we enter into heaven with Him). We cannot settle for a one-time experience, but must diligently seek Him daily. In pointing to this, Paul is not only saying to pursue life in the Spirit continually but also to seek after His will. We cannot claim to be His and yet abide by our will. James said it beautifully wherein he said, "Come now, you who say, 'Today or tomorrow we will go into such and such a town and spend a year there and trade and make a profit'— yet you do not know what tomorrow will bring. What is your life? For you are a mist that appears for a little time and then vanishes. Instead you ought to say, 'If the Lord wills, we will live and do this or that.' As it is, you boast in your arrogance. All such boasting is evil. So whoever knows the right thing to do and fails to do it, for him it is sin" (James 4:13-17). To arrogantly pursue our own will in place of His is a sin in His eyes. It is only by abiding according to His Spirit that His Fruit is manifested in us.

It is only after examining these three aspects regarding the Fruit of the Spirit that we can then approach the Fruit of the Spirit listed by Paul. To approach it before runs the risk of approaching it with an incorrect understanding that could unintentionally yield deception. What we receive from the Word is predicated by how we approach the Word.

It may seem that we got off track from our original subject, but I assure you we have not. In the original passage (and passages that bear similar statements) Jesus placed emphatic emphasis on bearing fruit and the consequences for those who do not bear good fruit. If Jesus placed such emphasis on it, it is crucially important that we truly understand it so that we can abide by His admonition. All that has been discussed regarding discipleship and the Fruit of the Spirit is perfectly in step with our focus subject. Truly abiding with Christ is to operate in discipleship and to bear the Fruit of the Spirit. Only now that we possess this understanding can we conclude our examination of this passage.

As stated previously, Jesus points to two different aspects of abiding with Him. First, He says that His Word must abide in us, then He says that we must abide in His love. We will begin by looking at His Word abiding in us, but before we do we must properly define what His Word is.

The Apostle John began his Gospel account with this: "In the beginning was the Word, and the Word was with God, and the Word was God…All things were made through him, and without him was not any thing made that was made…The light shines in the darkness, and the darkness has not overcome it" (John 1:1,3,5). Matthew begins his Gospel account by demonstrating where Jesus came from, Mark began his by demonstrating how He came to serve, and Luke began his by setting the historical stage by examining other events that were transpiring that correlated to His birth. John took a vastly different approach than his fellow Gospel writers and instead took us back to the beginning. The words of John at the start of his Gospel account echo that which is written at the very start of the Bible: "In the beginning, God created the heavens and the earth… And God said, 'Let there be light,' and there was light. And God saw that the light was good. And God separated the light from the darkness" (Genesis 1:1,3-4). By John beginning his Gospel this way he was not only emphatically demonstrating that Jesus was the One God manifest in the flesh (see John 1:14), but he was also conveying the nature of the Word.

The Greek word for "word" is "logos" which contains within it a multiplicity of meanings. "Logos" can refer to thoughts or plans that exist in the mind, then the utterance of those thoughts or plans into existence. Further, "logos" in the understanding of Greek culture refers to the governing authority behind all things. Finally, taking "logos" in context with John's usage, we find that "logos" is a creative power that gives life. The cohesive understanding we can ascertain from these definitions is: the Word sees in the mind's eye that which is not, and then calls into being that which it sees; and due to its power and authority, that which it calls into being comes to life. The Word sees, calls forth, and brings to life.

Scripture confirms to us the power and authority of His Word. For it says in Psalms 138:2, "For You have magnified Your word above all Your name" (NKJV). Further, we read, "For as the rain and the snow come down from heaven and do not return there but water the earth, making it bring forth and sprout, giving seed to the sower and bread to the eater, so shall my word be that goes out from my mouth; it shall not return to me empty, but it shall accomplish that which I purpose, and shall succeed in the thing for which I sent it" (Isaiah 55:10-11). Once His Word goes forth all of creation must bow in surrender to it. We read this in the creation account of Genesis 1. Eight times throughout Genesis 1 do we read of the relationship between Him speaking and creation surrendering. This is not limited to creation. We could present countless examples, but to fast-forward, we could look to the ministry of Jesus. Again, countless examples could be used, but we will look at John 11. Death itself could not resist the power and authority of His Word. For even after lying dead for four days, at the word of Jesus death had to lose its grip on Lazarus and let him go. In short, there is nothing more powerful than His Word and it never fails.

There are two applications regarding His Word abiding in us, both are integral. First, we will focus on the written Word of God. We must understand the scope of such. Since we live in the day and age of the new covenant many believe the Old Testament Scripture is not important for us to know. A simple reading of New Testament Scripture will quickly disprove such thinking. First, looking to the teaching of Jesus, He says, "For truly, I say to you, until heaven and earth pass away, not an iota, not a dot, will pass from the Law until all is accomplished. Therefore whoever relaxes one of the least of these commandments and teaches others to do the same will be called least in the kingdom of heaven, but whoever does them and teaches them will be called great in the kingdom of heaven" (Matthew 5:18-19). Additionally, Paul says, "For whatever was written in former days was written for our instruction, that through endurance and through the encouragement of the Scriptures we might have hope" (Romans 15:4). Finally, he says once more, "All Scripture is breathed out by

God and profitable for teaching, for reproof, for correction, and for training in righteousness, that the man of God may be complete, equipped for every good work" (II Timothy 3:16-17).

We need to understand that at the time of Jesus' words in Matthew 5, and Paul's words in Romans 15 and II Timothy 3 the New Testament did not exist. The only Scripture they had at that time was the Old Testament. Yet, Jesus said that not an iota or dot would pass from the Law before heaven and earth had passed away, and Paul says all that is written in the Old Testament was written for our instruction (writing to the New Testament Church in Rome), and (speaking of the Old Testament) said that it was breathed out (or divinely inspired) by God and profitable for us. Therefore, we cannot so easily dismiss the Old Testament but must hold it in the same regard as we do the New Testament. Both the Old and New Testaments must be taken together for a complete understanding to be fostered.

Further, the question must be asked, to what degree should we seek after the Word of God? First, it cannot be stressed enough that this isn't the proper attitude with which to approach the Word of God. Any aspect of our walk with Him approached out of religious routine and not a sincere heart is not what He truly desires. Samuel says concerning Saul's "great sacrifice," "Has the LORD as great delight in burnt offerings and sacrifices, as in obeying the voice of the LORD? Behold, to obey is better than sacrifice, and to listen than the fat of rams" (I Samuel 15:22). It is not religious adherence that He looks for, but the heart of one who humbly seeks to obey. A heart of sincerity.

Now returning to our posed question (with the right attitude in mind), we read wherein Jesus says, "It is written, 'Man shall not live by bread alone, but by every word that comes from the mouth of God'" (Matthew 4:4). Further, we read in Job 23:12, "I have not departed from the commandment of his lips; I have treasured the words of his mouth more than my portion of food." In essence, while there is not a strict layout that says we ought to read and study so much, there is a heart with which we ought to approach His Word. In the two quoted passages we see Jesus and Job draw a correlation between food and the Word. Food is our natural nourishment, it strengthens us and provides us with vital nutrients needed to lead a healthy life. The spiritual equivalent to that, then, is the Word. The Word is our spiritual nourishment which provides spiritual strength and spiritual nutrients necessary to lead a healthy spiritual life. What we learn from Jesus and Job is that our desire for spiritual nourishment should outweigh our desire for physical nourishment. Again, there is no strict layout that we are meant to follow, but a proper positioning of priority. At the end of the day, the Word should be given a greater place in our lives than even that which nourishes us physically.

Regarding His written Word abiding in us, Psalms 119 provides poetic insight into such. Psalms 119 is the longest chapter of the Bible, and it is entirely dedicated to honoring His Word, seeking understanding of His Word, and endeavoring to be in proper alignment with His Word. Since it is the longest chapter in the Bible we do not have time to examine it all, there is one passage however that speaks directly to our discussion here. The psalmist says, "How can a young man keep his way pure? By guarding it according to your word. With my whole heart I seek you; let me not wander from your commandments! I have stored up your word in my heart, that I might not sin against you" (Psalms 119:9-11).

The word "pure" is "zâkâh" and it refers to both make clean and keep clean. The word "guarding" is "shâmar" and it means "to make a hedge about; to protect; to take heed to." Therefore, we make and keep clean the path that we walk on by allowing the Word to form a protective hedge around us. Further, the psalmist gives us insight into how we do this. He says, "With my whole heart I seek you." "Whole heart" is "kôl" which rightly means, "the whole; the totality; everything." "Heart" is a complex word, it is "lêb" and it encompasses more than just the heart. It more rightly refers to the whole inward man, i.e. the heart, mind, and will of an individual. "Seek," then, is "dârash" and it means "to diligently seek with care." Therefore, we allow the Word to form a hedge around us by intimately pursuing His Word with our whole being (the heart, mind, and will). The psalmist then offers up a plea unto God: let me not wander from Your commandments! We must understand that it is not our discipline that keeps us, but our heartfelt desire mixed with

His grace at work in our lives. "For it is God who works in you, both to will and to work for his good pleasure" (Philippians 2:13).

Finally, the psalmist offers one last bit of wisdom. He says, "I have stored up your word in my heart, that I might not sin against you." "Stored up" is "tsâphan" which refers to treasuring something. In essence, it is not merely hoarding the Word, but storing up as much as we can of the Word because there is nothing more valuable to us. It is a hidden treasure of great price that a man found in a field, which he then sold all he had to purchase the field wherein the treasure lay (see Matthew 13:44). "Heart" is the same word as before, and "sin" is "châtâ'" which means, "to miss the mark; to incur guilt; to wander from the way." When we truly treasure the Word with all of our being and store it up within us, it keeps us on the path of righteousness for His name's sake (see Psalms 23:3).

This has all been said regarding His written Word. There is, however, another aspect of His Word. That is, His spoken, living Word. Regarding the written Word we have the Greek word "logos," which we examined. Regarding the living Word, we have the Greek word "rhēma." "Rhēma" is translated as, "that which is or has been spoken by the living voice." Another way we could define this word would be "the active Word." When speaking on what our approach to the Word ought to be we quoted Matthew 4:4 which says, "Man shall not live by bread alone, but by every word that comes from the mouth of God." "Word" here is "rhēma." Another use we could quote would be John 6:63, "It is the Spirit who gives life; the flesh is no help at all. The words that I have spoken to you are spirit and life."

We can see, then, the nature of the living Word in comparison to the written Word. It is by the written Word that we receive everyday direction, guidance, and wisdom. It is then by the living Word that we receive nourishment, strength, revelation, and even life itself. The written Word we partake of by opening the Bible and seeking after the truth so graciously presented to us. On the other end, the living Word is not something contained in a book but only comes directly from the mouth of God. In other words, tapping into the living Word requires us to engage in an intimate relationship with the Almighty wherein we seek after His voice. We define prayer as a conversation with God, yet if we are honest, we do 98% of the talking. Some may ask, "Does God speak to us conversationally like that?" Absolutely He does. However, it is not as simple as a conversation you could have with your friend or family member. We learn the voice of God by first engaging in the logos, the written Word. We then come to understand how He speaks. This, however, is still not the end of the matter. For then we must make it a habit to diligently seek after His voice and give Him space wherein He can speak.

This relationship is perfectly demonstrated in an interaction recorded by the Prophet Jeremiah: "Call to me and I will answer you, and will tell you great and hidden things that you have not known" (Jeremiah 33:3). "Call" is "qârâ'" which gives us insight into what this interaction should look like. It means two things of particular interest, that is, "to call by name," and "to meet together." Therefore, this calling is more than just a crying out to Him, it is to call Him by name to petition Him to meet with you. And we have this promise that if we call on Him in this way, He will answer. Further, Jeremiah gives us an understanding as to what this answer looks like, and it greatly resembles our understanding of "rhēma."

Jeremiah reveals that in this intimate encounter with Jesus, He "will tell you great and hidden things that you have not known." It is important to understand that the "rhēma" will never contradict the "logos," rather, the "rhēma" will bring revelation of the "logos." Both the "rhēma" and "logos" are of God and from God, therefore, if the living Word ever contradicted the written Word it would equate to God contradicting Himself.

Returning to our point of focus, His Word abiding in us: we can only truly reach the place of His Word abiding in us when both the "logos" and "rhēma" are present in our lives. The written Word apart from the living Word becomes merely a book of regulations, an extensive list of "dos" and "don'ts." However, the living Word cannot be apart from the written Word, for it is the written Word that teaches us His voice and vocabulary which then enables us to hear His living Word correctly. The living Word separated from the written Word is subject is misuse and abuse. Together they encompass the complete Word of God.

We then come to the second aspect of abiding with Him, that is, abiding in His love. Our discussion of love at this point will not be incredibly extensive, for we will continue to examine love in subsequent chapters. We will use this time to establish the foundation of love which we will spring-board off of in later discussions.

From the outset it is important to establish a vital point: God is love (see I John 4:8, 16). This is extremely interesting, for this is not merely indicating that He loves, but that He is the definition of love. We could take it even further and state that without Him there is no love. If you asked ten people to define love you would likely receive a varying number of definitions. Everyone has their own idea as to what love is based on their lived experience. However, experience does not define love, experience taints love. Why do I say that? Humanity is flawed. The Bible tells us in multiple places and in various terms that every human being ever has sinned and needs saving (see Romans 3:10-17, 23 as one example). Because of this truth, humanity has the habit of tainting whatever it engages in. I have heard Bro. Lee Stoneking say to this point, speaking specifically on the Gifts of the Spirit, that whenever humanity is involved in the operation of the Gifts of the Spirit, there will be misuse and abuse. Therefore, to define love based on the experiences we've had with others is to fall short of what love means. The only way to ascertain the true definition of love is to approach it with the understanding that He is the definition of such.

In I Corinthians 13 Paul gives us an in-depth look into what love is. We will only briefly look at it here but will take a greater look at it later on. It is important to understand the nature of love that he is writing about. "Love" in this passage is "agapē" which, in Scripture, is always used to refer to the love of God. Therefore, Paul is not defining love on a general level, but defining it according to the nature and character of Jesus Himself. Paul says that love according to Jesus is patient, and kind, does not envy or boast; is not arrogant, rude, or stubborn; is not irritable or resentful; does not rejoice with evil, but rejoices in the truth; love bears all things, believes all things, hopes all things, and endures all things. It is interesting that in his definition of love, Paul lists what it both is and isn't. By doing so he carefully guards against misunderstanding and misinterpretation.

Christianity: Putting the Christ Back in Christianity

In the previous chapter, Christians are Monotheistic, we quoted the verse from Deuteronomy 6:4, well the verses that follow are integral to this topic. It says, "You shall love the LORD your God with all your heart and with all your soul and with all your might. And these words that I command you today shall be on your heart. You shall teach them diligently to your children, and shall talk of them when you sit in your house, and when you walk by the way, and when you lie down, and when you rise. You shall bind them as a sign on your hand, and they shall be as frontlets between your eyes. You shall write them on the doorposts of your house and on your gates" (Deuteronomy 6:5-9). In the previous chapter, we talked about how integral Deuteronomy 6:4 was and is to the Jewish faith. It follows then, considering that verses 5-9 are placed in the same context as verse 4, that Deuteronomy 6:5-9 is just as integral. In Deuteronomy 6:4 He establishes how we are to understand Him, that is, He is absolutely One; Deuteronomy 6:5-9 then establishes how we are to approach Him and live in Him.

The word for "love" in this passage is "'âhab" which means more than to simply care for another, but to exhibit a great desire for them. This does not convey a casual relationship, but one of intensity and passion. It is immediately evident that our relationship with God is not meant to be something that we approach with casual disregard, but He desires our full attention. He wants to be the object of our passion. He wants to be the reason we wake up every morning. But not only this, for the word "'âhab" can also refer to His love for us. Therefore, He not only wants us to passionately pursue Him but He wants us to realize the great passion with which He pursues us. He wants us to lay our heads against His chest and hear His heart beating and realize that it beats for us. It is no accident that one of the metaphors that He employs in Scripture to describe our relationship with Him is that of a husband and a wife. One only needs to read the Song of Solomon to see how passionately He feels toward us.

He then continues and begins to define how we are to focus this passionate love. He proclaims that our love ought to be focused through our hearts, souls, and might (according to the English translation of the original Hebrew). However, if we examine the

Hebrew words behind heart, soul, and might, we will quickly arrive at a better understanding of what He is proclaiming here.

First, "heart" is "lêbâb" and its root is the same Hebrew word for "heart" that we looked at earlier, "lêb." Further, it means the same thing as "lêb," that is, it refers to the inward man, i.e. the heart, mind, and will of an individual. Second, "soul" is "nephesh" and "soul" really is a poor translation of this word. The most precise translation of "nephesh" is "throat," however, in ancient Hebrew, this word was often used to refer to the physical part of the individual or their flesh. Lastly, we have "might." "Might" is translated from the Hebrew word "me'od." "Me'od" being used in this context is very interesting because it is not a thing (as the inner man and flesh are) but a modifier. The word "me'od" is used to add emphasis to other words. To give an example, we see in Genesis 1 God calls every part of His creation "good" after He creates it. However, once humanity has been created and creation is complete, He then proclaims that it is "very good." The word "very" in this passage is "me'od." Some translations of "me'od" are "exceedingly; abundance; muchness; to a great degree." Therefore, translating it as "might" is not necessarily wrong, however, such a translation falls short of the true scope of the word. I feel that "muchness" presents the best translation of the word in terms of conveying its meaning. Therefore, what we see from translating these words is that our love for Him is to be present and focused through our inward man (heart, mind, and will), our flesh (our physical being), and everything our lives consist of (muchness).

Notice, immediately after He instructs us on how to abide in a loving relationship with Him, He then transitions to how we ought to obey and keep His Word and pass it on to the next generation. He says, "And these words that I command you today shall be on your heart. You shall teach them diligently to your children, and shall talk of them when you sit in your house, and when you walk by the way, and when you lie down, and when you rise. You shall bind them as a sign on your hand, and they shall be as frontlets between your eyes. You shall write them on the doorposts of your house and on your gates" (Deuteronomy 6:6-9). Therefore, where love is present there will be heartfelt obedience and the desire to impart that which we adhere to.

We see this truth confirmed by Jesus in John 14; He says, "If you love me, you will keep my commandments" (John 14:15). The Apostle John echoed this in his first epistle when he said, "In fact, this is love for God: to keep his commands. And his commands are not burdensome" (I John 5:3 NIV). What is this text saying? Is it impossible to keep His Word if you do not love Him? Yes and no. One could walk in obedience to Him without love being present, but this will be a short-lived journey. Notice that it is only when love is present that obedience is not a burden. Therefore, to walk in obedience apart from love will eventually cause that obedience to feel like a great weight. One will only carry such a weight for so long before they drop it out of exhaustion.

Abiding in His love is the only thing that will keep us. Yes, we can have His Word apart from love, but eventually, His Word will become a chore if love continues to be absent. When we abide in His love, understanding what His love looks like, nothing will be able to deter us. No storm, crisis, struggle, or tribulation, all will fade away in the presence of His great love.

Praise the name of the Lord Most High.

Focused Reflection

Nine times in John 15:4-10 do we read Jesus employ the use of the word "abide." We obtain a consistent understanding of this word when we examine Webster's Dictionary and Dictionary.com's definition of such; to abide refers to taking up an abode, or to having a permanent residence. Additionally, the Greek word "menō" further establishes this understanding of abiding with such translations as, "to dwell; to endure; to continue unchanged; to be permanent."

Further, it ought not to be overlooked that Jesus repeated this word nine times within a brief portion of dialogue. Repetition is a significant grammar tool used in the Hebrew culture to add emphasis or to signal great importance. Therefore, it is not a stretch to assert that to abide with Christ is absolutely essential to a Christian walk. We could even say it like this: one cannot have a Christian walk unless they abide with Christ.

Jesus makes it plain through the employment of the vine

and branches analogy. The vine is the source. The vine contains within it the necessary nutrients that the branches need to live and bear fruit. A branch disconnected from the vine ceases to live and, thereby, ceases to bear fruit. Thus our very life and the fruit we bear is dependent upon our state of abiding.

1. What does it mean to abide with Christ? How do we put into practice this act of abiding in Him?

2. Why is it so important that we bear good fruit? What is the good fruit that we are called to bear?

3. Is the good fruit that is birthed through abiding present in your own life?

> I am the vine, you are the branches. He who abides in Me, and I in him, bears much fruit; for without Me you can do nothing. If anyone does not abide in Me, he is cast out as a branch and is withered; and they gather them and throw them into the fire, and they are burned.
> -John 15:5-6

4

Christians Are Baptized in His Name and Spirit
Christians Abide with Christ II

Jesus answered him, "Truly, truly, I say to you, unless one is born again he cannot see the kingdom of God." Nicodemus said to him, "How can a man be born when he is old? Can he enter a second time into his mother's womb and be born?" Jesus answered, "Truly, truly, I say to you, unless one is born of water and the Spirit, he cannot enter the kingdom of God. That which is born of the flesh is flesh, and that which is born of the Spirit is spirit. Do not marvel that I said to you, 'You must be born again.' The wind blows where it wishes, and you hear its sound, but you do not know where it comes from or where it goes. So it is with everyone who is born of the Spirit."
~John 3:3-8

In the previous chapter, Christians Abide with Christ, we discussed a plethora of topics that were all directly or indirectly mentioned by Jesus in the focus passage, John 15:4-10. When diving into the discussion regarding bearing fruit we briefly examined the topic surrounding being baptized in His name and filled with His Spirit. However, this topic is of extreme importance for one who wishes to truly abide with Christ. Therefore, I do not feel that leaving it as a mere side topic is acceptable. It is for this reason that I've dedicated space for this topic here.

It could be debated as to whether or not this is a true chapter. It could, more rightly, be labeled as an excursion. Regardless of its rightful definition, we will endeavor to adequately convey the proper nature of these things and their essentiality.

In our passage of focus quoted above, we read of one of the Jewish religious leaders seeking an audience with Jesus. Nicodemus sought to meet him under the cover of darkness, likely due to the ridicule he would receive from his fellow leaders if they knew of this meeting. Nicodemus opens up the meeting by acknowledging that the works Jesus performed validated that He was indeed from God. This was a very cautious statement. For he was not confessing that Jesus was God manifest in the flesh, but merely that He was anointed by God.

Jesus, not being One to engage in small talk or religious pleasantries, completely bypassed Nicodemus' pleasant introductory remarks and cut to the heart of the matter. "Truly, truly, I say to you, unless one is born again he cannot see the kingdom of God." Nicodemus was just as perplexed by this statement as many of us are today. He responded, "How can a man be born when he is old? Can he enter a second time into his mother's womb and be born?" Nicodemus' response to Jesus' statement is quite telling regarding his spiritual state. His response was focused purely on the natural, thinking only of natural birth and how absurd it would be to experience that again when older. To this degree, he was correct. Yet, he should've immediately known that Jesus was not referring to the natural.

Jesus very directly points to the Kingdom of God. It is likely that Nicodemus, upon hearing this phrase, thought only of the physical restoration of Israel (such was the common frame of mind among first-century Jews, even Jesus' disciples). With this assumption, we could see why he responded with the natural in mind. Yet, as I said, this is telling of his spiritual state. As He did with His disciples, Jesus was trying to restructure Nicodemus' frame of mind, taking it off the natural and looking to the spiritual.

It was not merely Jesus' reference to the Kingdom of God that should've been evidence to Nicodemus, but also His careful word choice. The word "again" used by Jesus is "anōthen" which can also mean, "from above; from a higher place." This is a clear indication of the spiritual realm. In essence, He was saying that unless you are born of the Kingdom you cannot enter the Kingdom.

Jesus, being sympathetic to the ignorance of Nicodemus, offered a clarifying statement. Revealing what it meant to be "born again," He says, "Born of water and of Spirit." There are some scholars and theologians that approach this passage with a frame of mind somewhere in-between that of Nicodemus (focused on the natural) and Jesus (focused on the spiritual). They say that being "born of water" merely refers to the natural birth, while being "born of…Spirit" refers, obviously, to spiritual birth. Those who hold this view seek to downplay the role of water baptism in salvation. We will discuss this further momentarily. However, the "middle of the road" interpretative stance does not fit the context of the passage. Jesus approached the conversation focusing purely on the spiritual. It was Nicodemus who turned the focus toward the natural. Why, then, would Jesus' response justify Nicodemus' ignorance? The short answer is that Jesus would not compromise what He was trying to teach. We can examine Jesus' whole ministry and see definitive proof that Jesus was not a man of compromise. Therefore, keeping His character in focus, it should be apparent that Jesus' statement on being "born of water and of Spirit" directly correlated to being "born again."

For further evidence regarding Jesus' focus, we can look to the very next verse. He says, "That which is born of the flesh is flesh, and that which is born of the Spirit is spirit." If Jesus wished to allude to natural birth and spiritual birth in the previous verse as He did here, why did He not make it plain just as He did with this statement? Jesus here is drawing a clear line in the sand, so to speak. In the previous verses, He spoke on entrance into the Kingdom of God and how it required being born spiritually. Then, in this verse, He makes the explicit statement that if something is merely of the natural it, thereby, has no place in the spiritual (that which is born of the flesh is flesh). However, being born of the Spirit grants access to the spiritual.

The final statement of Jesus that we will examine from this passage has to do specifically with being "born of Spirit." Of the Spirit He says, "The wind blows where it wishes, and you hear its sound, but you do not know where it comes from or where it goes. So it is with everyone who is born of the Spirit." What is Jesus saying here? We are, in no way, in control of the Spirit. We do not dictate when it comes, how it comes, or where it comes from. The word translated as "wind" here is the same word, "pneuma," translated as "spirit" in earlier verses. The word "wishes" is "thelō" which is, "to will; to have in mind; to be disposed." Therefore, the Spirit blows where He so desires to. The only sign that we have regarding the arrival of the Spirit is that we "hear its sound." The word "sound" is "phōnē" which is "an articulate sound or voice; language; tongue; dialect." The arrival of the Spirit is always accompanied by the language of the Spirit.

We will come back to these things momentarily, for just a moment though we will put a pin in it. Before continuing further in our discussion it is of great importance that we address what must precede baptism of water and Spirit. We addressed this in the previous chapter as well, so we will attempt to not be repetitious. However, it is important to understand that before baptism in His name and Spirit, there must first be repentance.

Before Jesus, the bringer of salvation, arrived on the scene, we first read of the Prophet John who prepared the way for the salvific ministry of Jesus. How did he do this? It says of John, "In those days John the Baptist came preaching in the wilderness of Judea, 'Repent, for the kingdom of heaven is at hand.' For this is he who was spoken of by the prophet Isaiah when he said, 'The voice of one crying in the wilderness: Prepare the way of the Lord; make his paths straight'" (Matthew 3:1-3). Further, even Jesus when His ministry first began started by declaring, "Repent, for the kingdom of heaven is at hand" (Matthew 4:17). Finally, on the Day of Pentecost, after the initial outpouring of the Spirit, Peter gave His "altar call" by first declaring, "Repent..." (Acts 2:38).

"Repent" is the Greek word "metanoeō" which means two things that are both essential to true repentance. First, it means, "to undergo a change in frame of mind and feeling." Second, it means, "to make a change of principal and practice." Therefore, true repentance encompasses both the inward and the outward. Repentance can begin as a feeling of remorse for something that was said or done, but if it stays as a mere feeling of remorse there has not been true repentance. That feeling of remorse must grow and evolve to where it impacts the way that one lives.

Repentance is the vital first step of salvation because it is in repentance wherein the individual recognizes the need for salvation and endeavors to take the necessary steps toward salvation. One may be baptized before repenting, but in truth, all they did was get wet. Baptism is of no effect without repentance first being present. Additionally, Jesus will not fill an individual with the Spirit without their first being a change of heart, mind, and direction. Peter confirms these things to us in the mentioned Scripture, Acts 2:38: And Peter said to them, "Repent and be baptized every one of you in the name of Jesus Christ for the forgiveness of your sins, and you will receive the gift of the Holy Spirit."

Going back to our passage of focus, we will examine what it means to be "born of water." Understanding that being "born of water" was referring to one of the key aspects involved in being "born again," we can readily interpret this as water baptism. I mentioned earlier that some seek to downplay the role of water baptism in salvation. Therefore, before exploring the essential aspects of biblical water baptism, we will first address this idea to rightly convey its essentiality.

For those who seek to downplay water baptism's significance, they take the stance that it is merely a public confession of faith with no true ramifications regarding salvation. Those who hold this view either have to, one, completely ignore certain passages of Scripture, or two, grossly misinterpret them. First, we can look to a passage we have already quoted, Acts 2:38. In said verse, Peter states that it is both repentance and water baptism that grant "forgiveness of your sins." The word "forgiveness" here is "aphesis" which means, "deliverance; remission; forgiveness; pardon." Therefore, without water baptism, these things cannot be. Thereby, our sins would still hold us captive.

Further, in one of Jesus' final teachings to His disciples recorded in Mark 16:16, He says, "Whoever believes and is baptized will be saved, but whoever does not believe will be condemned." Those who contend that baptism is not necessary for salvation state that Jesus did not say, "Those who do not believe and are not baptized will be condemned." However, those who make such a statement are reading something into the text that is not there. Salvation starts with belief (or faith), and those who have faith will see it through and be baptized. However, those who have no faith will see no need for baptism. Therefore, it is implied that those without belief will also not be baptized. What we are left with, then, is a clear indication from Jesus Himself that baptism is a part of salvation.

Finally, the Apostle Peter writes and says, "Baptism, which corresponds to this, now saves you, not as a removal of dirt from the body but as an appeal to God for a good conscience, through the resurrection of Jesus Christ" (I Peter 3:21). The context of this passage is Peter was making a correlation between Noah and the Flood and water baptism today. The Flood simultaneously cleansed the earth of sin and saved Noah and his family. Likewise, baptism washes our inward man and saves us. The word "save" here is "sōzō" which means, "to save; to keep safe; to rescue from danger or destruction."

As I said, the only way in which one can claim that water baptism has no part in salvation is to either, one, completely ignore Scriptures such as these, or two, grossly misinterpret them. However, I find it hard to understand how exactly one could truthfully misinterpret them.

In our examination of the essentiality of baptism, we have already conveyed what exactly it does in our lives. Water baptism plays a key role in salvation in terms of cleansing us from sin (see Acts 2:38; I Peter 3:21). We can see this further demonstrated in Paul's recounting of his own salvation experience. Quoting the words of Ananias to him, he says, "And now why do you wait? Rise and be baptized and wash away your sins, calling on his name" (Acts 22:16).

There is, however, another key thing that baptism does in our lives. Paul says, "For as many of you as were baptized into Christ have put on Christ. There is neither Jew nor Greek, there is neither slave nor free, there is no male and female, for you are all one in Christ Jesus. And if you are Christ's, then you are Abraham's offspring, heirs according to promise" (Galatians 3:27-29). The word for "have put on" is "endyō" which refers to putting on clothes. Therefore, when we are baptized into Christ (which we will come back to momentarily) we are wrapped in Him like a garment. We are clothed in His name. After one is baptized in His name, thus putting on His name, they, thereby, become a part of His Kingdom family. In His family, there is no cultural or ethnic difference, for we are all one in Him. Further, it is only after being clothed with Him that we become heirs of the promise. The promise being in reference to eternal life and salvation with Him. Therefore, what is evident is that without baptism we are not a part of His family, and if we are not a part of His family, we have no place in His home.

This language of baptism correlating to putting on an article of particular clothing is not unique to Paul. More likely, Paul picked up this language from a parable of Jesus. In Matthew 22 we read the Parable of the Wedding Feast. Picking up in verse 8, we read, "Then he said to his servants, 'The wedding feast is ready, but those invited were not worthy. Go therefore to the main roads and invite to the wedding feast as many as you find.' And those servants went out into the roads and gathered all whom they found, both bad and good. So the wedding hall was filled with guests. But when the king came in to look at the guests, he saw there a man who had no wedding garment. And he said to him, 'Friend, how did you get in here without a wedding garment?' And he was speechless. Then the king said to the attendants, 'Bind him hand and foot and cast him into the outer darkness. In that place there will be weeping and gnashing of teeth'" (Matthew 22:8-13). The wedding feast of Heaven is open to all. However, while the invitation is sent to all, all those who would respond are expected to be clothed in particular apparel. Without this apparel being present, the individual has no place at the feast.

Understanding the essentiality of water baptism (its part in salvation), and what it does in our lives (washes our sins and clothes us in His name), we can now discuss the means of water baptism. Some believe that water baptism is administered merely through either sprinkling or splashing water on the individual. This line of thinking has no Scriptural support. First, we can look to the word "baptize" in Greek. It is "baptizō" which means, "to immerse; to submerge; to overwhelm." I find "to overwhelm" particularly interesting, for one could, by completely misinterpreting what it means to immerse or submerge, twist this to mean something other than being fully submerged in the water. However, one would be hard-pressed to misinterpret "to overwhelm" in such a way. Truly, to be overwhelmed means to be surrounded on all sides. Therefore, to be overwhelmed by water is to be completely surrounded by water.

Additionally, Paul equates baptism to us being buried with Christ (see Romans 6:3-4; Colossians 2:12-13). One is not considered to be buried after only having a few sprinkles of dirt spread across their body. Rather, they are deemed buried only after being fully covered by the dirt. Therefore, we can only be considered as having been buried with Him after we have been fully covered by the water.

Second, it is not the water that has the power. The power is in what is spoken over the one being buried in the water. If one is baptized with having nothing said over them, then all that transpired was them getting wet. The water only has the power to cleanse and clothe when it is coupled with His name.

The most prevalent baptismal formula in Christendom today is taken from Matthew 28:19, which reads, "Go therefore and make disciples of all nations, baptizing them in the name of the Father and of the Son and of the Holy Spirit." One reason this formula is so widely used is due to the fact that the majority of professing Christians are Trinitarians (which we addressed in the chapter, Christians are Monotheistic). In this verse, Jesus admonishes His disciples to baptize in the name of the Father, Son, and Holy Spirit. We have already demonstrated how Jesus was the Father made manifest, and that the Holy Spirit is His Spirit. We can also look to the grammatical structure of this Scripture for further evidence. We see that the singular word "name" is used here. Therefore, we can surmise that there is a single name attributed to these titles. As to what the name is, we can look to the Gospels for the answer to that. We see that Jesus came in the name of the Father (see John 5:43), the name of the Son is Jesus (see Matthew 1:21), and Jesus declared that the Holy Spirit would come in His name (see John 14:26). Therefore, this Scripture is only further confirmation of His Oneness.

Jesus' disciples clearly understood what Jesus was saying. For we can look to the Book of Acts and see that in every instance wherein baptism took place, it was done in the name of Jesus (see Acts 2:38; 10:48; 19:5; 22:16).

Some may ask, "Well, I've already been baptized with the titles Father, Son, and Holy Spirit spoken over me. What should I do?" To that, I would direct us to Scripture. Looking to the beginning of Acts 19, we see Paul come across a group (twelve in all) who were disciples of John the Baptist. Paul, being Paul, immediately gets down to business and says, "'Into what then were you baptized?' They said, 'Into John's baptism.' And Paul said, 'John baptized with the baptism of repentance, telling the people to believe in the one who was to come after him, that is, Jesus.' On hearing this, they were baptized in the name of the Lord Jesus" (Acts 19:3-5). In essence, he said, "You have been obedient to what you have known thus far, but now greater revelation has been given." Hearing this, they responded with the same level of obedience with which they had before. Therefore, I would say that Scripture indicates if one has been baptized in any other way other than in the name of Jesus then they need to be rebaptized.

Last but not least, we come to being baptized in His Spirit, or we could word it as being filled with His Spirit. The majority of Christendom asserts that there is indeed an infilling of His Spirit. However, what exactly this looks like greatly differs. Again, we will use Scripture as our authority regarding this much-debated topic.

First, before we dive into the various Scriptural aspects of Spirit baptism, we ought to address why it is necessary. To do this, we must look back to the beginning with Adam and Eve.

We read in Genesis 2:7, "Then the LORD God formed the man of dust from the ground and breathed into his nostrils the breath of life, and the man became a living creature." We looked at previously how "breath of life" refers to the Spirit of God. Therefore, we come to understand that man has a body, soul, and spirit. The spiritual aspect of our being is what directly connects to God, for it is from Him. After his creation, He then told man, "You may surely eat of every tree of the garden, but of the tree of the knowledge of good and evil you shall not eat, for in the day that you eat of it you shall surely die" (Genesis 2:16-17). Unfortunately, we all know how the story goes. Adam and Eve gave into the temptation of the serpent and sinned against God by eating from the very tree He told them not to. What is of interest is the fact that Adam and Eve did not drop dead. What happened? Did God lie? Not at all, for in that moment Adam and Eve did die, just not physically (although physical death now began with the introduction of sin into creation). Rather, the death they suffered in that moment was spiritual.

Jesus is life itself (see John 1:4), and in Him is no sin at all (see I John 3:5). In fact, because He is holy (see Leviticus 19:2) He cannot dwell where there is sin. Therefore, when Adam and Eve sinned it forced God to remove Himself from their lives. And since He is life, when His Spirit left them the result was spiritual death. As Paul said, the wages of sin is death (see Romans 6:23). This nature of sin that was birthed in Adam and Eve then began passing down to every generation. Every human being is born with an inclination toward sin. Which, thereby, keeps us bound in this place of spiritual death. The purpose of the Spirit, then, is to bring back to life those who were dead (which encompasses all of humanity). Since He is life and cannot abide with death, the only way we can abide with Him in heaven is to partake of His life.

Paul put it this way:

> We were buried therefore with him by baptism into death, in order that, just as Christ was raised from the dead by the glory of the Father, we too might walk in newness of life. For if we have been united with him in a death like his, we shall certainly be united with him in a resurrection like his.
> -Romans 6:4-5

And later in the same book, he says, "You, however, are not in the flesh but in the Spirit, if in fact the Spirit of God dwells in you. Anyone who does not have the Spirit of Christ does not belong to him. But if Christ is in you, although the body is dead because of sin, the Spirit is life because of righteousness. If the Spirit of him who raised Jesus from the dead dwells in you, he who raised Christ Jesus from the dead will also give life to your mortal bodies through his Spirit who dwells in you" (Romans 8:9-11).

Notice how Paul states that if we do not have His Spirit then we are not His. This is interesting when you keep in focus the truth that baptism places His name on us and grafts us into His family. Therefore, it is evident that one without the other is incomplete. One may wonder why we are not considered His unless we have

His Spirit. The answer to this can be found by looking back to our discussion of His life versus the death of sin. If we do not have His Spirit then we do not abide in His life, therefore, we are not His. We can, by no means, downplay the essentiality of the Spirit. Paul said it is Christ in us that gives us the hope of glory (see Colossians 1:27). Christ being in us is referring to His in-dwelling Spirit. Therefore, without such present in our lives, we have no hope of eternal glory.

The work of the Spirit in our lives goes far beyond the life it gives us. Our focus in this chapter is primarily His salvific work in our lives, but here are other ways in which the Spirit of Jesus works in our lives: He teaches us to give us a greater understanding of His Word and reminds us of what He has spoken (see John 14:26; John 16:13-15); convicts us of sin (see John 16:7-8); gives us the power to be His witnesses (see Acts 1:8); gives us Spiritual Gifts (see Romans 12:3-8; I Corinthians 12:1-11); manifests the Fruit of the Spirit (see Galatians 5:22-23); intercedes on our behalf (see Romans 8:26-27); and gives us strength to persevere (Jude 20-21). This is merely a quick look into the operation of the Spirit and not an exhaustive list, but we must understand the essentiality of the Spirit in our lives.

I mentioned earlier that the majority of Christendom recognizes the aspect of His Spirit in our lives. What is not widely agreed upon is the reception of His Spirit. Our focus is not going to be drawing attention to the beliefs of other denominations, but instead focusing on the teaching of Scripture.

When examining John 3:3-8 we highlighted the word "sound" in correlation to the Spirit and how in Greek the word "phōnē" refers to a spoken language or tongue. This teaching regarding the Spirit is not unique to John 3:8. In Mark 16:17 Jesus is speaking and states that there will be certain "signs" ("sēmeion" meaning, "a distinguishing mark") that accompany those who "believe" ("pisteuō" meaning, "to have faith; to trust"). One of the signs listed by Jesus is "They will speak in new tongues." "Tongues" is "glōssa" and one meaning it can have is, "a nation, as defined by its language." Keep in focus that these are "new tongues." Therefore, Jesus was indicating that the people who believed would become a new nation defined by their new tongue. Or in other words, they would become people of His Kingdom and they would speak His Kingdom language.

We can take this even further and go back to the Prophet Isaiah wherein he wrote, "For with stammering lips and another tongue He will speak to this people, to whom He said, 'This is the rest with which you may cause the weary to rest,' and, 'This is the refreshing'; yet they would not hear" (Isaiah 28:11-12 NKJV). People may try to explain away this passage, however, keeping the content in view, it is evident that Isaiah is prophesying of the Spirit. Isaiah specifically states that this thing that comes "with stammering lips and another tongue" will give "rest with which you may cause the weary to rest" and "the refreshing." These two identifiers are clear indicators of the Spirit, for the author of Hebrews equates the Spirit to rest (see Hebrews 4:1-11), and the Spirit is often equated to living water (see John 4:13-14; 7:38).

Therefore, before even stepping into the history of the first church (the Book of Acts) we can see that the coming of the Spirit is accompanied by the sign of speaking in tongues. The Book of Acts confirms this accompanying sign. We see this in Acts 2:1-4 when He first poured out His Spirit for the first time on the Jews, Acts 10:44-48 when He poured out on the Gentiles for the first time, and Acts 19:1-6 upon former disciples of John the Baptist. It is also strongly implied in Acts 8:14-19 because Philip explicitly knew that they hadn't received it yet, and then when they did receive it Simon the Sorcerer saw (meaning it was visible) it and wanted the power for himself. Therefore, Luke covers all people groups in his account: Jews, Gentiles (encompassing all Non-Jewish people), former followers whose understanding was incomplete, and Samaritans (people rejected by most Jews).

Some may ask, "Why speaking in tongues?" In James 3:3-8 the Apostle James speaks very specifically on the tongue. In this passage, he states that the tongue is a small member, yet it is the most unruly member. He equates it to a small fire that sets an entire forest ablaze. Further, he states that any animal on the earth can be tamed by man, but the tongue can be tamed by no one. Therefore, when we submit ourselves to Jesus and allow Him to enter in, He brings into submission the most unruly part of our being and causes it to glorify Him.

Earlier, in the chapter, Christians Abide with Christ, we also brought attention to how it was through tongues that He divided humanity who sought to do evil (see Genesis 11:4-9), therefore, it is through tongues that He brings humanity back into unity (see Acts 2:1-4). What we discussed regarding Mark 16:17 also correlates to this. For, as we demonstrated, the word for "tongues" in Greek, "glōssa," refers to a nation (unified people) defined by their language.

Therefore, to abide with Christ is to be baptized in His name and Spirit. Or, in other words, is to be born of water and of Spirit. It is only when we are baptized in His name and Spirit that we are then able to "see the Kingdom of God." The word "see" is "eidō" which has a various number of definitions, all of which pertain to experiencing something. Thus, we cannot experience His Kingdom if we forsake to be born into His Kingdom. How we can expect to abide with Him if we are not present with Him in His Kingdom?

It is with this question that I end this discussion.

Focused Reflection

We must understand that abiding with Christ is much more than just a position that we profess to hold, but a life we choose to live. In several places throughout the Bible, pertaining to various specific topics, we are told to not be people who are all talk and no walk (to put it in my own words). We are admonished time and time again to put into practice that which we profess. Or, as it is often said, "Practice what you preach."

The first vital step in the fulfillment of abiding with Christ is to be a humble partaker of His salvation. The truth of our need for salvation is something that is accepted and preached by the majority of professing Christians. However, where we have often failed is our understanding of salvation. We mustn't allow culture and private interpretation to define what biblical salvation looks like. Remember, we are not the authors of salvation, He is.

1. Do you understand the significance and importance of heartfelt repentance? Is heartfelt repentance a practice that is manifest in your life?

2. Have you been baptized? If so, how were you baptized? Did the baptism you experienced align with Scriptural baptism? If not, what would hinder you from obeying Scripture? Is your salvation worth the risk?

3. Have you received His Spirit since you believed? If so, how do you know? What is the evidence of His Spirit within you? Does your professed evidence align with Scriptural evidence?

> Then Peter said to them, "Repent, and let every one of you be baptized in the name of Jesus Christ for the remission of sins; and you shall receive the gift of the Holy Spirit. For the promise is to you and to your children, and to all who are afar off, as many as the Lord our God will call."
> -Acts 2:38-39

5

Christians Are People of Prayer
Christians Abide with Christ III

Now Jesus was praying in a certain place, and when
he finished, one of his disciples said to him, "Lord,
teach us to pray…"
~Luke 11:1

The nature of this entry is similar to that of the previous,
Christians are Baptized in His name and Spirit. That is, it's less of a
unique chapter and more of an excursion of what was briefly talked
about in the chapter, Christians Abide with Christ. In said chapter
part of our focus was Jesus' statement regarding His Word abiding
in us. In such discussion, I drew attention to both the written Word
(logos) and the living Word (rhēma). I defined engaging in the rhēma
as engaging in an intimate encounter with God in prayer. Similar
to how we treated the topic of being Born Again in the previous
entry, I want to take a moment and focus on prayer. The reason
being, prayer is a prevalent topic throughout the Gospels, not only
in verbal teaching regarding its operation but also in accounts of its
demonstration. We are made witness to several different prayers that
were prayed by Jesus throughout the various Gospels. Due to the
focused teaching on it and the demonstrative accounts of it, I felt it
pertinent to take time to hone in on it here.

We've mentioned this before, but it bears repeating here;
when approaching the topic of Jesus and His disciplined prayer
life, it is important to remember that while He was fully God, He
also willingly chose to become fully human. He was not merely a
theophany (a temporary, visible representation of the invisible), or
only partially human. Rather, the only way that He could truly atone
for our sins was to become fully human. In doing so, He took on the
aspect of humanity that desires to do things its way, which is the easy
and comfortable way. God's way calls for devotion and sacrifice,
which stands in direct contradiction to the desires of our humanity.

Since He clothed Himself in humanity, He had to discipline His humanity by faithfully engaging in spiritual disciplines such as prayer. The fact that Jesus prayed does not make Him any less God, it only highlights His humanity.

Therefore, I say all this to ask this question: understanding that Jesus was God made manifest in the flesh and had all the power of God at His fingertips, yet He still had to faithfully engage in prayer, how much more should we?

Let's take a moment and look back to our focus text for this excursion/chapter. Luke 11:1 presents us with an interesting scene. As Jews, Jesus' disciples were likely taught, from a young age, the ceremonial prayers of Judaism. They likely knew all the right words and nuances that made up the various intricate prayers. Further, they likely knew which particular prayer to pray in whatever situation they were in. Ceremonially, they were likely very familiar with the concept of prayer. However, the text implies that while Jesus was praying His disciples were listening in on it. It is not hard to imagine what this scene may have looked like. We can readily imagine Jesus praying with intimate passion and fervency, and then the scene pans over to the disciples who are mentally comparing His prayer and the way He prays to their ceremonial prayers. It was likely here that the disciples then realized that they did not truly understand prayer. Their approach to prayer was likely largely focused on ceremony, while His transcended mere religion and dove headfirst into relationship.

In the chapter, Christians Abide with Christ, we highlighted Jeremiah 33:3 to demonstrate the essence of prayer. It says, "Call to me and I will answer you, and will tell you great and hidden things that you have not known." We already examined the key points of this Scripture, so I won't do so again. If you need a refresher I invite you to look back at the chapter, Christians Abide with Christ. However, the essence of this Scripture is that prayer consists of relational communication.

Jesus expounded upon this principle. He says, "And when you pray, you must not be like the hypocrites. For they love to stand and pray in the synagogues and at the street corners, that they may be seen by others. Truly, I say to you, they have received their reward. But when you pray, go into your room and shut the door and pray to your Father who is in secret. And your Father who sees in secret will reward you. And when you pray, do not heap up empty phrases as the Gentiles do, for they think that they will be heard for their many words. Do not be like them, for your Father knows what you need before you ask him" (Matthew 6:5-8).

Jesus begins by implementing the standard of prayer. He does so ever so simply by saying, "And when you pray." The word "when" is "hotan" which can be translated as "frequently." Meaning, it is something that is engaged in regularly. It is such a norm in one's life that it becomes a habit, to the point where to not engage in it would be contrary to the norm. We keep saying how prayer is relational communication. Understanding such, let's draw the correlation to our relationship with our spouse or a dear friend. Relationships are built on communication. If you ceased to communicate with your spouse, you would soon cease to have a spouse. Further, if you ceased to communicate with your friend, you would eventually reach a point where the term "friends" would no longer apply to your relationship. Likewise, if we fail to frequently engage in relational communication with our Father, that intimate relationship will cease to be and He will say of us, "Depart from Me, I never knew you."

There exist in Scripture various analogies that represent the relationship between Jesus and His Church. One such analogy that is abundantly prevalent pertains to a husband and a wife. It is no accident that Jesus chose the most intimate relationship two humans can have with one another to represent His relationship with us. Speaking on marriage, the Bible tells us that the two become one flesh (see Genesis 2:24). Meaning, they are not merely two individuals living separate lives under one roof. Rather, their lives become intricately interwoven to the point where you could not discern where the one ended and the other began. Therefore, by Jesus employing this analogy, He is indicating that the same ought to be true regarding our relationship with Him. That when others look at us they should not be able to discern where we end and He begins.

After establishing the standard of prayer, Jesus dives into the mode of prayer. He begins this portion of His discourse by outlining how not to pray. Often, Jesus' rebukes were aimed toward the religious elite of the day because they were image focused. Thus, He frequently identified them as "hypocrites." The word "hypocrites" refers to a stage actor who wears a mask, thus concealing their true selves. Therefore, by calling the religious elites hypocrites, He was exposing them for what they were. That is, actors wearing a mask, hiding who they really were. Their image-focused, pride-driven motives led them to pray in the places where they would receive the most attention from the people. In essence, their prayers were less about communion with God and more about praise from men. In turn, man had become their god. To this, He said, "They have received their reward." Meaning, the attention they received from men would be all they received. There would be no heavenly reward for their mode of prayer.

After establishing how not to pray, Jesus then begins to demonstrate the proper mode of prayer. He says, "But when you pray, go into your room and shut the door and pray to your Father who is in secret. And your Father who sees in secret will reward you. And when you pray, do not heap up empty phrases as the Gentiles do, for they think that they will be heard for their many words. Do not be like them, for your Father knows what you need before you ask him."

First, the word "room" is "tameion" which refers to a place of privacy. However, Jesus calls us to go one step further than privacy, He calls us to a place of isolation in prayer. He admonishes us to "shut the door," thus closing us off from the rest of the world. In this place of isolation, we are not truly isolated, in truth, we are never more connected than in this place. For He says, "Pray to your Father who is in secret. And your Father who sees in secret will reward you." The word "secret" is "kruptos" meaning "hidden; concealed; secret." Therefore, when we partake of this isolation, God begins to truly unveil and reveal Himself to us. We begin to become acquainted with the hidden parts of His nature that cannot be made known apart from isolated intimacy. This truth points directly back to Jeremiah 33:3 where we learn that He reveals "hidden things that you have not known."

It is important to note, regarding these things, that it is

biblical to engage in corporate times of prayer where you join in unity with the Body of Christ. The truth that prayer is an isolated experience with you and God does not mean you have to physically isolate yourself. These truths speak more to the heart of man than the outward position that he is in. Truly, one could be physically isolated while still not being connected to Jesus. The point of these things is that when in prayer our focus ought not to be who is around us, or what so-and-so is doing. Prayer is time between you and God, no matter where you are physically. When the Body unites in genuine prayer, where all are intimately connected to Jesus, it creates a dynamic unity in the Spirit that shakes the very foundation of the world. Even though each is focused on God and not the other, we are all intimately connected to the One Spirit, thus connecting us all in one mind and one accord.

Jesus continues on the proper mode of prayer and states that numerous, repetitious phrases don't get the attention of God. This is likely pointed at the ceremonial prayers that were offered out of religious duty, not relationship. While we may not have set ceremonial prayers in our culture, we often fall into this same practice. We pray using religious phrases and terminology that we have heard other ministers or fellow Christians use. We think we need to use certain verbiage or a particular tone of voice to get the attention of God. Why don't we go ahead and address the elephant in the room: we all know Jesus doesn't speak in KJV verbiage right? If not, allow me to reveal to you that Jesus does not speak in KJV verbiage. Jesus speaks to us relative to our ability to understand. Meaning, He is not going to speak to someone in Spanish if they only speak French.

Again, prayer is a time of isolated intimacy between you and Jesus where you engage in relational communication. True prayer is genuine, not consisting of empty religious phrases, but it is a heartfelt expression unto God.

Some may ask, "If prayer does not consist of various religious terms and phrases, how then should I pray?" Thankfully, Jesus so graciously answered this question before we even asked. As He said, "For you Father knows what you need before you ask him."

Regarding how one ought to pray, Jesus put it like this:

In this manner, therefore, pray: our Father in heaven, hallowed be Your name. Your kingdom come. Your will be done on earth as it is in heaven. Give us this day our daily bread. And forgive us our debts, as we forgive our debtors. And do not lead us into temptation, but deliver us from the evil one. For Yours is the kingdom and the power and the glory forever. Amen.
-Matthew 6:9-13 NKJV

Before diving into the various aspects of Jesus' prayer outline, it is important to note that this was never meant to be a strict dialogue that we follow verbatim. If such was the case, it would fall under the category of "empty phrases" that Jesus spoke on. This outline for prayer given by Jesus was meant to be a guideline we used that we coupled with heartfelt expression. This prayer outline is merely meant to point us in the right direction of proper prayer, it was never meant to become a ceremonial prayer that we offer.

Keeping this understanding in view, Jesus demonstrates that prayer begins with recognition. This recognition is twofold. First, with the phrase, "our Father in heaven," we recognize Jesus' supremacy and authority over all things. For Heaven is above all, therefore, if He has authority in Heaven, then He has authority in the things under Heaven as well. However, He is a personal God who desires intimate relationship. Therefore, it is not good enough to keep the recognition to things outside our reach, we need to recognize such in our own lives. We do so by declaring, "Hallowed be Your name." The word "hallowed" is "hagiazō" which means things along the lines of, "to be holy; to set apart; to consecrate," however, it can also mean, "to render or acknowledge." Therefore, we recognize His authority not only from a distance but intimately as well.

After we recognize Him and His authority over all things, including our lives, we then align ourselves with Him. Jesus said to pray, "Your kingdom come. Your will be done on earth as it is in heaven." First, another way we could understand the phrase, "Your kingdom come," would be, "Manifest Your Kingdom here."

When we pray this prayer, we are seeking for all things to come into agreement with how they are in Heaven, or the seat of His authority. This includes our individual lives as well. When we pray this prayer, we are seeking for everything contrary to His Kingdom to be brought into subjection to it. This will likely include various aspects of our lives. Before God can manifest His Kingdom in your life, He may have to deal with some things that keep it at bay. The second part of this prayer is submitting yourself to His will and way. Again, we began by recognizing Him not only generally, but also intimately. Therefore, when we pray, "Your will be done," we are not saying it in a general sense only, but also in a personal sense.

We've already said it, but it is in prayer that Jesus reveals hidden things to you. Things that were not previously known. The only way that He can do so is if you are in alignment with Him and His Kingdom. If you weren't and He revealed a hidden thing to you, you would likely misconstrue that revelation and carry it in the wrong direction. However, aligning with Him and His will first, when He then reveals the secret thing we will interpret it correctly and pursue it in relation to His Kingdom.

Following aligning ourselves with His Kingdom, He then admonishes us to pray, "Give us this day our daily bread." This is an interesting portion of the prayer. Many throughout the ages have sought to allegorize this saying to refer to Jesus' presence in our lives (as the Living Bread) or the Word being revealed to us (as the Bread of Life). I don't think these understandings are necessarily wrong, for it is good to seek the Living Bread and the Bread of Life daily. However, I truly believe that Jesus was speaking of our daily necessities in life. We could reference Matthew 6:25-34 wherein Jesus is speaking on not worrying about daily necessities such as food or clothes. He deeply cares about even the most seemingly insignificant aspects of nature, so how much more does He care for us? At the close of that passage, He declares, "But seek first the kingdom of God and His righteousness, and all these things shall be added to you" (Matthew 6:33 NKJV). If we have followed His outline for prayer, then this is exactly what we have done. First, we recognize Him, then we align ourselves with Him and His Kingdom. By this, we "seek first the kingdom of God and His righteousness."

Why is it important to seek His Kingdom first before praying about our daily necessities? Aligning ourselves with Him births within us the right attitudes, mindsets, and desires. Without aligning ourselves with Him allows the carnal man and its attitudes, mindsets, and desires to run rampant. Therefore, if our carnal man is abounding, we will likely pray out of greed rather than need. By first aligning with Him, we are able to focus on our true daily needs, not our vain greed.

He continues and says, "And forgive us our debts, as we forgive our debtors." We won't dive too deep into this just yet because we are going to take a deeper look into forgiveness a little later. However, notice, our forgiveness is predicated on us forgiving. We receive mercy when we give mercy. Jesus said in an earlier portion, "So if you are offering your gift at the altar and there remember that your brother has something against you, leave your gift there before the altar and go. First be reconciled to your brother, and then come and offer your gift" (Matthew 5:23-24). We cannot expect forgiveness if we are withholding forgiveness.

After we seek forgiveness for the wrongs we have committed, He then admonishes us to pray, "And do not lead us into temptation, but deliver us from the evil one." Therefore, after we have sought forgiveness for our sins, we are then to pray for His grace to work in us to give us power over those sins. If we are coming to Jesus day after day, repenting over the same sins every day, that is a sign of spiritual immaturity. For if we were spiritually mature, we would be allowing His grace to work in us to grow us to a point where we overcome that which once held us bound. Paul said, "What shall we say then? Are we to continue in sin that grace may abound? By no means! How can we who died to sin still live in it" (Romans 6:1-2)? This by no means indicates that we will never mess up and sin. For we are still human and still battle with that human nature that is inclined toward sinful desires. What Paul is saying is that if His grace is truly at work in our lives we will no longer continue to struggle with the same sins and temptations, but we will die to those things which once held us captive and live in Him and His righteousness.

The final portion of Jesus' prayer outlines is not present

in many translations, this is due to it not being present in some of the earlier manuscripts that we have found. However, it is present in many of the more recent manuscripts and fits the context of the passage. That is why I chose the NKJV translation over the ESV for this passage, for the ESV omits the final portion.

I feel this final portion is a fitting end to Jesus' prayer outline, for it unifies with how the prayer begins. We begin with recognition and we end with recognition. Another way we could word this would be, we begin with a declaration of faith in who He is and His power, and we end by once again declaring our faith in Him and His power and authority. Thereby, our prayer is bookended by declarations of faith. Again, we will come back to faith later on and dive deep into it. But the author of Hebrews tells us, "And without faith it is impossible to please him, for whoever would draw near to God must believe that he exists and that he rewards those who seek him" (Hebrews 11:6).

I want to take a moment and focus on the portion of prayer wherein we pray for our daily necessities. We already demonstrated how before we petition Him for our needs we first need to align ourselves with Him, lest we seek out of greed rather than need. It is unfortunate, but many individuals' definition of prayer relates to us bringing to Him a laundry list of things we desire. We pray for and seek after things that we desire that would make our lives easier, more comfortable, and more enjoyable. The Apostle James spoke to this idea of prayer. He said, "You ask and do not receive, because you ask wrongly, to spend it on your passions. You adulterous people! Do you not know that friendship with the world is enmity with God? Therefore whoever wishes to be a friend of the world makes himself an enemy of God. Or do you suppose it is to no purpose that the Scripture says, 'He yearns jealously over the spirit that he has made to dwell in us'" (James 4:3-5)?

While Jesus desires to bless His people, His blessings do not always look how we imagine them. When we think of blessing our minds gravitate towards things either of a financial nature or things of luxury. However, never in His Word did He promise that His blessings were strictly financial or luxurious. God is more concerned with your salvation than your comfort. True prayer is not us bringing our laundry list of wants to Him, James declared that this mindset is at enmity with God. To greedily seek after the luxuries of this world is to declare that you desire them over the things of His Kingdom. This is why it is essential to first align ourselves with Him and His Kingdom and His will before we ever present a need unto Him. If we faithfully and genuinely align ourselves with Him first, that submission will naturally weed out many desires that do not align with His will for our lives.

Many quote Psalms 37:4 which says, "Delight yourself in the LORD, and he will give you the desires of your heart." They attempt to use this Scripture as evidence that He gives us whatever we desire as long as we love Him. However, those who use this Scripture in this way take it completely out of context with the rest of the chapter. The entirety of Psalms 37 is centered around putting one's trust in Him and not focusing on what the wicked of this world have or what they do. In fact, a later verse in the same chapter says, "Better is the little that the righteous has than the abundance of many wicked. For the arms of the wicked shall be broken, but the LORD upholds the righteous" (v.16-17). However, if we truly wanted to only hone in on Psalms 37:4, a thorough study of this Scripture and the Hebrew words used would reveal that it refers to submitting yourself unto God and allowing Him to mold and shape you. When you allow Him to do this, the desires of your heart change from being focused on yourself and the world to being Kingdom focused.

The Apostle John affirms this truth of being aligned with His will regarding the things we ask for. He says, "And this is the confidence that we have toward him, that if we ask anything according to his will he hears us" (I John 5:14). Therefore, prayer is not you sitting on Santa's lap, reading off your Christmas list. Prayer is aligning yourself with the heart and mind of Jesus and His will and praying according to His will so that the things that He desires for you and those around you will be made manifest.

In the preceding excursion, we spoke on the New Birth and how the infilling of His Spirit is always accompanied by the outward sign of speaking in tongues. It is important to know that tongues is not restricted to the New Birth experience. Speaking in tongues should consistently be present in the life of every Christian. Paul said, "I thank God that I speak in tongues more than all of you" (I Corinthians 14:18). There will be times in prayer wherein we feel the need to pray, but don't know what we ought to pray. We feel the Spirit leading us to it, but are at a loss for words regarding what needs to be prayed about. Paul speaks on these things too. He says, "Likewise the Spirit helps us in our weakness. For we do not know what to pray for as we ought, but the Spirit himself intercedes for us with groanings too deep for words" (Romans 8:26). Again, prayer is aligning yourself with Him and praying according to His will. There will be times, however, when we struggle to pray according to His will how we ought. But praise be to God that He sees us in our time of weakness and does not forsake us, but reaches down and bridges the gap (intercession) between our heartfelt desire and our inability.

In short, every facet of prayer is centered around being aligned with Him and His Kingdom. Looking to Jeremiah 33:3, "call" is "qârâ'" which not only means calling out to one by name, as we mentioned, but also a meeting. Therefore, prayer is meeting Him which requires us to seek His Kingdom. Further, as Jesus demonstrated in Matthew 6, proper prayer is predicated upon establishing His Kingdom on earth and in our lives. Finally, again as Jesus conveyed, and John as well, He hears our prayers when we align ourselves with His will.

Kingdom prayer is essential in the life of every professing Christian.

Focused Reflection

Prayer is an integral part of a Christian's walk. We could define prayer very simplistically as our communication with God. However, we also cannot limit our understanding of prayer to simply, "Communicating with God." We must understand that true prayer is birthed out of a heartfelt desire to truly interact with Jesus. If we approach prayer as a mere duty, then we will get little to nothing out of it. It is when we approach it in sincerity, love, and devotion that we truly begin to experience God in our midst.

The Apostle James said, "You ask and do not receive, because you ask wrongly, to spend it on your passions" (James 4:3).

It is essential that our hearts are right when we approach God in prayer. That is why, in teaching us to pray, Jesus demonstrated that before we begin asking for things, we first need to ensure that we are alignment with His Kingdom and His will.

1. Do you have a daily prayer life? If so, what does it look like?

2. How would you describe your heart (your mindset and attitude) when you approach God in prayer? Is it one of duty or desire?

3. After you have prayed, do you feel like God has heard you? If not, why do you think that is?

Pray without ceasing.
-I Thessalonians 5:17

6
Christians Are Worshippers

God is spirit, and those who worship him must
worship in spirit and truth.
~John 4:24

In Christendom the practices of praise and worship are
widely recognized, even though the definitions of these practices
vary from denomination to denomination, and even church to church
within the same denomination. One thing that I have noticed, from
my own church experience, is that the terms praise and worship are
often used interchangeably. Both praise and worship are biblical
mandates that we ought to engage in, but they are not the same thing
and they ought to be understood properly. When we possess a proper
understanding of a particular subject we are, then, able to operate
in it in a greater way. Therefore, we will begin by examining what
praise is and how it relates to us. Afterward, we will dive into the
biblical mandate of worship.

The Webster's Dictionary defines praise in four different
ways: "1. To commend; to applaud; to express approbation of
personal worth or actions; 2. To extol in words or song; to magnify;
to glorify on account of perfections or excellent works; 3. To
express gratitude for personal favors; 4. To do honor to; to display
the excellence of." The Book of Psalms is well-known for being
replete with poems and songs that are filled with lyrics that mirror
these very definitions provided above. Some examples are Psalms
95:1-2, "Oh come, let us sing to the LORD; let us make a joyful
noise to the rock of our salvation! Let us come into his presence
with thanksgiving; let us make a joyful noise to him with songs
of praise!" Psalms 117:1-2, "Praise the LORD, all nations! Extol
him, all peoples! For great is his steadfast love toward us, and the
faithfulness of the LORD endures forever. Praise the LORD!" And,
of course, the ever-popular Psalms 150, "Praise the LORD! Praise
God in his sanctuary; praise him in his mighty heavens! Praise him
for his mighty deeds; praise him according to his excellent greatness!

Praise him with trumpet sound; praise him with lute and harp! Praise him with tambourine and dance; praise him with strings and pipe! Praise him with sounding cymbals; praise him with loud clashing cymbals! Let everything that has breath praise the LORD! Praise the LORD" (v.1-6)!

Furthermore, the concept of praise is not unique to Psalms or the Old Testament alone but is present in the New Testament as well. We read in Colossians 3:16, "Let the word of Christ dwell in you richly, teaching and admonishing one another in all wisdom, singing psalms and hymns and spiritual songs, with thankfulness in your hearts to God." Also, in Hebrews 13:15, "Through him then let us continually offer up a sacrifice of praise to God, that is, the fruit of lips that acknowledge his name." And in James 5:13, "Is anyone among you suffering? Let him pray. Is anyone cheerful? Let him sing praise." Finally, we can look to Jesus and see this same call to praise in Luke 19:37-40: "As he was drawing near—already on the way down the Mount of Olives—the whole multitude of his disciples began to rejoice and praise God with a loud voice for all the mighty works that they had seen, saying, 'Blessed is the King who comes in the name of the Lord! Peace in heaven and glory in the highest!' And some of the Pharisees in the crowd said to him, 'Teacher, rebuke your disciples.' He answered, 'I tell you, that if these were silent, the very stones would cry out.'"

Notice the words of Jesus. If His followers ended the song of praise unto Him, then even the most inanimate aspect of creation would pick up where they left off. David admonished everything that has breath to praise Him (see Psalms 150:6), but He is so abundantly worthy of praise that if the living ceased to give it, then even the lifeless would begin to offer it. Praise is a mandate because of how abundantly worthy of it He is.

Looking to the Hebrew word for "praise" (using Psalms 150), it is the word "hâlal." In its original usage "hâlal" did not mean or refer to praise, but came to be associated with it through usage. Its meaning points to focusing on something that is a ways off and being led by it. An example of this word is how, in ancient times, travelers would be led by the stars at night. Interestingly, this word has come to be associated with the concept of praise. From this, we can ascertain that praise is giving our focus and attention to a thing and as we do so, we are led by that very thing. David said, "Yet you are holy, enthroned on the praises of Israel" (Psalms 22:3). The word "enthroned" is "yâshab" which, in its truest meaning, refers to turning or pressing toward a place of dwelling. Therefore, the fact that He is "enthroned on the praises" ("praises" being the same word from before, "hâlal") demonstrates that when we give our focus and attention to Him, seeking to be led by Him ("hâlal"), He then turns toward us and our praise and presses toward us to abide therein. Praise gets the attention of Jesus.

Continuing into the New Testament, in Hebrews 13:15 the word "praise" is "ainesis" which means, "a thanks offering." In Luke 19:37 it is "aineō" which is, "to celebrate; to extol; to honor." The word "extol" according to Webster's Dictionary simply means, "to magnify." Therefore, the definition of praise (in relation to God) that we derive from these New Testament words is, to exuberantly lift up Jesus with an offering of thanksgiving. This concept of thanksgiving being central to praise is present in an earlier quoted verse as well, "Let the word of Christ dwell in you richly, teaching and admonishing one another in all wisdom, singing psalms and hymns and spiritual songs, with thankfulness in your hearts to God" (Colossians 3:16).

Often, when people think of thanksgiving, their minds go to the end of the matter. Someone does something nice for you and you express thankfulness toward them. Indeed, this is an important aspect of thankfulness that should not be neglected. The psalmist David himself declared that we ought to "praise Him according to His mighty deeds." The issue, however, comes when this is our only understanding of thanksgiving. There is another aspect of thanksgiving that is just as, if not more, important when it comes to giving thanks unto Jesus. That is, offering thanksgiving before He has done His mighty deeds.

One example of this concept is found in II Chronicles 13. We read, "Jeroboam had sent an ambush around to come upon them from behind. Thus his troops were in front of Judah, and the ambush was behind them. And when Judah looked, behold, the battle was in front of and behind them. And they cried to the LORD, and the priests blew the trumpets. Then the men of Judah raised the battle shout. And when the men of Judah shouted, God defeated Jeroboam and all Israel before Abijah and Judah. The men of Israel fled before Judah, and God gave them into their hand. Abijah and his people struck them with great force, so there fell slain of Israel 500,000 chosen men. Thus the men of Israel were subdued at that time, and the men of Judah prevailed, because they relied on the LORD, the God of their fathers" (v. 13-18).

One may wonder how this correlates to our point. For one, the name "Judah" ("yehûdâh") means to praise or celebrate. Therefore, the story revolves around a group of praisers. Then, those same people, who were known for their praise, began to do just that. They lifted up a cry, blew the trumpets, and shouted. Sounds like an Apostolic praise session to me. The key, though, is the situation these people were in when the praise was sent forth. There was an enemy, Jeroboam, who had Judah surrounded on every side. Judah was dead to rights…but God. If Judah had not offered up praise (thanksgiving) when they did (before He showed up), would He have shown up? We can speculate, but considering the context we could safely surmise that the answer would be, no. Remember, praise gets His attention and draws Him close to us.

This is merely one Old Testament example, there are a plethora more that could be brought to light. Instead, we will take our focus to the New Testament. Again, the New Testament is replete with possible examples, but one immediately comes to mind. Looking to the Book of Acts we read of when Paul and Silas were imprisoned. It reads, "Having received this order, he put them into the inner prison and fastened their feet in the stocks. About midnight Paul and Silas were praying and singing hymns to God, and the prisoners were listening to them, and suddenly there was a great earthquake, so that the foundations of the prison were shaken. And immediately all the doors were opened, and everyone's bonds were unfastened" (Acts 16:24-26). The story continues with the jailer awakening to find the cells open and thinking they had all escaped. Knowing the punishment that awaited, he sought the easy way out and prepared to kill himself. Paul, still present with all the others, stopped the man. This led to the salvation of him and his whole house (see v. 27-34).

Depending on who you might ask, some would say that Paul and Silas were in no position to be singing songs of praise. They were previously beaten and then thrown in jail. What did they have to be thankful for? Remember, praise is keeping your focus and attention on Him. Therefore, Paul and Silas weren't focused on the chains that had them bound temporarily, but on the One who held them eternally. And from this not only were Paul, Silas, and the whole jail delivered, but salvation came to an entire household.

Therefore, taking all of this into consideration, how might we collectively define praise? In my own words, praise is an exuberant declaration of exaltation and thanksgiving toward Jesus, whether the work is already done or not yet manifest; praise keeps Him at the absolute center of all focus and attention, no matter what is transpiring around about; and praise is an invitation from us unto Him for Him to come abide with us, whether things are good or bad.

Now, transitioning to our main topic, we come to worship. We've attempted to concisely yet thoroughly define praise, but now we must ask, "What is worship, then?" Looking to our focus text, John 4:24, the word "worship" in this Scripture is "proskyneō" which, in its truest meaning, refers to kissing the hand of another as a sign of reverence. This word has also come to refer to bowing or kneeling also as a sign of reverence. In essence, every meaning of this word points to showing reverence toward another. "Reverence," according to Oxford Languages, means, "a deep respect for someone or something." In essence, reverence points to esteeming someone higher than yourself.

With this understanding, we can see how there is an aspect of worship associated with singing. Truly, one does not have to think hard to bring to mind various songs that revolve around exalting who God is. Some may focus on His power, His love, or any of His various attributes.

Looking back to Psalms 95 quoted earlier, we see a few verses later, "Oh come, let us worship and bow down; let us kneel before the LORD, our Maker! For he is our God, and we are the people of his pasture, and the sheep of his hand" (Psalms 95:6-7). The word "worship" is "shâchâh" which means, "to bow down; to prostrate one's self." Further, "bow down" is "kâra'" meaning, "to kneel; to bend the knee; to bow down." Finally, "let us kneel" is "bârak" which means, "to kneel or to bless." It is no accident that the psalmist used three different words that all echo the same meaning. The psalmist is emphatically declaring that we are to live a life of reverence unto our King. This is not meant to be a momentary affair, but a consistent lifestyle. In other words, while there is an aspect of worship that encompasses singing, the true extent of worship far surpasses singing and transcends into the way we live.

Paul spoke on this very thing. He writes, "I appeal to you therefore, brothers, by the mercies of God, to present your bodies as a living sacrifice, holy and acceptable to God, which is your spiritual worship. Do not be conformed to this world, but be transformed by the renewal of your mind, that by testing you may discern what is the will of God, what is good and acceptable and perfect" (Romans 12:1-2).

The NKJV words this same passage like so:

> I beseech you therefore, brethren, by the mercies of God, that you present your bodies a living sacrifice, holy, acceptable to God, which is your reasonable service. And do not be conformed to this world, but be transformed by the renewing of your mind, that you may prove what is that good and acceptable and perfect will of God.
> -Romans 12:1-2 NKJV

Between the different translations of the Bible, there is always some variability in wording. However, the difference here is quite interesting. The wording the ESV offers regarding Paul's point of focus is, "spiritual worship," but the NKJV words it as, "reasonable service." It would seem as though there was a mess up somewhere because it does not seem that these two phrases are pointing to the same thing. However, the word translated "spiritual" by the ESV and "reasonable" by the NKJV is "logikos" which can, in fact, be translated as either referring to the inner man or that which is reasonable or logical. Additionally, the word translated "worship" by the ESV and "service" by the NKJV is "latreia" which can either refer to worship, or an act of service unto another.

Taking these things into consideration, I believe it would nurture a greater understanding if we combined these two translations. For example: instead of simply saying "spiritual worship" or "reasonable service," we could say, "this spiritual thing you do, which is your reasonable service, is worship."

So we know that Paul is writing about worship here, but what is his definition of worship? Looking to the quoted passage, he begins by admonishing us to "present your bodies as a living sacrifice." "Present" is "paristēmi" which can be translated as "to dedicate, consecrate, or devote." Therefore, this not merely saying half-heartedly, "Here ya go." Rather, it is sincere, heartfelt, and intentional. This "presenting" is not performed out of religious routine or duty, but out of great love. Second, the word "bodies" is "sōma." Generally, this word refers to a physical body of a human or animal, whether it be living or dead. However, the word can also be used to refer to the appetites and passions of the flesh that lead to sin. As the Apostle James said, "But each person is tempted when he is lured and enticed by his own desire. Then desire when it has conceived gives birth to sin, and sin when it is fully grown brings forth death" (James 1:14-15). Therefore, we are admonished to sincerely hand over the part of our being that draws us away from Him so that we can draw closer to God.

The way that we are to do this is by being a "living sacrifice." The word "living" is "zaō" which can be translated as, "full of life." On the flip side, the word "sacrifice" is "thusia" which refers to both the act of sacrifice and the thing which is sacrificed. These two words seem to stand in contradiction to one another. On the one end, Paul states that we are to be full of life, yet he immediately follows that by saying that we are to die. If you look up the meaning of "sacrifice" according to either Oxford Languages or Webster's Dictionary, some words that you will see associated with it are kill, slaughter, suffer, destroy, burn, and so on. In other words, the death Paul is calling for us to experience is not a peaceful death where we simply lay our heads down and don't wake back up. No, the death that he is calling us to is brutal and gruesome. Why is that? It is because the flesh does not want to die. There is an innate survival instinct that is present within each one of us that works to preserve us from death or harm. Therefore, when we start talking about death, the flesh will do all it can to fight succumbing to that very thing. The death that we are called to endure cannot be a passive thing, for our flesh would never allow it. This is why it is described in such gruesome terminology. The fight that will be endured to come to that place of death will be an all-out war.

We can look to Jesus as a perfect example. As we have discussed already, Jesus was YAHWEH manifest in the flesh. His entire purpose for manifesting Himself among us was to save us from our own sinfulness that we could not escape. The only way that He could do so was to die in our place, for the wages of sin is death (see Romans 6:23). However, truly being God manifest in the flesh, He possessed that same innate survival instinct that we do. His death was not easy because He was God. He had to fight for it. We see that clearly in His prayer in the Garden of Gethsemane.

We read, "And he withdrew from them about a stone's throw, and knelt down and prayed, saying, "Father, if you are willing, remove this cup from me. Nevertheless, not my will, but yours, be done." And there appeared to him an angel from heaven, strengthening him. And being in agony he prayed more earnestly; and his sweat became like great drops of blood falling down to the ground" (Luke 22:41-44). Jesus had to war so hard against His flesh that blood begin to drip from His brow. I can't imagine how hard He must have been praying at that moment, but this is the image Paul is creating in his writing.

Circling back, we still have this seeming contradiction presented to us by Paul: to be full of life, yet to die brutally. There are a couple of ways that we could understand this. First, Paul could be implying that we are not "full of life" until we first die. The part of our being that we are sacrificing is our carnal man ("thusia"), the part of us that is drawn to that which is sinful. This part of us is what propels us into death, again, the wages of sin is death. Therefore, as long as we entertain this carnal part of our being we have no life, only death.

Jesus put it like this:

> Remember Lot's wife. Whoever seeks to preserve his
> life will lose it, but whoever loses his life will keep it.
> -Luke 17:32-33

The "Remember Lot's wife" line is so simple yet so telling. Lot and his family were rescued by God from Sodom and Gomorrah and simply told to not look back on the city. In essence, they were commanded to sacrifice their carnal selves. Yet Lot's wife could not. Her desire for that which pleased her carnal self was too great, so she turned back and died. This "life" that Jesus is referring to is not our breath, but the life that we live in relation to the world. Whoever seeks to preserve the life they have made for themselves here will, in the end, have no life at all. Nothing in this world can give life, only death. It is only when we lose our worldly lives that we then come to have life.

Jesus makes it even more plain in the Gospel of Mark:

> And calling the crowd to him with his disciples, he said to them, "If anyone would come after me, let him deny himself and take up his cross and follow me. For whoever would save his life will lose it, but whoever loses his life for my sake and the gospel's will save it. For what does it profit a man to gain the whole world and forfeit his soul? For what can a man give in return for his soul? For whoever is ashamed of me and of my words in this adulterous and sinful generation, of him will the Son of Man also be ashamed when he comes in the glory of his Father with the holy angels."
> -Mark 8:34-38

To seek after this world and the things it has to offer is to forfeit eternal life with Him. But when we forfeit this world and the things it has to offer, that is when we will truly experience life.

We could also look to the Gospel for further demonstration of this truth. Jesus first died, then was buried, and then rose on the third day. Therefore, those of us who seek to partake of His Gospel must first repent (which is dying to the self), be buried (baptism in His name), and then we will experience new life in His Spirit. In His Kingdom, death proceeds life.

The second manner in which we could interpret this phrase would be that Paul is calling us to continual sacrifice. When we sacrifice our carnal man, we are not physically dying, but killing the desires of the flesh. Unfortunately, because we are stubborn creatures that don't like to stay down, we can easily get back up off the altar of sacrifice. Since the sacrifice of our carnal man is not a one-and-done deal, it must be done continually. Or, to word to precisely, it must be done daily.

Again, looking to the words of Jesus, He says, "If anyone would come after me, let him deny himself and take up his cross daily and follow me" (Luke 9:23). The word "daily" is "hēmera" which means, "day to day; continually." What are we to do daily? One, "deny" ourselves. "Deny" is "aparneomai" which means, "to deny; to disown; to disregard." Two, we are to take up our "cross." What does this mean? "Cross" is "stauros" which figuratively refers to exposure to death.

This is, then, the second way in which we could interpret this phrase: as long as we are living, moving, and breathing we are to continually sacrifice ourselves afresh. Every day, first thing in the morning, sacrifice yourself again. Any day that we neglect to engage in self-sacrifice, we run the risk of allowing our flesh to rear its ugly head and take control of us.

Paul declares, "I have been crucified with Christ. It is no longer I who live, but Christ who lives in me. And the life I now live in the flesh I live by faith in the Son of God, who loved me and gave himself for me" (Galatians 2:20). The only way that we can, in like fashion with Paul, declare that Jesus lives in us is by endeavoring to be a "living sacrifice." It is by this that we engage in "spiritual worship" unto God.

From our examination of what worship is and the Scriptures we looked at that correlate to it, we can surmise two key aspects that directly tie to worship. That is, humility and surrender. A thorough discussion of both of these topics will aid us in garnering a greater understanding of worship and how to apply it to our lives.

Christianity: Putting the Christ Back in Christianity

We will focus on humility first, but it would be beneficial for us to begin our look into humility by first examining pride. Why would it be beneficial for us to examine pride? When we are seeking to understand something in its proper light, it is helpful to also examine what it is not. By outlining what it is not, it creates safe parameters for us regarding what a thing is and helps us to stay within the defined parameters. Another reason why it would be beneficial to examine pride is that pride is an ever-so-prevalent issue across the whole world, and there is a reason for it.

Speaking on humility and its connection to right relationship with God, the Apostle James says, "But he gives more grace. Therefore it says, 'God opposes the proud but gives grace to the humble.' Submit yourselves therefore to God. Resist the devil, and he will flee from you. Draw near to God, and he will draw near to you. Cleanse your hands, you sinners, and purify your hearts, you double-minded. Be wretched and mourn and weep. Let your laughter be turned to mourning and your joy to gloom. Humble yourselves before the Lord, and he will exalt you" (James 4:6-10).

The word "opposes" used by James here is "antitassō" which does not merely refer to disagreeing with someone, but it more rightly refers to a great army being arrayed against an opponent. In other words, God actively goes to war against the spirit of pride. The word "proud" is "hyperēphanos" which means, "assuming; haughty; arrogant." Webster's Dictionary defines "assuming" as, "taking or disposed to take upon one's self more than is just." In essence, "assuming" refers to thinking that you are due more than other people and that you deserve more. Why? Simply because you are better and more worthy than everyone else. "Haughty," also according to Webster's Dictionary, is "having a high opinion of one's self, with some contempt for others." Meaning, you exalt yourself to a lofty pedestal and force all others to stand beneath you. Having a haughty spirit is to belittle others for the express purpose of making yourself bigger. Finally, "arrogant" is "making or having the disposition to make exorbitant claims of rank or estimation; giving one's self an undue degree of importance" (Webster's Dictionary). Meaning, you usurp yourself into positions and place upon yourself titles that you feel you are deserving of, regardless of the opinion of others.

Solomon spoke on these very things when he penned, "Pride goes before destruction, and a haughty spirit before a fall" (Proverbs 16:18). "Destruction" is "sheber" and it directly refers to the process of placing grain on the threshing floor or in a millstone and then crushing it. It is a very descriptive and powerful word. He is saying that those who live by pride will soon be crushed with great force and violence. Whenever the harvester took grain to the threshing floor or placed it in the millstone, it was for the express purpose and crushing it so it would burst forth and reveal what is within (the seed). To live by pride is to subject oneself to brutal crushing until the seed of such is revealed within us. Further, "fall" is "kishshâlôn" which is often used to refer to the tumbling or ruin of buildings or cities. It is a toppling over of something once great and tall. When we live according to a haughty spirit, everything that we endeavored to build and amass will come tumbling down and be brought to ruin. How do these things happen exactly? Because God actively goes to war against the proud, and who can stand against the Lord?

One may ask, "Why does God so actively war against a proud spirit? There are several different reasons we could list as to why exactly He takes such an aggressive stance against such. However, rather than listing all these various reasons, we will go directly to the heart of the matter.

At various points throughout Scripture, God often gave revelation to those He wrote through regarding things that transpired long ago in times past. For example, many believe that it was when God passed before Moses and showed him His hinder glory that Moses received revelation of the events that transpired before his birth, particularly of the things involving creation (see Exodus 33:18-23; 34:5-7). In this same way, He revealed to different prophets the things that led to the fall of Lucifer.

God spoke through three different prophets regarding Lucifer, and it is by considering each account that we form a cohesive understanding of the events that led to his demise. First, read from the Prophet Isaiah:

How you are fallen from heaven, O Day Star, son of
Dawn! How you are cut down to the ground, you who

laid the nations low! You said in your heart, I will ascend to heaven; above the stars of God I will set my throne on high; I will sit on the mount of assembly in the far reaches of the north; I will ascend above the heights of the clouds; I will make myself like the Most High.' But you are brought down to Sheol, to the far reaches of the pit. Those who see you will stare at you and ponder over you: "Is this the man who made the earth tremble, who shook kingdoms, who made the world like a desert and overthrew its cities, who did not let his prisoners go home?"
-Isaiah 14:12-17

Second, we read from the Prophet Ezekiel:

Moreover, the word of the LORD came to me: "Son of man, raise a lamentation over the king of Tyre, and say to him, Thus says the Lord GOD: "You were the signet of perfection, full of wisdom and perfect in beauty. You were in Eden, the garden of God; every precious stone was your covering, sardius, topaz, and diamond, beryl, onyx, and jasper, sapphire, emerald, and carbuncle; and crafted in gold were your settings and your engravings. On the day that you were created they were prepared. You were an anointed guardian cherub. I placed you; you were on the holy mountain of God; in the midst of the stones of fire you walked. You were blameless in your ways from the day you were created, till unrighteousness was found in you. In the abundance of your trade you were filled with violence in your midst, and you sinned; so I cast you as a profane thing from the mountain of God, and I destroyed you, O guardian cherub, from the midst of the stones of fire. Your heart was proud because of your beauty; you corrupted your wisdom for the sake of your splendor. I cast you to the ground; I exposed you before kings, to feast their eyes on you. By the

multitude of your iniquities, in the unrighteousness of your trade you profaned your sanctuaries; so I brought fire out from your midst; it consumed you, and I turned you to ashes on the earth in the sight of all who saw you. All who know you among the peoples are appalled at you; you have come to a dreadful end and shall be no more forever."
-Ezekiel 28:11-19

Finally, the Apostle and Prophet John gave us insight into his casting out:

Now war arose in heaven, Michael and his angels fighting against the dragon. And the dragon and his angels fought back, but he was defeated, and there was no longer any place for them in heaven. And the great dragon was thrown down, that ancient serpent, who is called the devil and Satan, the deceiver of the whole world—he was thrown down to the earth, and his angels were thrown down with him.
-Revelation 12:7-9

Taking these three passages into consideration, this is the cohesive understanding we can garner: Lucifer was once a high-ranking angel in the heavenly realm. He had beauty, wisdom, and position. At some point though, the beauty, wisdom, and rank went to his head. He looked at himself, then looked at God. He then had the most destructive thought, "What is so great about that Guy? Look at me! I could easily be just like Him, maybe even better." Unfortunately, Lucifer was not content with keeping this perverse thought to himself but endeavored to share his message with his fellow angels for the purpose of creating a new divine order. Even more unfortunate, one-third of the angels bought into his twisted vision and sought to bring it to pass (see Revelation 12:4). Of course, we all know what Lucifer seemed to have forgotten, Jesus is the Almighty. Therefore, Lucifer and the angels he deceived never stood a chance but were quickly dealt with and cast out of the heavenly realm.

Once again, we come to an "unfortunately." For the story does not end here. Lucifer has been cast out and he is overwhelmed with bitterness, resentment, and hatred toward God. He wants to get back at Him and hit Him where it hurts, so to speak. But how do you hit God where it hurts? Lucifer soon saw his opportunity.

The Bible begins with Jesus, the One who holds all power, bringing all things into being. He calls forth and it manifests. His Word has life-giving power. He creates the world, the atmosphere, the environment, and the various creatures that inhabit nature. But for what purpose? It all comes to a head on day six. Jesus looks at His creation and is pleased with what He has created, but now it is time to bring into being what all this has been for. We read in Genesis 1:26-28, "Then God said, 'Let us make man in our image, after our likeness. And let them have dominion over the fish of the sea and over the birds of the heavens and over the livestock and over all the earth and over every creeping thing that creeps on the earth.' So God created man in his own image, in the image of God he created him; male and female he created them. And God blessed them. And God said to them, 'Be fruitful and multiply and fill the earth and subdue it, and have dominion over the fish of the sea and over the birds of the heavens and over every living thing that moves on the earth.'"

There it was. The opportunity Lucifer had been looking for to hit God where it hurts. He saw the care and love that He put into creating these things He called humanity. He knew that these were His prized creation. That is when he devised within himself to attack them to get back at God.

We all know how this part of the story goes. We all know how Lucifer tempted Eve and she fell and she and Adam sinned together. But notice with what Lucifer tempted Eve. He said, "You will not surely die. For God knows that when you eat of it your eyes will be opened, and you will be like God, knowing good and evil" (Genesis 3:4-5). He tempted Adam and Eve with the same sin that caused him to fall: pride. It is sad really, for Adam and Eve were already as much like God as they could be. They were created in His image and given dominion over His creation. They forsook the position they already had in Him for the sake of assuming a loftier position that did not exist.

So why does Jesus so actively go to war against a proud spirit? Because pride is at the heart of every sin, and it is pride that separated Him from His beloved creation. It was pride that brought sin and death into the His creation.

The flip side of all this though is to walk in the spirit of humility. Looking back to the passage from James, we read that God "gives grace to the humble." "Grace" is "charis" which does not necessarily have a straightforward meaning. Rather, it is a far-reaching word that encompasses the total work of God in our lives to do in us and through that which we could never do alone. In essence, to those who walk in humility, God pours out in their lives in abundance. However, we need to understand what it means to be humble that way we can then walk in the grace of Jesus.

The word for "humble" from this passage is "tapeinos" and a literal translation of this word is, "not rising far from the ground." Or, in other words, not elevated. Webster's Dictionary defines "humility" as, "in theology, humility consists in lowliness of mind; a deep sense of one's own unworthiness in the sight of God, self-abasement, penitence for sin, and submission to the divine will." Therefore, one who walks in humility fully embraces the truth of John 15:5 wherein Jesus says, "Apart from me you can do nothing." Those who are humble recognize that any good or perfect thing in their lives is not of themselves, but only of God.

Paul said, "For I know that nothing good dwells in me, that is, in my flesh. For I have the desire to do what is right, but not the ability to carry it out" (Romans 7:18). James added to this truth and said, "Every good gift and every perfect gift is from above, coming down from the Father of lights, with whom there is no variation or shadow due to change" (James 1:17). Humility is a sincere recognition of our utter dependency upon God for everything good in us. Humility recognizes that it is by Him that we live and move and have our being (see Acts 17:28).

True humility, however, is not merely with God, but with our fellow man as well. For Paul said, "Do nothing from selfish ambition or conceit, but in humility count others more significant than yourselves. Let each of you look not only to his own interests, but also to the interests of others" (Philippians 2:3-4). To walk in the spirit of humility is to walk into a room full of people and, regardless of your position or their positions, consider them higher than yourself. Just as humility, in relation to Jesus, is a recognition of our utter dependency upon Him, so humility, in relation to others, is a recognition of our utter dependency upon them.

Paul put it well wherein he said,

"For just as the body is one and has many members, and all the members of the body, though many, are one body, so it is with Christ. For in one Spirit we were all baptized into one body—Jews or Greeks, slaves or free—and all were made to drink of one Spirit. For the body does not consist of one member but of many. If the foot should say, 'Because I am not a hand, I do not belong to the body,' that would not make it any less a part of the body. And if the ear should say, 'Because I am not an eye, I do not belong to the body,' that would not make it any less a part of the body. If the whole body were an eye, where would be the sense of hearing? If the whole body were an ear, where would be the sense of smell? But as it is, God arranged the members in the body, each one of them, as he chose. If all were a single member, where would the body be? As it is, there are many parts, yet one body. The eye cannot say to the hand, 'I have no need of you,' nor again the head to the feet, 'I have no need of you.' On the contrary, the parts of the body that seem to be weaker are indispensable, and on those parts of the body that we think less honorable we bestow the greater honor, and our unpresentable parts are treated with greater modesty, which our more presentable parts do not require. But God has so composed the body, giving greater honor to the part that lacked it, that there may be no division in the body, but that the members may have the same care for one another. If one member

suffers, all suffer together; if one member is honored, all rejoice together. Now you are the body of Christ and individually members of it."
-I Corinthians 12:12-27

Jesus created His Church to resemble a body. A body cannot function properly with just one member in operation. Each member of the body is dependent on each other. No man is an island. A man alone on an island will eventually die. However, a body that works in unison is a flourishing body that can accomplish great feats. Concerning the Body of Christ, we will only come to a place of unison when we walk in humility, esteeming one another more highly than ourselves.

Further, we have a promise from Jesus that if we walk willingly in humility, He will reward us. Looking once more to the passage from James, he writes, "Humble yourselves before the Lord, and he will exalt you" (James 4:10). The word "exalt" is "hypsoō" and it refers to elevating one to a high, and lofty position. In essence, the position, power, and prestige that the prideful selfishly seek after, God will freely give to those who recognize their dependency upon Him and others.

Jesus also gave us a parable speaking on this very thing. He says:

"When you are invited by someone to a wedding feast, do not sit down in a place of honor, lest someone more distinguished than you be invited by him, and he who invited you both will come and say to you, 'Give your place to this person,' and then you will begin with shame to take the lowest place. But when you are invited, go and sit in the lowest place, so that when your host comes he may say to you, 'Friend, move up higher.' Then you will be honored in the presence of all who sit at table with you. For everyone who exalts himself will be humbled, and he who humbles himself will be exalted."
-Luke 14:7-11

When we operate out of pride and seek to elevate ourselves, we will, inevitably, be humiliated when it is revealed that we are not worthy of that lofty position. However, if we humbly accept a lowly position and don't assume we are deserving of anything more, He will come and say, "Come up higher, My friend."

The second aspect of worship, then, is that of surrender. The word "surrender" is defined by Oxford Languages as, "to cease resistance…and submit to authority." Webster's Dictionary defines it as "to yield; to give up one's self into the power of another." In essence, to surrender is to lay down one's life and to place it in the hands of another. In doing this, we are indicating that the one whose hands we are placing our life into is greater than ourselves.

Earlier we quoted Mark 8:34-38 wherein Jesus says, "If anyone would come after me, let him deny himself and take up his cross and follow me. For whoever would save his life will lose it, but whoever loses his life for my sake and the gospel's will save it. For what does it profit a man to gain the whole world and forfeit his soul? For what can a man give in return for his soul? For whoever is ashamed of me and of my words in this adulterous and sinful generation, of him will the Son of Man also be ashamed when he comes in the glory of his Father with the holy angels." This falls right in line with the topic of surrender, but other key passages speak on this topic of surrender.

One well-known account from the Gospels is between Jesus and the rich young ruler. We read:

> And as he was setting out on his journey, a man ran up and knelt before him and asked him, "Good Teacher, what must I do to inherit eternal life?" And Jesus said to him, "Why do you call me good? No one is good except God alone. You know the commandments: Do not murder, Do not commit adultery, Do not steal, Do not bear false witness, Do not defraud, Honor your father and mother.'" And he said to him, "Teacher, all these I have kept from my youth." And Jesus, looking at him, loved him, and said to him, "You lack one thing: go, sell all that you have and give to the poor, and you will have treasure in heaven; and come,

follow me." Disheartened by the saying, he went away sorrowful, for he had great possessions.
-Mark 10:17-22

The young ruler sought from Jesus what it takes to inherit eternal life. According to the Law, the young man lived a very devoted life, however, Jesus longed for him to have more. The text says that He "loved him." The word "loved" is "agapaō" and one meaning it can have is, "to be well pleased with." Jesus was proud of what this young man had done and the life he had lived. Therefore, He wanted him to have more. However, the path to more came by the way of surrender.

The rich young ruler was just that, rich. To be rich is not wrong or evil, the Bible often says that Jesus desires to bless His children in many ways, one of which is financial. However, while wealth can be a wonderful tool for the growth of His Kingdom, it can also be a subtle poison that slowly eats away at us from the inside out. The rich young ruler outwardly lived a life of sincere devotion, but this call to surrender revealed the state of his inner man. Jesus called him to surrender, but the young ruler had already surrendered to another power: wealth.

Jesus spoke on this war between God and monetary gain. He said:

"Do not lay up for yourselves treasures on earth, where moth and rust destroy and where thieves break in and steal, but lay up for yourselves treasures in heaven, where neither moth nor rust destroys and where thieves do not break in and steal. For where your treasure is, there your heart will be also. The eye is the lamp of the body. So, if your eye is healthy, your whole body will be full of light, but if your eye is bad, your whole body will be full of darkness. If then the light in you is darkness, how great is the darkness! No one can serve two masters, for either he will hate the one and love the other, or he will be devoted to the one and despise the other. You cannot serve God and money."
-Matthew 6:19-24

To surrender to money is to surrender to the world and its corrupt system. In doing so, we fill our whole inward man with darkness. However, to surrender to God and diligently pursue the things of His Kingdom is to bask in His life and light. Just as light and dark cannot coexist, one cannot surrender to both God and monetary gain.

Furthermore, surrender reaches beyond our wealth. At the close of Luke 9, we read of three short interactions between Jesus and would-be disciples. It says:

> "As they were going along the road, someone said to him, 'I will follow you wherever you go.' And Jesus said to him, 'Foxes have holes, and birds of the air have nests, but the Son of Man has nowhere to lay his head.' To another he said, 'Follow me.' But he said, 'Lord, let me first go and bury my father.' And Jesus said to him, 'Leave the dead to bury their own dead. But as for you, go and proclaim the kingdom of God.' Yet another said, 'I will follow you, Lord, but let me first say farewell to those at my home.' Jesus said to him, 'No one who puts his hand to the plow and looks back is fit for the kingdom of God.'"
> -Luke 9:57-62

What should we surmise from this text? One question: are we willing to live a life of surrender unto Him even when it is not comfortable, convenient, and easy? To surrender is to yield to the authority of another. It is to place our lives in the hands of one greater than ourselves. So when we can't stay in a 5-Star hotel but are forced to sleep under the stars, will we remain surrendered? Or if His will does not align with how we have things planned out, will we remain surrendered? Finally, when the work we do for His Kingdom is tiresome and hard, will we remain surrendered?

Whoever said surrender was easy? Jesus understood it wasn't and He also understood that most people don't understand what they are doing when they claim to surrender. Jesus spoke on these things when he said:

"If anyone comes to me and does not hate his own father and mother and wife and children and brothers and sisters, yes, and even his own life, he cannot be my disciple. Whoever does not bear his own cross and come after me cannot be my disciple. For which of you, desiring to build a tower, does not first sit down and count the cost, whether he has enough to complete it? Otherwise, when he has laid a foundation and is not able to finish, all who see it begin to mock him, saying, 'This man began to build and was not able to finish.' Or what king, going out to encounter another king in war, will not sit down first and deliberate whether he is able with ten thousand to meet him who comes against him with twenty thousand? And if not, while the other is yet a great way off, he sends a delegation and asks for terms of peace. So therefore, any one of you who does not renounce all that he has cannot be my disciple"
-Luke 14:26-33

One thing I have seen a lot of people trip up over is this statement from Jesus saying that we are to hate our own family. It is important to understand that Jesus is not actually calling us to hate our families. We will discuss this in a subsequent chapter, but He calls us to love even our worst enemy, never to hate. What Jesus was indicating was that our devotion and surrender unto Him ought to be so profound that every other relationship, even with those closest to us, ought to pale in comparison. It is a call to place Him as supreme priority, high above all others.

Jesus goes on to discuss how anyone who does not think about what they set out to do before they do it is setting themselves up for failure. He calls us all to a life of surrender, but are we prepared to surrender? Do we know what that means? He tells us exactly what that means: "Any one of you who does not renounce all that he has cannot be my disciple." "Renounce" is "apotassomai" which means, "to renounce; to forsake; to withdraw one's self from." The only way we can ever truly claim to be His followers is by taking our lives and saying, "I yield it all to You." Anything less is not enough. We must, at a moment's notice, be prepared to lay everything aside for Him. If there is anything that causes us to hesitate then we have not surrendered unto Him and surrendered unto another.

Paul put it this way,

> "But whatever gain I had, I counted as loss for the sake of Christ. Indeed, I count everything as loss because of the surpassing worth of knowing Christ Jesus my Lord. For his sake I have suffered the loss of all things and count them as rubbish, in order that I may gain Christ and be found in him, not having a righteousness of my own that comes from the law, but that which comes through faith in Christ, the righteousness from God that depends on faith— that I may know him and the power of his resurrection, and may share his sufferings, becoming like him in his death, that by any means possible I may attain the resurrection from the dead."
> -Philippians 3:7-11

Bringing this all into one train of thought: while worship may be expressed through songs that magnify Him and exalt His nature, it is more perfectly understood as a lifestyle. Worship is self-sacrifice. To worship is to continually die daily to our carnal man and its desires while exalting Him and His desires. To worship is to live a life of humility, understanding that everything good in us is of Him and apart from Him we can do nothing. Finally, to worship is to surrender it all to Him. To be willing at a moment's notice to lay everything aside. It is to count everything as dung compared to Him and His will.

I want to take a brief moment here and discuss fasting, for it directly correlates to a lifestyle of worship and ought to be practiced by every professing Christian.

Jesus said, "And when you fast, do not look gloomy like the hypocrites, for they disfigure their faces that their fasting may be seen by others. Truly, I say to you, they have received their reward.

But when you fast, anoint your head and wash your face, that your fasting may not be seen by others but by your Father who is in secret. And your Father who sees in secret will reward you" (Matthew 6:16-18). First, regarding fasting, Jesus said, "when you fast." The word "when" is "hotan" implying both expectancy and frequency. Therefore, contrary to the popular belief of some, fasting is not something only for the religious elite but is expected for all people who claim to follow Him.

After setting the standard for fasting, Jesus continues by demonstrating how we are to carry ourselves as we fast. The religious leaders of the day were all about receiving attention from the people. They did this in various ways, from the way they prayed (see Matthew 6:5), to how they gave (see Matthew 6:2), and, as demonstrated above, how they fasted. The religious leaders took spiritual disciplines that were meant to be practiced in a place of private intimacy with God and made them a public spectacle. That is why, after drawing attention to their wrong way of doing things, He said, "They have received their reward," implying that the only reward they would receive was the attention of men, but not the attention of God.

Fasting is not meant to be a public spectacle that you announce on Facebook. If you fast properly, no one should even know that you are, indeed, fasting. That is what Jesus demonstrated in the second half of this passage. Don't allow your countenance to be lowly and depressed, but carry yourself as you normally would before those around you. Again, seek the attention of God and not of man.

But what does it mean to fast and what is its purpose? The traditional view regarding fasting is to abstain from food for a duration of time. The Greek word for "fast," "nēsteuō," agrees with this assessment. The reason that food is often the primary focus of a fast is because of the body's need for it. When you deny the body food you are denying it a basic necessity. Some may ask, what is the point of that? Without starting down a theological rabbit trail, because of the sinful nature we were all born with in our flesh, we must work to deny that sinful nature while, simultaneously, glorifying the spiritual nature within us that is aligned with Christ. By denying a basic necessity of the body we, thereby, gain control over it, therefore allowing us to better abide by His holy nature and not our sinful nature. To this point though, we must note that it is not merely about denying the flesh. If all we do is deny the flesh and nothing more, then what have we gained? The flesh will rise right back up to its former place. Rather, when we fast, we need to simultaneously feed our spiritual man through increased intake of His Word and increased engagement in prayer.

Jesus demonstrated this for us. After His baptism (which was not unto repentance but a humbling of Himself, in His flesh, unto what He was called to do) at the close of Matthew 3, the narrative transitions at the start of Matthew 4 to Him being led by the Spirit into the wilderness. We are told that it was in this setting that He fasted for forty days and forty nights (see Matthew 4:2). We must understand that since He was manifest in human flesh, He now had within Him the ability to sin. Thus, before He began His earthly ministry, He had to bring His flesh into submission to the Spirit of YAHWEH within Him.

Jesus fasted for forty days and forty nights, then, at the end of said fast, was tempted by Lucifer. It was a test of His submission that was brought through fasting. Was He truly submitted to the Spirit in His flesh? We all know the answer to that question was yes. But if Jesus had not fasted and brought His flesh into submission the way that He did, would His ministry have been as impactful?

Now I place the attention on you and me; how much more impactful would we be as Christians if we regularly denied our flesh and brought it into submission to His Spirit? Follow-up question: would we better exemplify a lifestyle of worship if we frequently engaged in fasting? I believe the answer to that question is an emphatic, "Yes."

Bringing all this to final focus; we opened this chapter by quoting John 4:24: "God is spirit, and those who worship him must worship in spirit and truth." We understand what it means to worship now, but how do we worship in spirit and truth?

Looking to Greek, the word "spirit" is "pneuma" which is typically translated as "spirit," however, it can refer to various other things all of which pertain to the inward man or the inward part of our being. "Truth" is "alētheia" which can refer to sincerity or to truth that has been revealed. From my own experience, when I have heard a great man or woman of God teach from this passage they have always approached it as referring to two different aspects of worship. I do not discount the various interpretations of this Scripture, but during my study, I was drawn toward a different conclusion. It seems to me that to "worship in spirit and truth" is not referring to two different aspects of worship, but rightly defining how worship ought to be expressed.

As we demonstrated, the word for "spirit" ("pneuma") always pertains to the inward part of our being, and "truth" ("alētheia") can be defined as, "sincerity." One way this could be understood is that worship is not meant to be an outward spectacle or show for those around. Worship is not meant to draw the attention of men but of God. Therefore, worship does not begin outwardly, but rather inwardly. For as He told Samuel, while men look at the outward, He looks at the heart (see I Samuel 16:7). Additionally, He does not want worship that is performed out of obligation or duty, but love. Or, in other words, sincerity. To offer insincere worship is to not worship at all. Therefore, when we come to Him in worship, it needs to begin in our inward man where only He can see it and be given sincerely.

Do we esteem Him worthy of our worship? We need to ask ourselves this question in light of its proper understanding.

Focused Reflection

Worship is not a concept foreign to the majority of people. Take a glance all around the world to the various cultures and their various religions and you will see people engaging in what they prescribe to be worship. But what does it mean to offer biblical worship? If you sought to ask various professing Christians, you would likely receive a plethora of answers. The various answers you receive may not necessarily be wrong, but they also may not truly encompass what it means to worship.

Biblical worship is sacrifice. Sacrifice in our day and age is somewhat of a foreign topic. In our culture, we do not regularly engage in acts of sacrifice. For the Jews, however, sacrifice was embedded into the heart of all that they did. It is no accident that Leviticus (the third book of the Torah) is largely dedicated to the topic of proper sacrifice. While we may no longer be required to engage in animal sacrifice (and thank God for it), we are still called to engage in sacrifice.

1. When you think of "sacrifice," where does your mind go?

2. If you were to engage in an act of sacrifice, what would that look like?

3. How often would you say that sacrifice is present in your life?

I appeal to you therefore, brothers, by the mercies of God, to present your bodies as a living sacrifice, holy and acceptable to God, which is your spiritual worship.
-Romans 12:1

7
Christians Are People of Sacrifice
Christians Are Worshippers II

Jesus looked up and saw the rich putting their gifts into the offering box, and he saw a poor widow put in two small copper coins. And he said, "Truly, I tell you, this poor widow has put in more than all of them. For they all contributed out of their abundance, but she out of her poverty put in all she had to live on."
~Luke 21:1-4

We would be remiss if, in our discussion of worship, we failed to touch on sacrifice. In the previous chapter we, indeed, touched on sacrifice. However, our focus pertained to being a living sacrifice (as Paul put it) and how we live that out in our everyday lives. There remains an additional aspect to sacrifice that bears discussion. That is, sacrificing things in our possession.

Before we dive into how this vein of sacrifice plays out in our lives, it is pertinent that we examine the concept behind our sacrifice. A common question revolves around why we are admonished to sacrifice our possessions. Part of the issue is the word "possession." Oxford Languages defines this word as, "the state of having, owning, or controlling something." Speaking to the mindset of Western culture (because it is what I am accustomed to), we are all about possession. In our way of thinking, the more one possesses, the more important or powerful they are. If someone possesses a large amount of money, we regard them as high class and seek to live in like manner as them. If someone possesses a large quantity of books, we esteem them to be studious and learned. These are just two brief examples of this mindset regarding numerous possessions. However, the opposite is also true in our way of thinking. If someone possesses little money, we regard them as poor and destitute, having no desire to be anything like them. In essence, we judge a person not by who they truly are, but by what they possess. This is a very interesting state of mind for several reasons, one being that many individuals in Western culture own very little of what they seemingly "possess." In truth, much of what is "possessed" is owned by another, and the "possessor" pays the one who owns the thing. Thus, our measuring stick is not based in truth, but in falsehood.

There remains another interesting point regarding this concept of "possession." That is, even if one truly owns a thing (according to how Western authorities determine such things), that thing is still not theirs. What do I mean? How is it not theirs if they possess it?

The psalmist David recorded, "The earth is the LORD's and the fullness thereof, the world and those who dwell therein, for he has founded it upon the seas and established it upon the rivers" (Psalms 24:1-2). Further, in case we attempted to relegate this statement to merely refer to things in nature, He declares, "The silver is mine, and the gold is mine, declares the LORD of hosts" (Haggai 2:8). Some may ask how God can claim ownership rights over all things. He establishes the answer to such at the very beginning. "In the beginning, God created the heavens and the earth" (Genesis 1:1). The remainder of Genesis 1, and the first part of Genesis 2, give us insight into how He brought all of creation into being. Being the One who brought everything into existence, does it not, therefore, follow that He possesses unique ownership rights over all things? When an artist crafts a new work of art, do they not stamp it with their signature signifying that the rights to that work are theirs? Others may enjoy that work, but they cannot claim it as their own. It is the same way with Jesus and His creation. He created all things, placed His signature on it all that points back to Him (see Romans 1:20), and allows others to enjoy His creation while maintaining ownership of it.

The question becomes, if He exercises ownership over all things, allowing us to enjoy His handiwork, what, then, does that make us? To put it simply: stewards. What is a steward? Webster's Dictionary defines "steward" as "a man employed in great families to manage the domestic concerns, superintend the other servants, collect the rents or income, keep the accounts." To put it simply, a steward is one who is trusted by another to keep watch over and carefully manage their possessions. What a steward manages is not their own, upon the return of the owner the steward is expected to return the possessions to the owner. However, while the steward manages the possessions, they are expected to manage them with care as if they were their possessions.

Jesus gave us the Parable of the Talents which demonstrates for us the relationship between a master and a steward. It reads:

"For it will be like a man going on a journey, who called his servants and entrusted to them his property. To one he gave five talents, to another two, to another one, to each according to his ability. Then he went away. He who had received the five talents went at once and traded with them, and he made five talents more. So also he who had the two talents made two talents more. But he who had received the one talent went and dug in the ground and hid his master's money. Now after a long time the master of those servants came and settled accounts with them. And he who had received the five talents came forward, bringing five talents more, saying, 'Master, you delivered to me five talents; here, I have made five talents more.' His master said to him, 'Well done, good and faithful servant. You have been faithful over a little; I will set you over much. Enter into the joy of your master.' And he also who had the two talents came forward, saying, 'Master, you delivered to me two talents; here, I have made two talents more.' His master said to him, 'Well done, good and faithful servant. You have been faithful over a little; I will set you over much. Enter into the joy of your master.' He also who had received the one talent came forward, saying, 'Master, I knew you to be a hard man, reaping where you did not sow, and gathering where you scattered no seed, so I was afraid, and I went and

hid your talent in the ground. Here, you have what is yours.' But his master answered him, 'You wicked and slothful servant! You knew that I reap where I have not sown and gather where I scattered no seed? Then you ought to have invested my money with the bankers, and at my coming I should have received what was my own with interest. So take the talent from him and give it to him who has the ten talents. For to everyone who has will more be given, and he will have an abundance. But from the one who has not, even what he has will be taken away. And cast the worthless servant into the outer darkness. In that place there will be weeping and gnashing of teeth.'"
-Matthew 25:14-30

This is a lengthy parable, so we won't go through it like a fine-toothed comb. The main points of the parable are readily obvious: the master bestowed to the servants parts of his possessions for them to manage in his absence; two of the servants acted respectively and obediently to their master by multiplying what he had given them for his kingdom sake, one, however, out of unjustified fear, forsook what had been entrusted to him; upon his return, the servants returned what had been entrusted to them and he blessed the two who were faithful and cursed the unfaithful one.

It is interesting to note how even though what was given to the servants was not theirs to keep, at his return the master blessed the two who were faithful by bestowing upon them more than what they had before. Therefore, instead of losing what had been entrusted to them, they multiplied. That is an interesting concept. Their faithfulness toward what was not even theirs produced a multiplied blessing in their lives. This is a key point to keep in remembrance. When we demonstrate our faithfulness to God by living as obedient stewards, He abundantly blesses us.

In another place, Jesus said, "One who is faithful in a very little is also faithful in much, and one who is dishonest in a very little is also dishonest in much. If then you have not been faithful in the unrighteous wealth, who will entrust to you the true riches? And if you have not been faithful in that which is another's, who will give you that which is your own? No servant can serve two masters, for either he will hate the one and love the other, or he will be devoted to the one and despise the other. You cannot serve God and money" (Luke 16:10-13). One thing my pastor, Pastor Brian Lane, says is that our checkbooks are theological documents. Why? Because one can easily discern who we serve, be it God or money, based on how we manage our finances.

How, then, do we become good and faithful stewards of the finances that He blesses us with? The immediate response most people have is tithing. Tithing can be traced back to the time of Abraham. We read of an interaction between Abram (later Abraham) and Melchizedek (who many believe was a theophany of God). Melchidezek bestows upon Abram a mighty blessing, and Abram responds by giving Melchidezek a tenth of everything (see Genesis 14:18-20). A tithe is just that, a tenth of a thing. Further, we find the principle of tithing all throughout Scripture (see Genesis 28:20-22; Leviticus 27:30; Malachi 3:10; Matthew 23:23 just to list a few examples).

One vitally important point that needs to be considered when discussing tithing is the focus of such. What do I mean? How should we be practicing tithing? Solomon in his wisdom gave us insight into this. He said, "Honor the LORD with your possessions, and with the first fruits of all your increase; so your barns will be filled with plenty, and your vats will overflow with new wine. (Proverbs 3:9-10 NKJV). The key point from this passage is found in the phrase, "first fruits of all your increase." The word "firstfruit" is "rê'shîyth" which can be translated as "first; beginning." Furthermore, the Hebrew word for "of all" is "kôl" meaning, "all; whole; any; each; every; totality." Finally, the word "increase" is "tebû'âh" which means, "income; revenue; gain." Therefore, the proper practice of tithing is to take the first tenth off of any and every source of financial increase. Meaning, before the government takes their share, you give God His share. What do I mean? To honor Him with the first fruits is to tithe off gross, not net. Further, it is not just increase from paychecks, but all increase (as the word for "all" indicates). Meaning, even if it is a financial gift bestowed upon you by another, tithe on it.

While tithing is a critical way we practice good stewardship, it is not sacrifice. Allow me to make it plain: tithing is expected, therefore, it is not sacrifice. Looking back to what was said at the start; all that we seemingly have is His, not ours. What we seemingly possess is a gift from God to us. Tithing is merely us honoring the One who blesses us by giving Him back a portion of what is His. That is why Solomon said to "Honor the LORD" by tithing.

If, then, tithing is not sacrifice but is expected, how do we engage in this level of sacrifice? Jesus reveals to us another principle of giving in Malachi 3:8, "Will a man rob God? Yet you have robbed Me! But you say, 'In what way have we robbed You?' In tithes and offerings" (NKJV). The second principle of giving presented to us is that of "offerings." What is an offering? I have heard and read various ministers make different assessments regarding what an offering is. I have even heard some say that there is a specific percentage amount attributed to offerings. I confess I have not uncovered such in my own study. However, I likewise confess that these are more learned men than I and I humble myself before their wisdom. All I can convey to you here is what I have come to understand, by the grace of God, through my own study.

Through my own study, I have not come to find a particular number or percentage associated with the giving of offerings. There is, however, an underlying principle that makes up the core of this giving principle. The word "offerings" (as from Malachi 3:8) is "terûmâh" which, on the surface, merely means, "an offering." Looking beyond the mere surface of the word we find that it refers to something that is high, exalted, lofty, and such the like. The concept that this word then creates revolves around giving something of great value.

The Bible is replete with example after example of individuals bestowing unto God offerings of great value. We will look at this example more in-depth in a subsequent chapter, but the story of Cain and Abel reflects this truth. We see that Abel brought the firstborn out of his flock (see Genesis 4:4). How is this an offering of great value? The text implies that Abel showed no partiality in his offering. Meaning, even if the firstborn showed signs of being the strongest and had the best potential, he did not waiver on his covenant promise. Even if it meant losing a great specimen, he honored Jesus with his offering of great value.

Another example we could use is that of Abraham and Isaac (see Genesis 22:1-14). We all know the story well; God calls to Abraham and tells him that he is to offer his promised son, whom he loves, unto Him. Talk about an offering of great value. Despite the seemingly insurmountable task presented to him, Abraham diligently set out to do what he felt God had commanded him to do.

This concept of offering something of great value is not relegated only to the Old Testament. We can look to the New Testament as well and readily find numerous examples of this same practice. We read in the Book of Acts, "And all who believed were together and had all things in common. And they were selling their possessions and belongings and distributing the proceeds to all, as any had need" (Acts 2:44-45). And we again read just a few chapters later, "Now the full number of those who believed were of one heart and soul, and no one said that any of the things that belonged to him was his own, but they had everything in common…There was not a needy person among them, for as many as were owners of lands or houses sold them and brought the proceeds of what was sold and laid it at the apostles' feet, and it was distributed to each as any had need" (Acts 4:32,34-35).

Additionally, we could look to Paul's second epistle to the Corinthian Church and read his praise attributed to the Church of Macedonia. We read of how they experienced a severe test of poverty, yet, despite their poverty, gave willingly above their means (see II Corinthians 8:1-5).

Therefore, what we come to understand about the sacrifice of offering is that it is not truly an offering unless it is something of great value in our lives. Another, more direct, way we could word this would be: it is not a sacrificial offering unless it hurts. It all points back to who you choose to serve. When you understand that Jesus owns everything you are no longer concerned about hoarding your possessions for security's sake. When you place your finances in His hands you understand that He has the power to multiply them beyond your understanding. We discussed in the previous chapter how, in His Kingdom, death proceeds life. The same is true regarding sacrificial offering: giving proceeds getting. However, if you refuse to sacrificially give and instead choose to hold onto what you think you possess, one, it shows that you truly serve money and not God, and two, you will end up losing that which you thought you had. Remember, everything we seemingly possess is simply gifted to us by Him who owns it all.

Thus, we come full circle and return to our focus text for this discussion. It reads:

> Jesus looked up and saw the rich putting their gifts into the offering box, and he saw a poor widow put in two small copper coins. And he said, "Truly, I tell you, this poor widow has put in more than all of them. For they all contributed out of their abundance, but she out of her poverty put in all she had to live on."
> -Luke 21:1-4

To someone who looked only at the quantity of the gift and not the quality, it would have seemed as if the rich were offering more than the widow. Surely, in terms of monetary estimation, they did give more. However, while their gifts were of great monetary value, they were of little sacrificial value. In truth, what they were offering was not great at all. For to them, what they offered was mere pocket change. Looking to the poor widow, however, we see a very different story. By the standard of quantity, her gift was next to nothing. If you study it out, the two coins she gave would equal close to the value of two pennies in American culture. Yet, those two pennies are all she had. If you merely looked at the gift in terms of monetary value, hers would be scoffed at. But her gift was a true sacrificial offering.

I am not saying that we need to pull all our life savings out of the bank this very second. However, if He calls you to do that, then do it. What I am saying is that to truly live a life of worship is to live a life of sacrifice. This life of sacrifice is not only relegated to the denial of our flesh, as we discussed in the previous chapter, but in freely giving unto Him that which we value. Whatever we keep a firm hold of in our lives conveys what we live for and worship. If we hold onto Him then we will trust Him with our finances and know that He will always provide. Likewise, if we hold onto our money then it demonstrates that we trust the systems of this world more than the One who owns it.

I've heard it said, "I can't afford to give," but I say to you, "You can't afford not to give."

Focused Reflection

Throughout various cultures around the world, possessions hold great value for a plethora of reasons. Some attribute possessions to status, others even to deity. Whatever the precise ideology is regarding possessions within the various cultures around the world, the fact of the matter is that possessions are of high value to us as human beings.

This high level of value that is placed on possessions is extremely dangerous, as it can create a system of idolatry surrounding a particular possession or possessions as a whole. Jesus said very plainly, "No one can serve two masters, for either he will hate the one and love the other, or he will be devoted to the one and despise the other. You cannot serve God and money" (Matthew 6:24). Culture says to place value on and pursue possessions, whereas God says to place value on the things of His Kingdom and to pursue Him. Despite what we might desire, we cannot have both.

1. Is there a particular possessions (or multiple possessions) in your life that you place a high value on? If so, why?

2. Think about that thing (or those things) in your life that you hold in high esteem; how would you respond if God asked you to give them up sacrificially?

3. To what do we attribute the greater level of value, God or possessions? And to what do we bestow a greater level of love, God or possessions? Which do you pursue?

But seek first the kingdom of God and his righteousness, and all these things will be added to you.
-Matthew 6:33

8

Christians Are People of Rest
Christians Are Worshippers III

"Come to me, all who labor and are heavy laden, and
I will give you rest. Take my yoke upon you, and
learn from me, for I am gentle and lowly in heart, and
you will find rest for your souls. For my yoke is easy,
and my burden is light."
~Matthew 11:28-30

What a fantastic seeming contradiction.

In the previous two chapters, Christians are Worshippers
and Christians are People of Sacrifice, our main focus has been
living a life of worship. We have endeavored to demonstrate how
to live a life of worship is to live sacrificially. In the former chapter,
Christians are Worshippers, we sought to convey how this life
of sacrifice plays out in everyday living. We talked about how it
requires a death to self, and how, in His Kingdom, death proceeds
life. Further, we illustrated how this death is a perpetual affair, not
a one-time occurrence. This death to self must be played out daily,
lest that carnal man rears its ugly head within us. Furthermore, in
the latter chapter, Christians are People of Sacrifice, we focused
our attention on our finances. We showed how everything is His
and we are merely stewards of it. Relating to this, we demonstrated
how giving tithe is our way of honoring Him by returning to Him a
portion of what is already His. However, giving tithe is not sacrifice,
it is expected. To sacrifice is to give an offering. This is when it
truly becomes an act of worship. For an offering is not given out of
abundance, but out of need. To give an offering is to emphatically
declare to Jesus that you trust Him and His ability to provide more
than you do in this world's systems.

In both chapters, the worship discussed required great effort,
intentionality, and even pain. Consequently, there seems to be little
to no rest involved with worship. Regardless of how it may seem,

rest is an integral aspect of worship. In fact, I would go so far as to say that one cannot truly exercise worship unless they engage in rest. But what does it mean to worship through rest?

To understand this vital aspect of worship, we need to go back to the beginning. As we demonstrated in the chapter, Christians are Monotheistic, the Christian faith is birthed out of the Jewish faith. The truths presented in the Old Testament are still true for us today because they serve as a type and shadow of the various aspects of the New Testament. Therefore, we see the practice of rest first demonstrated by God Himself.

Looking to the creation account, we read:

> And God saw everything that he had made, and behold, it was very good. And there was evening and there was morning, the sixth day. Thus the heavens and the earth were finished, and all the host of them. And on the seventh day God finished his work that he had done, and he rested on the seventh day from all his work that he had done. So God blessed the seventh day and made it holy, because on it God rested from all his work that he had done in creation.
> -Genesis 1:31-2:3

The word "rested" in Hebrew is "shâbath." Look familiar? It should. Although, we more readily recognize it as Sabbath, the official day of rest in Judaism. God Himself demonstrated this practice of rest for us. He observed all He had done, declared it "very good" and then proceeded to simply bask in what He had done. The words used in "very good" are telling regarding what God thought of His handiwork. The word "very" is "me'od" which always refers to an abundance of a thing, or "muchness," and "good" is "ṭôb" which does not just mean that something is pleasing or acceptable, but more perfectly refers to a thing being fully complete and functional. Therefore, we could define "very good" as "abundantly complete." Meaning, that He saw nothing lacking, but everything perfectly positioned and functional.

When revealing the Law to Moses, one of the Ten

Commandments given to him was:

> "Remember the Sabbath day, to keep it holy. Six days you shall labor, and do all your work, but the seventh day is a Sabbath to the LORD your God. On it you shall not do any work, you, or your son, or your daughter, your male servant, or your female servant, or your livestock, or the sojourner who is within your gates. For in six days the LORD made heaven and earth, the sea, and all that is in them, and rested on the seventh day. Therefore the LORD blessed the Sabbath day and made it holy."
> -Exodus 20:8-11

Why did God call the Israelites to partake of this act of rest? It all revolves around those two words, "very good," or "abundantly complete." He declared that nothing was lacking in His creation, therefore, He simply basked in it. Likewise, He called Israel to recognize that all that He had done was perfect and complete, nothing lacking, and to simply bask in it. The Sabbath Day was given to the people as a day of refocusing and re-centering. The previous six days of the week had been filled with work, turmoil, stress, anxiety, and so on. The previous six days were all focused on doing. What needs to be done? This mindset forces our attention off of God and what He has done and fixes it on what we are doing. In essence, the attention is placed more on us than it is on Him. God recognized the need for work. The people needed to work the land and tend the animals in order to thrive and prosper. However, He did not want His people to become consumed in their work, but to take time and refocus on Him.

Keeping our focus solely on what needs to be done creates this prison within our own minds. There is no peace or enjoyment because there is always something lacking. However, when we stop, and turn our attention to Him, we come to realize that it is all "very good."

Unfortunately, as time went on, certain groups within Israel took the Law and turned it into something that it was never meant to be. To fully understand the background to all this would require a full-on history lesson. Such is not our focus here. However, a brief explanation proves beneficial. In short, Israel was given the Law but then continuously abandoned the Law. In time, Israel and Judah (as they were split) were conquered by two different nations. Through self-reflection, some of the people came to understand that their exile was a result of their forsaking the Law. Thereby, this group endeavored to emphatically return to the Law and go above and beyond in keeping it so that they would never be exiled again. This led to the formation of the group known as the Pharisees.

One of the Laws that the Pharisees twisted from its original intent was the Sabbath. The Sabbath, as mentioned above, was intended to be a day of peace wherein you re-centered and refocused on Jesus. The Pharisees, however, took this idea of "no work" to the extreme. Through their over-emphasizing of Scripture, so many tedious things became defined as "work." In essence, the Sabbath Day became a day where you had to sit there and do nothing, or else you were guilty of "work." They failed to understand that by "work" God meant self-focused productivity.

We then fast-forward to Jesus' day; time and time again it is recorded throughout the Gospels Jesus doing "work" on the Sabbath. There are countless examples of this we could use, but one, I feel, demonstrates the spirit of the Sabbath the best. We read, "One Sabbath he was going through the grainfields, and as they made their way, his disciples began to pluck heads of grain. And the Pharisees were saying to him, 'Look, why are they doing what is not lawful on the Sabbath?' And he said to them, 'Have you never read what David did, when he was in need and was hungry, he and those who were with him: how he entered the house of God, in the time of Abiathar the high priest, and ate the bread of the Presence, which it is not lawful for any but the priests to eat, and also gave it to those who were with him'" (Mark 2:23-26)?

The Pharisees created such restrictions surrounding the Sabbath to the point of self-harm. They utterly failed to recognize the heart of God. In Matthew's account, he adds at the end, "And if you had known what this means, 'I desire mercy, and not sacrifice,' you would not have condemned the guiltless" (Matthew 12:7). We will address the meaning of this Scripture momentarily.

Returning to the text from Mark; after dismantling the Pharisees argument, He then says, "The Sabbath was made for man, not man for the Sabbath. So the Son of Man is lord even of the Sabbath" (Mark 2:27-28). What is He saying? By Him saying that the "Sabbath was made for man, not man for the Sabbath," He is conveying that the Sabbath was meant to benefit the people, not restrict them. The Sabbath Day was never meant to be a day full of begrudging due to the numerous restrictions, but a day of peace. Again, the Sabbath Day was given so that the people would re-center their attention on Him and simply bask in what He had done. As to His statement, "So the Son of Man is lord even of the Sabbath," this was a testament to His deity and to the truth that He implemented the Sabbath. Thereby indicating that He was the Creator. If you need a refresher on Jesus being the ultimate revelation of the One true God, I would recommend revisiting the second chapter of this book, Christians are Monotheistic.

Continuing with this story, Mark 3 picks up immediately after this interaction and says, "Again he entered the synagogue, and a man was there with a withered hand. And they watched Jesus, to see whether he would heal him on the Sabbath so that they might accuse him. And he said to the man with the withered hand, 'Come here.' And he said to them, 'Is it lawful on the Sabbath to do good or to do harm, to save life or to kill?' But they were silent. And he looked around at them with anger, grieved at their hardness of heart, and said to the man, 'Stretch out your hand.' He stretched it out, and his hand was restored" (Mark 3:1-5). Again, this points us back to what was recorded in Matthew, "I desire mercy, and not sacrifice." Jesus, in essence, echoed this phrase by asking the question, "Is it lawful on the Sabbath to do good or to do harm, to save life or to kill?" Would it be breaking the Sabbath if you saved the life of someone who would die without your intervention? Remember, this is absolutely key, the purpose of the Sabbath was to refocus on Jesus and bask in His goodness. Keeping this in mind, we return to the question posed by Jesus. If someone was in dire need of help on Sabbath, what would cause them to bask in His goodness more readily, if you ignored them or if you helped them? I pray the answer is clear.

The Sabbath Day was never about the strict abolition of all "work," but was a day given so that we would bask in His goodness. It was a call to turn from self-focus to Him-focus.

The question becomes, what does this have to do with us? We are not under the Old Covenant, therefore, we do not observe the Sabbath. Well, yes, that is true, but also, no, that is wrong. Remember, everything written of old was a type and shadow of things to come. Meaning, the Sabbath is for us today, just not in the same sense.

The author of Hebrews, who I believe to be Apollos, had much to say about this rest throughout the epistle. There is much too great a quantity of passages regarding this for us to discuss here. Drawing attention to one, however, we read, "So then, there remains a Sabbath rest for the people of God, for whoever has entered God's rest has also rested from his works as God did from his. Let us therefore strive to enter that rest, so that no one may fall by the same sort of disobedience" (Hebrews 4:9-11). There is much that could be said regarding this passage, but we will make it plain; the author of Hebrews here is conveying that His Spirit (which is where we find our rest) allows us to rest from salvation through works (for He has fulfilled those works of righteousness and now imputes that righteousness to us by His Spirit).

However, this is not the end of the matter. We cannot close our discussion here, for we still have not fully presented this idea of rest. It is of the utmost importance that we understand that we no longer practice salvation through works. This concept places salvation in the hands of men, not God. We could never save ourselves. That is why He came and lived the life we could not and died the death we had ought for the pure sake of our salvation. However, this does not mean we are no longer required to work. How can this be? Is this a contradiction? No, and allow me to explain why that is.

One of the most commonly quoted Scriptures is found in Ephesians 2:8-9, "For by grace you have been saved through faith. And this is not your own doing; it is the gift of God, not a result of works, so that no one may boast." This passage indeed refers to salvation no longer being by works but by grace through faith. However, many misconstrue the meaning of this text to present the idea that all works are now abolished. Those who use this passage for such a purpose overlook the very next Scripture, "For we are his workmanship, created in Christ Jesus for good works, which God prepared beforehand, that we should walk in them" (Ephesians 2:10). It is abundantly clear that there are still works that we are called to after experiencing grace. Notice, however, the flow laid out by Paul. First, we experience His grace through faith. We are saved by believing and participating in His work. We receive the result of His work, salvation, by His grace, which is His Spirit. Only after we have received His grace are we then able to operate in the "good works" that we are called to. Meaning, we are utterly unable to perform these works apart from Him.

Paul further demonstrates this dependency upon His grace in our lives to accomplish that which He calls us to. Paul, speaking on a constant struggle he endures, said that he prayed three times to Jesus to remove this struggle (thorn) from his life. He couldn't bear it. Jesus' response was, "My grace is sufficient for you, for my power is made perfect in weakness," Paul, then, exclaimed, "Therefore I will boast all the more gladly of my weaknesses, so that the power of Christ may rest upon me" (II Corinthians 12:9). There was a thorn in Paul's life that he was struggling to deal with and could not understand why God wasn't lifting it. His misunderstanding was due to his thinking that he had to deal with this thorn alone. In truth, he could never deal with the thorn. Jesus, then, corrected Paul's way of thinking by conveying that His grace is sufficient to give us power in the midst of our every weakness.

Elsewhere, we read Paul say, "Therefore, my beloved, as you have always obeyed, so now, not only as in my presence but much more in my absence, work out your own salvation with fear and trembling, for it is God who works in you, both to will and to work for his good pleasure" (Philippians 2:12-13). Notice how Paul admonishes the Philippian Church to "work out" their "own salvation." What is this? Is this salvation through works? Not at all. For Paul continues, "for it is God who works in you, both to will and to work for his good pleasure." Meaning, we work out our salvation by allowing the grace of God to manifest in us which bestows upon us the desire and ability to pursue salvation. Again indicating, that apart from Him we are unable to do the works required of us. But there are works required of us.

Finally, looking back to a verse quoted in the chapter, Christians Abide with Christ, we read Jesus say, "Apart from me you can do nothing" (John 15:5). That word "nothing" is "oudeis" which is an absolute negative. Without Jesus, we are completely unable to do a single thing. We are utterly dependent upon Him for all that we do. For ask Paul said to the people of Athens, "In him we live and move and have our being" (Acts 17:28).

These truths are absolutely essential for us to understand. It is for this reason that we will reiterate them in the Epilogue.

We are called to work, but the work we are called to could never be obtained by our own merit. We emphatically need His grace to enable us to walk in the manner that He has called us to walk.

If we, then, are called to work, wherein is this rest? I once again draw our attention back to our earlier point: the purpose of the Sabbath was to refocus the people's attention on Him, basking in the goodness of all that He had done.

When we pursue the Christian walk with the mindset of having all this work that we need to do, we forsake His rest. When we endeavor to place the weight of this work upon our own shoulders, we forsake His rest. When we think that these things are dependent upon us, we forsake His rest. Therefore, we abide in His rest by understanding that it is Him that does the work through. That it is Him that carries the weight of the work on our behalf. That it is Him we are solely dependent upon. This is when we enter His rest: when we refocus our attention on Him and bask in all the goodness He is doing through us.

Returning to our focus passage here at the close, we read, "Come to me, all who labor and are heavy laden, and I will give you rest. Take my yoke upon you, and learn from me, for I am gentle and lowly in heart, and you will find rest for your souls. For my yoke is easy, and my burden is light." Notice that Jesus never once says those who "labor and are heavy laden" should cease to work. No, He says that He would give them rest. They had borne the heavy yoke of works for so long, a weight that they could not truly bear. Therefore, He says, "Take my yoke upon you…for my yoke is easy, and my burden light." Notice, again, He never says that there would be no yoke or no burden, but that He would remove the yoke they bore themselves and in its place put His yoke and burden upon us. The yoke and burden He places upon us is intertwined with His grace, making it "easy" and "light."

To walk the Christian walk, we must understand that there is work to do. The first half of the chapters, up until this current chapter, have all pertained to the works we are called to regarding our relationship with Him. The second half of chapters, beginning with Christians Have a Servant's Heart and ending with Christians Are a Light, all pertain to the works we are called to regarding our relationships with others. No one, who was a true Christian, ever said that this walk was easy. If we idly sit back and do not engage in what He has called us to, we run the risk of following out of His grace. We are called to work. But thanks to be God in the highest who does not place upon us more than we can bear, but bestows upon us His great grace which is sufficient in our every weakness.

Bask in the rest of Jesus by acknowledging every good work He does through you. In Jesus' name.

Focused Reflection

Rest is something void within Western culture. It doesn't take long to figure out, talk to a random individual for five minutes and they will likely mention how exhausted they are for this or that reason. Western society is not structured around rest, but productivity. For those immersed in such a culture, rest can become a foreign concept, but it is an essential one.

Often, when we think of rest, we think of kicking back in the recliner and getting a few minutes of shut-eye. This, however, is not quite what God meant when He said to engage in rest. Embedded within the biblical teaching of rest is this underlying premise of trust. To engage in rest is to let go of the reigns, to stop trying to be in control, and to trust in God as your Provider and your Abba. To engage in rest is to understand that when it is in His hands, all things will be good.

Christianity: Putting the Christ Back in Christianity

1. How would you describe your current state of rest (physical, mental, emotional, and spiritual)?

2. What do you internally experience when you think about letting go of the reigns of your life and allowing God to have control? Does it bring you peace or turmoil?

3. How would you describe your level of trust in God? Would you say that you trust God?

Cast all your anxiety on Him, because He cares for you.
-I Peter 5:7 (BSB)

9
Christians Have a Servant's Heart

A dispute also arose among them, as to which of them was to be regarded as the greatest. And he said to them, "The kings of the Gentiles exercise lordship over them, and those in authority over them are called benefactors. But not so with you. Rather, let the greatest among you become as the youngest, and the leader as one who serves. For who is the greater, one who reclines at table or one who serves? Is it not the one who reclines at table? But I am among you as the one who serves."
-Luke 22:24-27

The debate regarding who is the greatest is a debate that is prevalent in many different aspects of American culture (it is likely equally present in other cultures, but I can only speak directly to American culture). One of the most popular debates revolves around who is the GOAT (Greatest Of All Time) regarding the NBA. Two popular candidates are Michael Jordan and LeBron James, but other names have been thrown into the arena. Arguments go back and forth, these statistics are in favor of one, while those statistics are in favor of the other. At the end of the day, the argument is still not settled. Regardless of who ought to be dubbed the GOAT, everyone readily agrees that they are two of the greatest to ever play.

Due to their place of greatness, they are constantly in the spotlight, the focus of various articles, and receiving attention and accolades of various natures. You don't even have to be an avid NBA fan (as I am not) to know of these two players. Due to their greatness, their names have become household names to the point that a hermit living under a rock would likely say, "Oh yeah, I've heard of them!"

The idea of being regarded as great and receiving the

attention that comes along with that is extremely appealing to most people. Everyone wants to be recognized. This need for recognition has become so abundant in our culture that we've done away with only awarding those who have done the best at something and have begun to give awards to all, simply for participating. Participation Awards are what we call these. All this does is feed the desire to be recognized.

However, this hunger for recognition is not unique to our culture or our day and age. In truth, the desire for recognition has been present since the dawn of time. In the previous chapter, we took the time to highlight pride and its roots. We demonstrated how pride was the first sin committed by Lucifer in heaven that ultimately led to his casting out (see Isaiah 14:12-17; Ezekiel 28:11-19; Revelation 12:7-9). Further, we showed how after his fall he attacked God's beloved creation with the same sin that he committed himself, pride (see Genesis 3:4-5). Lucifer tempted Adam and Eve with the lie that if they ate of this particular fruit then they would become just like God. Talk about a need for recognition. Unfortunately, because Adam and Eve gave into this temptation, it did not end with them.

We can flip just one chapter over to Genesis 4 and read the brief story revolving around Cain and Abel (see Genesis 4:1-8). From the text, we can see that Abel was a man of integrity who sought to restore right relationship with God. It says of him that for his offering he brought unto God the "firstborn of his flock and their fat portions" (v.4). Meaning, he didn't look around at his flock and find the weakest, sickest, or ugliest and say, "Yeah…you'll do." Rather, regardless of how good of a specimen it was, he brought the first fruits of his flock and offered them to God. In doing so, he acknowledged His favor in his life which resulted in a blessed and abundant flock. Cain, however, was not so diligent.

Scripture tells us that Cain brought to God "the fruit of the ground" (v.3), but God "had no regard" (v.5) for his offering. We are not told explicitly in Scripture why God did not receive his offering, but we can piece together a likely reason based on the clues presented in the text. Regarding Abel's offering, as we mentioned, the Word says that he brought the "firstborn." Meaning, regardless of how valuable that offspring could have been did not sway Abel's devotion. Even if it presented the greatest potential, if it was the first, he offered it. However, regarding Cain and his offering, no such description is given. Due to this absence, it is likely that Cain was not so diligent in his offering, but merely gave what he felt like giving. In essence, Abel gave out of devotion, while Cain gave out of obligation.

We are not told how God's disregard for Cain's offering was shown, but it must have been apparent, for we are told that Cain understood that his offering was not accepted and "so Cain was very angry, and his face fell" (v.5). This phrase "his face fell" presents the imagery of defeat or discouragement. If one's face was lifted high it would imply that they were full of joy, full of encouragement, and generally in good spirits. Therefore, for one's face to fall presents the opposite of these things. God did not pity Cain and his temper tantrum, for He was not showing unjust partiality, but was responding justly to what each had offered. God, therefore, called Cain out for his poor behavior. He said, "Why are you angry, and why has your face fallen? If you do well, will you not be accepted? And if you do not do well, sin is crouching at the door. Its desire is contrary to you, but you must rule over it" (Genesis 4:6-7). God rebuked Cain for his bad behavior, but He did not rebuke him out of disdain, but love. God wanted Cain to be right and do right, that is why He followed His rebuke with a warning of what would follow if he continued down the path he was heading toward.

Unfortunately, we all know the story. Cain did not heed the warning of Jesus and allowed sin to overtake him instead of him overtaking it. What was his sin? A prideful need for recognition that led him to envy and hatred. This spirit of envy and hatred that overtook him refused to allow Abel to be greater than he was. Thereby, he set out to remove his competition. We may think that accounts such as these do not have much ramifications in our lives today, but that is where we would be wrong. Jesus, in Matthew 5:21-26, alluded to the spiritual truth that hatred for another is equivalent to murder. The Apostle John picked up on what Jesus was saying and made it plain. He writes, "Everyone who hates his brother is a murderer, and you know that no murderer has eternal life abiding in him" (I John 3:15).

It is unfortunate to say, but this pattern of giving heed to the prideful need for recognition was not a one-time, isolated event. Rather, several biblical accounts present this same theme. We will look at two additional examples, the first being that of Saul, king of Israel. We don't have the time or space to examine every facet of Saul's life, so our focus will be regarding his relationship with David. However, before we dive into the Saul\David dynamic, we need to lay a brief foundation that sets the stage for the events that were to follow.

Scripture tells us that Saul was a good, stereotypical definition of an earthly king. He was a head taller than everyone else and was considered more handsome than all the other men. Scripture goes so far as to say, "There was not a man among the children of Israel more handsome than he" (I Samuel 9:2). However, despite his impressive stature and good looks, Saul did not think very highly of himself. The reason for this low self-esteem was due to the tribe that he was born into, that is, the tribe of Benjamin. After first meeting and talking with the Prophet Samuel, it is recorded that Saul said, "Am I not a Benjaminite, from the least of the tribes of Israel? And is not my clan the humblest of all the clans of the tribe of Benjamin? Why then have you spoken to me in this way" (I Samuel 9:21)? Therefore, Saul had very humble beginnings, but that humility would soon dissipate.

The story continues that Saul officially becomes the first king of Israel and begins to perform mighty deeds. We aren't told at what point exactly Saul lost the humbleness of mind that he had at first, but he did lose it. Later on, in the narrative of his life, we read of a war against one of the oldest enemies of Israel, the Philistines. Somewhere along the way, Saul lost sight of the Word of God and began to follow after what seemed best to him in his own wisdom. He forsook the wisdom of God and considered self greater than God. This was his first step into pride. Due to his loss of humility and embracing of pride, we read Samuel prophesy to Saul, "You have done foolishly. You have not kept the command of the LORD your God, with which he commanded you. For then the LORD would have established your kingdom over Israel forever. But now your kingdom shall not continue. The LORD has sought out a man after his own heart, and the LORD has commanded him to be prince over his people, because you have not kept what the LORD commanded you" (I Samuel 13:13-14). Saul failed to fulfill the stipulation of being "a man after His (YAHWEH's) own heart." Therefore, He turned His eyes toward another who would truly walk after the heart of God.

The story goes, as we know well, God had Samuel anoint David as the next king of Israel (see I Samuel 16:11-13). Of course, Samuel knew if Saul knew he had anointed another to be king, he would be furious. Therefore, Samuel did these things in secret so that Saul would be completely unaware of the anointing on David's life. Unfortunately, even if Saul didn't know that David was the next king in waiting, he did know that God was with him and he was jealous of it. That destructive spirit of prideful recognition consumed Saul to the point of trying to kill David while he played the lyre (see I Samuel 18:10-12). This was not the only time he attempted this, for just one chapter later he attempts the same thing (see I Samuel 19:9-10). Eventually, his pride consumed him to the point where he wasted time, energy, and resources attempting to hunt down David and kill him. Yet, even while Saul unjustly sought to kill David, David has two different opportunities to do to Saul that which he wanted to do to him. But he did not. Some may ask he didn't seize the opportunity. There is a simple answer to such an inquiry: David operated out of honor.

Eventually, Saul's lack of humility and honor led to not only his death but also to the death of Jonathan and his other sons (see I Samuel 31:1-7). Saul's heart of pride resulted in the death of his entire family. We looked at pride and humility in the previous chapter, so we won't repeat it all here. If you need a refresher I invite you to glance back and reread our discussion on pride and humility. However, the relationship between Saul and David is a perfect example of James 4:6, "God opposes the proud but gives grace to the humble."

The life of Saul not only exemplifies God's response to pride and humility but also reveals another crucial aspect of living with a servant's heart: honor. Oxford Languages defines "honor" as, "regard with great respect." Further, they define "respect" as, "admire (someone or something) deeply, as a result of their abilities, qualities, or achievements." Concerning the narrative of Saul and David: Saul was not a good man, this was evident. David did not honor Saul because he looked up to him. Rather, there was a different, more profound reason for the honor that David gave Saul.

Following the death of Saul and his sons, a servant of Saul took the crown and ran to David to tell him the news. The servant likely thought David would be joyous and praise the servant, however, David lamented and wept over the news he had received (see II Samuel 1:11-12). After the time of weeping, David further questioned the servant on how he came by this information. That is when David learned that the servant had killed Saul at this request. David's response was, "How is it you were not afraid to put out your hand to destroy the LORD'S anointed" (II Samuel 1:14)? And then had the servant executed for his actions (see II Samuel 1:15-16).

This interaction between David and Saul's servant reveals why David so greatly honored Saul: because YAHWEH had anointed him. It was that simple. In David's mind, to rise up against Saul would have been to rise up against God Himself. Therefore, it was not so much that David was honoring Saul, but honoring the One who had anointed and positioned him.

Some may ask, "But God had now anointed David and removed His anointing from Saul. Why then did David continue regarding Saul as His anointed?" While all this is true, it is also true that God had not yet removed Saul and positioned David. Therefore, if David had taken matters into his own hands and risen up against Saul, would God have honored such an action? Would David have been right in the eyes of God? That was not something he was willing to risk. Thereby, he continued to honor the man who held the position and allowed God to work in His timing. David knew that he was anointed and that God would appoint him when God so willed.

Keeping all this at the forefront of our minds, I feel it imperative to take a moment and discuss honor before diving into servanthood. Humility and honor are vital components of abiding in a true spirit of servanthood. Therefore, what is honor, and how do we operate in it toward others?

Jumping back momentarily, Oxford Languages' definition of honor directly correlates to respect. Respect can sometimes be a touchy subject in our culture. One phrase I have heard or seen countless times is: "Respect is earned, not given!" Or some variation of that statement. Such a statement aligns perfectly with the world and its mindsets and attitudes. However, such a statement stands in direct contradiction to the life born-again Christians are called to live. To say that we only give respect to those who earn it is equal to saying that we judge everyone based on the works they do. Sound familiar? We were once judged according to our works, and we failed every time to measure up. But thanks be to Jesus Christ for His loving kindness and great grace that He showed us. Because of Him and His work, we are no longer judged by works, but His grace has become sufficient.

Therefore, we have been redeemed from salvation through works and now live in grace. Why, then, would we judge another according to their works? If we could not measure up, then how could we expect someone else to be able to? Jesus spoke on this very thing when He said, "Judge not, that you be not judged. For with the judgment you pronounce you will be judged, and with the measure you use it will be measured to you. Why do you see the speck that is in your brother's eye, but do not notice the log that is in your own eye? Or how can you say to your brother, 'Let me take the speck out of your eye,' when there is the log in your own eye? You hypocrite, first take the log out of your own eye, and then you will see clearly to take the speck out of your brother's eye" (Matthew 7:1-5).

First, we see that if we decide to take it upon ourselves to judge, we will, therefore, be judged according to how we judged others. Meaning, if we have entered into the law of grace, freed from salvation by works, but then judge others according to their works, we will then be judged also according to our works. Second, Jesus reveals that this judgmental attitude is birthed out of prideful hypocrisy. He uses the analogy that compares a speck to a log. Think about the significant difference between a speck and a log. In essence, He is saying that His grace has covered and removed massive flaws from your life. Yet, you are quick to draw attention to the minor flaw (the speck) that your neighbor has. Jesus says that there is nothing wrong with wanting to help your neighbor with their issues, but only with the right heart and through His grace can one truly do so.

Therefore, as Christians, our view of respect should never be, "Respect is earned, not given!" Rather, it should be, "Respect is a gift of grace." The Christian's approach to honor should mirror that of David: they may not be your favorite person in the world, but they are anointed by God. One professing to be Christian should have the same motive as David: David honored Saul because he first honored God. The path to true honor and respect is through right relationship. Jesus must be first, for if your eyes are not firmly fixed on Him then every other relationship will suffer. However, if He is positioned properly in our lives as our main focus and priority, then every other relationship will flourish.

To give honor is a biblical mandate, both in the Old and New Testaments. Looking to the Ten Commandments once again; the first four commandments given by God all deal with our relationship with Him, while the final six all directly deal with our relationship with others. It is telling, then, that the first commandment He gave us concerning how we interact with each other is, "Honor your father and your mother, that your days may be long in the land that the LORD your God is giving you" (Exodus 20:12). Further, not only is this commandment the bedrock of the horizontal commandments, but Paul also pointed out how this is the first commandment given with a promise (see Ephesians 6:2). The word "honor" in this verse is "kâbad" which simply means, "to be heavy." In our day and age, such an idea does not make much sense. The only way we understand the word "heavy" refers to something possessing a great weight. Nothing more. However, sometimes to properly understand the true meaning of biblical concepts you have to, to the best of your ability, remove yourself from your present cultural mindset and tap into the ancient cultural mindset. This is not always easy, but extremely beneficial where we can. In ancient Hebraic culture, how heavy a thing was did not merely refer to its weight, but its value. Therefore, His first commandment to us regarding our relationships with one another was to attribute great value to one another.

Some may try to argue and say, "Well, that was only

concerning our father and mother." My rebuttal would be to direct our attention to the New Testament. Paul, writing to the Church in Rome, said, "Love one another with brotherly affection. Outdo one another in showing honor" (Romans 12:10). It is important to approach this Scripture with the understanding that Paul was a Jew. Thus, his understanding of honor would have been birthed from what the Law had declared. Further, not only would Paul have approached the topic of honor with a Hebraic mindset, the word used here for "honor," "timē," holds a similar meaning to the Hebrew word, "kâbad," that is, it refers to something of value. Notice, though, Paul did not keep honor confined to parental relationships but extended it to every relationship that we have. He took what the Law had declared and then set the bar even higher. The raising of the bar, so to speak, is not unique to this passage or Paul. It began with Jesus who would draw attention to an Old Testament precept and the Jew's interpretation of it, and then call them to come up higher. Because we live in the covenant of grace, as discussed earlier, we are called to a higher level of living because we have His Spirit now abiding within us, aiding us in our walk.

Additionally, Paul addresses the level at which we are to honor one another. Paul admonishes us to "outdo one another." The word "outdo" is "proēgeomai" which can refer to two things. One, it can mean, "to give precedence to," and two, it can refer to leading the way. "Precedence," according to Oxford Languages, means, "the condition of being considered more important than someone or something else; priority in importance, order, or rank." Therefore, with just one word, Paul states that we are to bestow a greater rank of importance to one another by showing them honor, and when we do so, we set the standard for those who come after us and they will then do likewise.

Why is all this important to discuss? We alluded to it earlier, but we will make it plain here: if you do not honor them you will not serve them. If we do not serve them, we are not abiding by the character of Christ and have failed to be Christians. Understanding all of these things, we can now return to our chapter text and discuss what it means to operate with the heart of a servant.

After the dispute broke out between the disciples regarding

who was the greatest among them (which is quite sad when taken in context, for this argument directly followed Him revealing that one would betray Him [see Luke 22:21-23]), Jesus began His correction by drawing attention to the world with its systems and governments. First, He says, "The kings of the Gentiles exercise lordship over them, and those in authority over them are called benefactors." The word "benefactor" merely refers to one who benefits. Therefore, Jesus is indicating that those in the world seek loftier positions and titles because with them comes a greater level of benefit. Often the higher you climb in the world's system, the greater the compensation. The irony of this is that, in the world, the higher you go the more you are served. Therefore, even though you are compensated more, you are doing less. Of course, this idea appeals to every human being. Do less, but get more? Sign me up! However, Jesus quickly squandered this mindset and attitude in His disciples. He says, "But not so with you." In essence, He said, "Everything the world does regarding the flow of their systems and governments, you will do the opposite." He, then, goes on to explain what this looks like.

First, He says, "Let the greatest among you become as the youngest." Jesus points back to the argument they were all having moments before, who was the greatest, and says that whoever is deemed as such, this is what they shall truly be. In our culture today this statement may not make much sense. In our day and age, being the youngest is sometimes preferred. It is often joked about how the youngest is always babied and spoiled the most. However, it was quite the opposite in the day and age in which this statement was made. In Jewish culture, the youngest child received little to no honor. It was the eldest child who received the greatest honor, blessing, and favor. One example of this is found in the life of David. When God instructed Samuel to anoint a new king from the sons of Jesse, Jesse did not initially think to present David before Samuel. As the youngest, Jesse likely thought that there was no way that David would be anointed over his older brothers (see I Samuel 16:11-13).

Often, when we give of our time, talent, or treasure, we do so with the intent of getting back something in return. We all do this. What we seek after may differ, such as attention, recognition, blessing, and so on, but we seek, in some way, to be honored for what we did or gave. However, to operate with such a motive, we operate in the spirit of the eldest brother. To abide by this instruction from Jesus we need to embrace the spirit of the youngest brother. When you do or give something, do not do it expecting to be given back in return. As Paul said, quoting Jesus, "It is more blessed to give than to receive" (Acts 20:35).

One thing of importance to note regarding these things: abiding in the spirit of the youngest and abiding by the truth that it is more blessed to give does not mean we are to reject gifts offered to us by others. Looking back once more to David; David did not reject the anointing of God by the hands of the Prophet Samuel because he was the youngest and not initially honored by his father. He readily received what was being given to him. When a gift is rejected, the one rejecting is often attempting to convey a spirit of humility, and aiming to honor the giver by deeming themselves unworthy to receive what is being given. However, when we reject a gift we are, in truth, operating out of pride and dishonor. Even Jesus, the One who came to serve, willingly received when others sought to give to Him. There are several different examples we could use to demonstrate this, but perhaps the most beautiful was when the woman (who John identified as Mary, the sister of Martha and Lazarus) anointed Jesus with the costly perfume, washed His feet with her tears, and dried them with her hair (see Matthew 26:6-13; Mark 14:3-9; Luke 7:36-50; John 12:1-8).

Jesus continues His lesson on servitude and says, "The leader as one who serves." First, the word "leader" is "hēgeomai" which can mean a few different things depending on its usage. However, in essence, this word refers to one who exercises chief authority. Second, the word "serves" is "diakoneō" which refers to waiting upon someone, such as a waiter in a restaurant or a host at a party. Further, "diakoneō" is where we get our word for "deacon."

Typically, when one thinks of a leader, they think of one who sits atop the proverbial totem pole and issues out commands and edicts. "Come here. Go there. Do this. Do that." Often, our thinking regarding leadership more so pertains to what they say, rather than what they do. However, Jesus called for an upheaval of the traditional operation of leadership. Don't misconstrue this, Jesus was not calling for an abolishment of leadership, but a change in how it is presented and acted in. Rather than being more focused on saying over doing, Jesus admonished would-be leaders to focus more on doing rather than saying. Or, as the saying goes, "Lead by example." Jesus is calling for those who lead to step out from behind their fancy desks, put their boots on the ground, and use their hands to work the fields.

Of course, those who lead need to make decisions and sometimes need to issue commands. However, Jesus is saying that in His Kingdom the primary mode of leadership is through being a servant unto the people. The decisions that are made, the moves that are taken, and the words that are said are all done so through the heart of a servant. We do not exist to be served, we exist to serve.

One point of clarification before moving on: while we operate with a servant's heart toward the people, we do not serve the people. That statement seemingly stands in contradiction to all that I have said, but allow me to explain. Paul said, "For am I now seeking the approval of man, or of God? Or am I trying to please man? If I were still trying to please man, I would not be a servant of Christ" (Galatians 1:10). We operate with a servant's heart through humility and honor and willingly serve them. However, this does not mean we serve them. Again, a seemingly contradictory statement. Serving has two implications. The first is what we have discussed: aiding others, waiting upon others as a waiter or host would, considering others of greater honor than ourselves, and so on. The second more so pertains to servitude, as with a master and a servant. We have only One Master and no other. First, we serve Him and live a life of servitude unto Him. Only then can we operate with a heart of a servant unto the people. Priorities must be kept in proper order. Only by keeping Him first can we truly serve the people. This is why the preceding chapters are all about right relationship with Him. Only after coming into right relationship with Him can we then abide in right relationship with others (see I John 4:7-21).

Continuing, Jesus ends this passage by drawing attention to Himself. First, He asks a question: "For who is the greater, one who reclines at table or one who serves? Is it not the one who reclines at table?" In the culture of Jesus' day, and ours as well, it is typically thought that the one who serves is of lesser importance than the one who sits. The one who sits is not having to do anything other than partake of what is given to them. However, who is the greatest of all? Is it not God Himself? That is why Jesus then says, "But I am among you as the one who serves." He is far greater than the greatest human to ever live. Was He the One sitting or serving? Serving.

Perhaps one of the most beautiful examples of His servitude is recorded in the Gospel of John. We read:

> Jesus, knowing that the Father had given all things into his hands, and that he had come from God and was going back to God, rose from supper. He laid aside his outer garments, and taking a towel, tied it around his waist. Then he poured water into a basin and began to wash the disciples' feet and to wipe them with the towel that was wrapped around him... When he had washed their feet and put on his outer garments and resumed his place, he said to them, "Do you understand what I have done to you? You call me Teacher and Lord, and you are right, for so I am. If I then, your Lord and Teacher, have washed your feet, you also ought to wash one another's feet. For I have given you an example, that you also should do just as I have done to you."
> -John 13:3-5, 12-15

Several things from this passage are key to understanding what it means to operate with a servant's heart. To understand the first thing Jesus does, we, as we have discussed previously, need to step out of our cultural mindset and step into first-century culture. Particularly, the Jewish culture of the day. Jews were extremely modest people. Jews did not wear one garment only. Jews wore an outer garment and an undergarment. To the Jews, to be seen only in one's undergarment was to be considered naked. They were by no means even close to being naked, for even the undergarment was sufficient covering. However, to the Jews, to be seen in one's undergarments was a shame. Therefore, Jesus began displaying a servant's heart by making Himself completely vulnerable. He opened Himself completely to those He served and allowed them to see a part of Him that most people would never see. Shifting the attention to us in our displaying a servant's heart; we cannot serve if we are closed off and distant. Those we are seeking to serve will never receive us in their hearts if we do not bear our hearts. Our act of service only begins after we make ourselves vulnerable before those we endeavor to serve.

After Jesus made Himself vulnerable by taking off His outer garment, the second thing He did was take a towel and tie it around the waist of His undergarment. What transpired here is very symbolic. The towel that Jesus wrapped around Himself substituted for His outer garment. Therefore, symbolically, Jesus took on a new identity when He was clothed with the servant's towel. The outer garment symbolized one way in which He was known, but He shed that identity and took on the identity of a servant. Therefore, a heart of a servant is not conveyed through a momentary act of service, but it only comes to pass when we willingly lay ourselves aside and readily take up the mantle of a servant. People will never see you as one who has a heart of a servant if they only see you serve in moments. Such a realization will only transpire through a change of identity.

After making Himself vulnerable and taking on a new identity, He then begins His act of service unto His disciples. How He served His disciples cannot be overlooked. In our day and age, the idea of washing someone's feet is gross enough, the feet are typically considered one of the dirtiest parts of the body even when clean. If anyone reading this has ever experienced a foot-washing ceremony, you know what exactly I am talking about. Engaging in such an act truly requires a great level of humility, as we have already talked about. However, once again, we cannot merely read this from a twenty-first-century state of mind but must position ourselves with a first-century understanding. In our society, it is very uncommon to see someone in public with no shoes on. Shoes are a commonality. Not only are shoes a commonality, but most people wear shoes that completely cover their feet. Occasionally you will see someone wearing flip-flops or sandals, but that is really only seen in certain environments, in certain seasons. The people of the first century did not have that same luxury. It was not uncommon to see someone without shoes, and even those who did wear shoes wore sandals that left much of the foot uncovered. Therefore, the feet of the people were heavily exposed to the ground they walked on. Further, in our society, we are blessed with paved roads and sidewalks. However, if we were to stray off into an open field, it is likely relatively tame and we are still protected from the ground by our shoes. Those of the first century, again, did not have these luxuries. The ground they walked on likely almost always consisted of dirt, mud, and animal feces.

Understanding this, we come back to Jesus' act of service. It is not hard to imagine how filthy the disciples' feet were at this moment, and Jesus knew this. He was not ignorant regarding what He was signing up to do. In fact, we can surmise that it was because of the filthiness of the disciples' feet that He endeavored to do this. Constantly throughout His ministry, Jesus was seen among the "scum" of the land: lepers, tax collectors, prostitutes, and such the like. The religious leaders of the day were appalled by the crowd that Jesus chose to surround Himself with and to be honest, many of us would have responded the same way they did. We have become so concerned with image that we are afraid of anything that may taint it. Such was the sin of the religious leaders, vain hypocrisy. We read of interaction between Jesus and some of the religious leaders wherein they questioned Him about His choice of followers. Jesus sharply responded, "Those who are well have no need of a physician, but those who are sick. I have not come to call the righteous but sinners to repentance" (Luke 5:31-32). It was Jesus' custom to get His hands dirty, so to speak, so why would this interaction with His disciples be any different?

As we operate with a servant's heart, there will be times when we may get a little dirty. There may be times when we are called to, figuratively or literally, wash the feet of one who has walked a rough road barefooted. The work will not always be glamorous, in fact, it likely will rarely be so. The work of a servant is not always pleasant, but it is always beneficial. The only way that we can readily demonstrate Jesus' servant heart is by serving just as He did; by doing the work that may not be glamorous, but that will benefit either the Body as a whole, or even just one member of the Body.

Some may wonder, "Do we really need to go that far just because Jesus did?" Jesus answered this question and questions like it. After finishing what He had set out to do, He said, "Do you understand what I have done to you? You call me Teacher and Lord, and you are right, for so I am. If I then, your Lord and Teacher, have washed your feet, you also ought to wash one another's feet. For I have given you an example, that you also should do just as I have done to you." The work Jesus performed with a servant's heart was meant as an example for us, that we would look at Him and see what He did and then do the same ourselves.

When we embrace the servant's heart and allow it to be demonstrated through our lives is when the Body of Christ will cease to be merely many members and truly become one Body. It is the servant's heart, garnered through humility and honor, that cultivates an atmosphere of unity. We can read all throughout the New Testament epistles where the various Apostles wrote that we are to be one Body, united together (see Romans 12:4-5; I Corinthians 12:12-31; Colossians 3:14-16 just to give three examples, there are many more). Jesus, in His high priestly prayer, declared that His will is for us to be one (see John 17:20-21). The word "one" from the Greek "heis" is interesting because it can refer to figuratively being one through unity, however, it more directly refers to actual oneness, as in, only one. Therefore, the oneness He desires for us to dwell in transcends "common unity" and reaches for a place where there is no division or separation between us but where we abide in true oneness together. Only one. Absolutely one. We will never achieve such without a servant's heart being demonstrated through our words and our actions.

Focused Reflection

The mentality of a servant, or the heart of a servant, is something not common within our culture. Most people operate in the spirit of the master (and I don't mean The Master), not the servant. Even the strongest of Christians have moments of weakness where, in their flesh, they embrace more of that "master" spirit than the heart of a servant. However, Jesus called us to serve.

Operating in a servant's heart requires that one take up a very humble position and be no respecter of persons. Operating in a servant's heart means being willing to give without the guarantee of a return on your investment. Operating in a servant's heart requires that one truly love His Kingdom and truly desire to point all men to Him.

1. A servant's heart is formed out of a deep love for Him that overflows and impacts our relationships with others. Would you say that you abide in that place of deep, overflowing love?

2. To truly serve requires a heart of humility. Humility is to make one's self low. Are you willing to take up such a position before God and others?

3. When you think of operating with a servant's heart toward another, where does your mind go? How do you picture that?

> Do nothing from selfish ambition or conceit, but in humility count others more significant than yourselves. Let each of you look not only to his own interests, but also to the interests of others.
> -Philippians 2:3-4

10
Christians Are People of Communion
Christians Have a Servant's Heart II

And he said to them, "I have earnestly desired to eat this Passover with you before I suffer. For I tell you I will not eat it until it is fulfilled in the kingdom of God." And he took a cup, and when he had given thanks he said, "Take this, and divide it among yourselves. For I tell you that from now on I will not drink of the fruit of the vine until the kingdom of God comes." And he took bread, and when he had given thanks, he broke it and gave it to them, saying, "This is my body, which is given for you. Do this in remembrance of me." And likewise the cup after they had eaten, saying, "This cup that is poured out for you is the new covenant in my blood."
~Luke 22:15-20

The nature of this chapter is going to resemble that of Christians Are Baptized in His Name and Spirit and Christians Are People of Prayer. Therefore, it is less of a complete chapter and more of an excursion used to build upon a previous point.

In the previous chapter, Christians Have a Servant's Heart, we ended by discussing how it is through abiding in the heart of a servant that there is unity in the Body. Abiding with a servant's heart is to consider others more highly than yourself. This type of atmosphere edifies, encourages, and emboldens. When individuals become more concerned with those around them than they are with themselves, it creates an atmosphere of powerful unity that can, truly, change the world.

I want to take a moment here and focus on this aspect of unity within the Body. In relation to Christ's example in our lives, there is no better way to demonstrate this than by taking a close look at communion.

Looking to our focus text, we see that Jesus had been longing for the arrival of this moment. He says, "I have earnestly desired to eat this Passover with you." "You" is an interesting word, for it can have both a singular and a plural focus without changing a single letter or pronunciation. One could readily call to a single individual and say, "I need you to help me," and the individual would feel that pointed petition. However, at the same time, one could gesture to a group of people and say the same, "I need you to help me," and each individual within that group would feel that beckoning. It is, however, human nature to think more so of ourselves than others. When we hear, "you," we are more likely to think of ourselves first than those in the group. Therefore, we come to the words of Jesus, how He said, "I have earnestly desired to eat this Passover with you," and first think of a singular focus. However, at no point did Jesus single out one disciple from the twelve. At no point did He say, "Peter, I've been looking forward to this time with you," or any such thing. No, the "you" employed by Jesus was directed at the group as a whole. It was a unified reference.

In "More Like Him," Dr. James A. Littles Jr. rightly asserts the unfortunate truth that many approach communion as a private experience. Many think of communion as a intimate time between themselves and Jesus and they quickly forget about everyone else in the room. However, never in any account of this Passover feast do we read that Jesus called for a private experience. Rather, He passed the cup around, each one passing it on to the next, partaking of the cup together. Likewise, after breaking the bread, it says that He "gave it to them." It was shared amongst them, partaking of the bread together.

During this intimate time together, Jesus revealed to His disciples that the cup represented His blood "that is poured out for you is the new covenant in my blood." Further, He said that the bread "is my body, which is given for you." After having each partake of the cup and the bread, He then said, "Do this in remembrance of me."

Let's take a moment to reflect on that. The supper that

He shared with His closest friends during His last night was representative of the things He would soon endure, the spilling of His blood and the breaking of His body. These things were not endured without purpose but brought about our salvation. While it is true that we are individually saved, the focus cannot be kept on just the individual. For the individual who is saved is grafted into something bigger than themselves. That is, we are grafted into the Body of Christ.

Paul said it like this, "The cup of blessing that we bless, is it not a participation in the blood of Christ? The bread that we break, is it not a participation in the body of Christ? Because there is one bread, we who are many are one body, for we all partake of the one bread" (I Corinthians 10:16-17). Paul pointed to the many individuals that partake of communion but then indicated that they are not merely individuals, but one. There is more we need to understand about being in and partaking of communion, but first I want to expound upon us being one body.

Later in the same epistle, Paul wrote in 1 Corinthians 12, "For just as the body is one and has many members, and all the members of the body, though many, are one body, so it is with Christ. For in one Spirit we were all baptized into one body—Jews or Greeks, slaves or free—and all were made to drink of one Spirit. For the body does not consist of one member but of many. If the foot should say, 'Because I am not a hand, I do not belong to the body,' that would not make it any less a part of the body. And if the ear should say, 'Because I am not an eye, I do not belong to the body,' that would not make it any less a part of the body. If the whole body were an eye, where would be the sense of hearing? If the whole body were an ear, where would be the sense of smell? But as it is, God arranged the members in the body, each one of them, as he chose. If all were a single member, where would the body be? As it is, there are many parts, yet one body. The eye cannot say to the hand, 'I have no need of you,' nor again the head to the feet, 'I have no need of you.' On the contrary, the parts of the body that seem to be weaker are indispensable, and on those parts of the body that we think less honorable we bestow the greater honor, and our unpresentable parts are treated with greater modesty, which our more presentable parts do not require. But God has so composed the body, giving greater honor to the part that lacked it, that there may be no division in the body, but that the members may have the same care for one another. If one member suffers, all suffer together; if one member is honored, all rejoice together" (v.12-26).

In human culture, numerous aspects create distinctions and divisions. Some examples are ethnicity, race, gender, language, religion, and so on. However, in Kingdom culture, the disunifying aspects of human culture are of no more effect. As humans, we have drawn the lines of distinction between people. However, Jesus calls us to see how He sees. In I Samuel 16:7 He instructs the Prophet Samuel to look on the outward appearance, for that is how humanity views each other, but He looks at the heart of man. Paul echoes that sentiment here. For he draws attention to the various distinguishing aspects of different people but then indicates that these no longer matter. "For just as the body is one and has many members, and all the members of the body, though many, are one body, so it is with Christ."

After Paul establishes that the cultural differences of humanity that once separated us are no longer applicable, he then endeavors to demonstrate the necessity of the body as a whole. As mentioned above, we often have an isolated mindset, thinking only of ourselves and how things impact us. We can deny it all we like but it is an unfortunate truth. We have to change our way of thinking in order to take the focus off of ourselves only and include others in it. The idea that we could make it alone is absurd and Paul conveys this to us. In the above passage, he addresses three false mindsets that lead to isolation. One, that you are not good enough, and two, that others are not good enough. Therefore, he addresses both insecurity and conceitedness, both of which are rooted in pride. The third deception is that some parts of the body are more desirable than others.

The idea that a foot could operate on its own apart from the rest of the body is absurd and we know it is. We imagine a lone foot attempting to hop around on its own and we chuckle because we know it is unrealistic. Yet, this is exactly what we do when we isolate ourselves from the rest of the Body. Some may have the mindset of, "A foot? I don't want to be a foot! Who wants to be a foot?" However, such an individual fails to recognize the importance of the feet in relation to the body, regardless of how they are perceived. For without the feet standing would be near impossible, and you can forget trying to walk. The feet balance and provide support from the rest of the body. Therefore, even though it is not a glamorous part of the body, it is absolutely essential.

When a body is out of unity, the various parts not working together as they should, that is when sickness and disease become present. A disunified body is an unhealthy body. It is likewise so with the Body. Christians dwelling in unity with one another create a healthy and strong Body that is able to work for His Kingdom purpose. However, a disunified Body is unable to adequately perform the work of the Kingdom because it is too busy warring with itself.

The word "communion" in Scripture is not directly tied to the act of partaking of the cup and bread, however, the word has been connected traditionally to the act due to the meaning the word holds. Webster's Dictionary offers a few good definitions of the word "communion:" one, "fellowship; intercourse between two persons or more; interchange of transactions, or offices; a state of giving and receiving; agreement; concord," and two, "mutual intercourse or union in religious worship, or in doctrine and discipline." One can readily see from these two definitions that communion strictly refers to a coming together, not just in duty, but in sincerity.

The sincerity aspect cannot be overlooked. Communion and mere duty do not coexist. To approach communion out of mere duty and not sincerity is to bring judgment upon yourself. Paul talked about this very thing in I Corinthians 11:17-32. I won't quote the whole passage here but reference a few key verses within the passage.

Paul began by addressing wrong mindsets and attitudes that individuals had when approaching communion. First, he addresses disunity in the Body. He says, "For, in the first place, when you come together as a church, I hear that there are divisions among you. And I believe it in part, for there must be factions among you in order that those who are genuine among you may be recognized" (v.18-19). But what were these divisions? There may have been multiple divisions within the Church of Corinth, however, Paul strictly addressed one in particular. That is, there were individuals approaching communion with a selfish, self-seeking, and lustful spirit. He says, "When you come together, it is not the Lord's supper that you eat. For in eating, each one goes ahead with his own meal. One goes hungry, another gets drunk. What! Do you not have houses to eat and drink in? Or do you despise the church of God and humiliate those who have nothing? What shall I say to you? Shall I commend you in this? No, I will not" (I Corinthians 11:20-22).

Often when we think of "lust" our minds gravitate toward that of a sexual nature. James said, "But every man is tempted, when he is drawn away of his own lust, and enticed. Then when lust hath conceived, it bringeth forth sin: and sin, when it is finished, bringeth forth death" (James 1:14-15 KJV). The word "lust" here is "epithumia" which refers to a passionate and impure desire. This desire is often associated with a sexual nature, however, one can have a passionate and impure desire for anything they please. John picked up on this truth when he wrote, "For all that is in the world— the lust of the flesh, the lust of the eyes, and the pride of life—is not of the Father but is of the world" (I John 2:16 NKJV). Those whom Paul called out had fallen into the trap of lust. Notice how John pinpointed that lust has two entrance points in our lives: our flesh and our eyes. John felt it pertinent enough to point out this distinction, therefore I feel it pertinent enough to expound upon this distinction.

"Flesh" is "sarx" which refers to our carnal nature. Some translations of this word are, "flesh; human nature; carnality; flesh as the seat of passion and frailty; material as opposed to the spiritual." In essence, "sarx" points to the longings of our flesh which are geared toward that of a sinful inclination due to the sinful nature we are born in. Greed, gluttony, fornication, and things the like are birthed out of the lust of the flesh, the desire to satisfy self.

On the other side, "eyes" is "ophthalmos" which very simply points to the eye itself or the vision of the eye. In seeking to acquire an understanding of the lust of eyes, it is useful to take Jesus teaching from Matthew 6:22-23 into consideration. He says, "The eye is the lamp of the body. So, if your eye is healthy, your whole body will be full of light, but if your eye is bad, your whole body will be full of darkness. If then the light in you is darkness, how great is the darkness!" In essence, He is saying that that which we focus on and give our attention to fills our inward man. If we focus on that which is pure and holy, our inward man will mirror that purity and holiness. On the flip side of this though, if we endeavor to focus on that which is impure and wicked, our inward man will become consumed in impurity and wickedness. This is why Paul admonishes us, "Set your minds on things that are above, not on things that are on earth" (Colossians 3:2). We could put it this way: your focus determines your direction. To focus on the things of this world is to pursue the world which puts you at enmity with Jesus. To focus on the things above, then, is to pursue His Kingdom and righteousness which leads to abiding with Him.

Returning to our focus text from I Corinthians 11, to wrongfully partake in communion with the Body is not merely discouraged and frowned upon. It is not simply that others will look down upon you. No, Paul informs us that to approach this practice of unity incorrectly is to entice judgment upon yourself. Paul says, "Whoever, therefore, eats the bread or drinks the cup of the Lord in an unworthy manner will be guilty concerning the body and blood of the Lord. Let a person examine himself, then, and so eat of the bread and drink of the cup. For anyone who eats and drinks without discerning the body eats and drinks judgment on himself. That is why many of you are weak and ill, and some have died" (I Corinthians 11:27-30). As we have said, communion is an act of sincere unity. Therefore, to approach communion with any other motive than to grow in unity is to be a hypocrite. When we operate in this hypocritical manner, we judge ourselves unworthy to partake in the unity. Paul went so far as to say that this hypocritical, lustful motive brought about sickness and even death. Paul, then, follows this warning with an admonishment to judge ourselves and our motives first before we endeavor to partake (see v.31).

Our aim here has been to unveil the essentiality of unity and the proper approaches we need in seeking it. This discussion, while drawing much attention to communion, is less about the act of communion and more about the purpose of communion. No man is an island. One who attempts to walk the Way alone is like a foot attempting to function apart from the rest of the body. We must strive for unity in the Body, for that is when we will be truly healthy.

Before ending this brief discussion here, we must discuss one final point. While unity with the Body is of the utmost importance, it is not the only manifestation of unity we need to have in our lives. Unity with the Body is a horizontal unity. Accompanying horizontal unity, we also need to possess vertical unity in our lives. I won't belabor this point too greatly, for in truth, what we discussed in the chapters Christians Abide with Christ through Christians are Worshippers establishes what it looks like to be in unity with Jesus. However, we must recognize this great necessity.

Paul, referencing once more the passage from I Corinthians, said, "For I received from the Lord what I also delivered to you, that the Lord Jesus on the night when he was betrayed took bread, and when he had given thanks, he broke it, and said, "This is my body, which is for you. Do this in remembrance of me." In the same way also he took the cup, after supper, saying, "This cup is the new covenant in my blood. Do this, as often as you drink it, in remembrance of me." For as often as you eat this bread and drink the cup, you proclaim the Lord's death until he comes" (v.23-26). Notice how Paul quoted Jesus saying twice, "Do this in remembrance of me."

It is essential that we maintain unity with the Body, I pray that has been thoroughly demonstrated. However, allow me to add this: unity with the Body apart from unity with Him is fruitless. If we take Christ out of the unity, then all we have left is a social club. Christ absolutely must be at the center of all that we do, lest all that we do be in vain. That is why I positioned the aspects of the Christian walk that pertain to right relationship with Him at the start of this book. If we don't have that relationship right and set properly, then every other relationship with utterly fail.

I love each and every one of my brothers and sisters, even those I have yet to meet. How can I say I love those I've never met? Because Jesus has joined us together in one family and we abide in unity with Him. Abiding in unity with Him makes every other relationship perfect. We would do well to remember the words of the Apostle John, "We love because he first loved us" (I John 4:19).

Focused Reflection

When people think of communion, their thoughts likely revolve around what is partaken of during communion. That is, the grape juice and bread. For many, communion is nothing more than a free snack during a particular service. However, the true meaning and purpose of communion is powerful and essential. Communion is all about unity.

Unity is a powerful spiritual truth that many do not quite grasp to its full extent. Unity is so powerful that even those who are not living in covenant with God can boast of powerful feats brought about by their unity (see Genesis 11). How much more, then, could be accomplished when a unified body is in covenant with God?

The unity of communion is particularly special because it has two parts. That is, we are coming into unity as one Body. We come into alignment with what was said about the church in the Book of Acts, "one mind and one accord" (Acts 2:1 KJV). The second is that we are coming into unity with God and His covenant promises that He has given to us.

1. How would you define "unity"?

2. Do you understand the power behind unity? What do you think that power looks like?

3. Would you say that you abide in a place of unity with your brothers and sisters and with God?

> And the LORD said, "Behold, they are one people, and they have all one language, and this is only the beginning of what they will do. And nothing that they propose to do will now be impossible for them.
> -Genesis 11:6

11
Christians Love Their Neighbors

And one of them, a lawyer, asked him a question to test him. "Teacher, which is the great commandment in the Law?" And he said to him, "You shall love the Lord your God with all your heart and with all your soul and with all your mind. This is the great and first commandment. And a second is like it: You shall love your neighbor as yourself. On these two commandments depend all the Law and the Prophets."
~Matthew 22:35-40

In the chapter, Christians Abide with Christ, we spoke on abiding in His love and how the first and great commandment is that He is One and that we are to love Him with our whole being, as Jesus stated in Mark 12:28-30, echoing Deuteronomy 6:4-5. However, Jesus did not end the statement there. Rather, He continues and says, "And a second is like it." That is an extremely interesting statement that shouldn't be overlooked. The Greek word for "like" is "homoios." "Homoios" can be translated as, "similar; resembling; like manner." In essence, Jesus was saying that understanding His Oneness and loving Him sincerely proceeds all things, however, we must allow that sincere, relational love to flow from our relationship with Him and into our relationship with others.

Notice the question that was posed to Jesus: "Which is the great commandment in the Law?" The lawyer (which refers to an expert on the Law) did not ask Jesus for a top ten ranking of the Law, but which was the greatest. Many look at Jesus' reply as a ranking of the top two. This is not at all what Jesus was doing. Though Jesus' answer may seem twofold, it is, in truth, two parts to one whole. It begins with loving Him, as we discussed, but then flows into loving others. In essence, Jesus was saying to operate in a state of love, toward God first then toward man, is the greatest commandment.

Here in this chapter, we are going to be examining three aspects of loving our neighbors: one, why it is important, two, how we display this love, and three, who our neighbor is. However, before we deep dive into these discussions, I want to take a look at a portion of Jesus' response in our focus passage.

Jesus' response regarding displaying love toward others states that we are to love our neighbors as ourselves. Jesus here is quoting from Leviticus 19:18 which reads, "You shall not take vengeance or bear a grudge against the sons of your own people, but you shall love your neighbor as yourself: I am the LORD." Verses 9 through 18 of Leviticus 19 deal with how to abide in right relationship with those around you. God highlights things such as being considerate of those in need (v.9-10), not seeking to take advantage of others through deception (v.11-12), being honest and living righteously before God (v.13-16), and harboring no hatred or resentment in your heart toward others, for to do so leads to sin, but to love those around you (v.17-18).

In both Leviticus 19:18 and Matthew 22:39, it is recorded, "Love your neighbor as yourself." I find the latter portion of this commandment of particular interest. Rarely do I think we truly take notice of it. I feel we have become so accustomed to this Scripture that we take little thought of it. If you would be so kind as to indulge me here for a minute, truly think about what this Scripture is saying: "Love your neighbor as yourself." What does it mean to love one as yourself?

I imagine some may scoff at this question, thinking it is elementary. Of course, to love one as yourself is to afford to them the same level of care, attention, and devotion that you afford to yourself. However, this is where I believe we fail to grasp the reach of this command. While we do show ourselves love, rarely, if ever, do we truly bestow upon ourselves the full level of love and care that we ought to. Rarely are we devoted to feeding ourselves properly with the right foods, granting ourselves the proper amount of sleep our bodies need, or giving ourselves time and space in which we can process our thoughts and emotions, or things such as these. In essence, rarely do we actually love ourselves. Therefore, if we were to approach this text and understand it as merely instructing us to give others the same care we give ourselves, the care that we would be giving them would not be a great display of love.

We will discuss here in a little bit what love looks like. However, one thing I want us to keep in the forefront of our minds as we discuss what love looks like is, how do we expect to bestow that level of love on others if we are not willing to bestow it upon ourselves? I am not saying we ought to be self-centered. Quite the contrary. As we have discussed previously, walking in humility is key to a Christian walk. Keeping this in mind, we need to understand that we will not be willing to freely give to someone that which we are not willing to give ourselves. If we don't care about ourselves and our own well-being, why do we think we will care about others and their well-being? Again, I am not saying we need to prioritize ourselves over others, but if we take a depressive stance regarding our own life, why do we think that depressive mindset will suddenly lift when involving others? We can put on a good face and smile and make a nice appearance, but what matters the most is the heart, not the outward appearance. To outwardly appear warm and caring, but to inside be cold and indifferent is to be a hypocrite. Therefore, the warmth and care we show others will be fake and in-genuine. Thereby, for the love we show others to be genuine, we first need to allow ourselves to experience it. As my pastor says, "You cannot lead others into an experience that you, yourself, have not yet had." We must keep this at the forefront of our thinking as we delve into this chapter.

Transitioning to the first part of our three-part discussion, the first thing we need to understand is why it is important to love our neighbor as ourselves. Speaking honestly, it is not easy to abide by this commandment. To walk in sincere obedience to this command requires great effort on our part, again, we will understand why that is when we discuss who our neighbor is. We (speaking of humanity as a whole) have this habit of "tapping out" when things become difficult. We prefer comfortability, ease, and things that require as little excursion as possible. In truth, there are only two ways in which we are able to step outside of this "tapping out." That is, one, having a great desire for that thing. Desire is a powerful tool.

Genuine, heartfelt desire can trump any innate instinct within us that drives us toward the comfortable and easy way out. The second is when we understand the importance or severity of a thing. However, responding properly concerning something of great importance requires maturity. Someone immature does not care about what is important, only what is desired. Therefore, this second way in which we break outside of the easy way requires growth mentally, emotionally, and spiritually. Thereby, beginning by laying out why we must adhere to this command aids us in breaking outside what is comfortable and easy, as long as we are mature. One final note I will add to this before moving on, being "mature" does not refer to a place in which we arrive at. To be "mature" means consistently traversing the path of growth ahead of us that leads us closer to God. Therefore, there are varying degrees of maturity, but all are on the path of maturity as long as they adhere to that path of upward growth.

Diving into why we need to adhere to this commandment of loving our neighbors as ourselves, we will be examining what the Apostle John had to say in I John 4. We are going to pick out key verses from this passage that relate to our topic here. Starting with verses 7-8, we read, "Beloved, let us love one another, for love is from God, and whoever loves has been born of God and knows God. Anyone who does not love does not know God, because God is love." John begins with the admonition to love one another, but he does not keep it so simple. Rather, he then quickly turns the attention from our relationship with each other, to God. He says, "for love is from God." The word "from" is "ek" which denotes the origin of a thing. Therefore, love originates in God. Thereby, as John concludes, "whoever loves has been born of God and knows God." Since love finds its origins in Him, to be born of Him (which alludes to the New Birth) and to know Him (which alludes to consistently walking in relationship with Him) is to display His love. If He is in us and we are in Him, then His love being shown forth from us will be a natural byproduct of that relationship. However, John also presents the flip side of this truth. That is, since He is the origin of love and abiding with Him and in Him would produce love in us, then those who do not display His love do not abide in Him. For if they did, they would display His love, for He is love.

John continues a couple of verses later and says, "Beloved, if God so loved us, we also ought to love one another. No one has ever seen God; if we love one another, God abides in us and his love is perfected in us" (v.11-12). First, John begins by implementing a love mandate. Another way one could word this would be: "Freely you received, freely give" (Matthew 10:28 NASB). We have done nothing to earn the love of God. In fact, we are told that He loved us even in our sins and willingly died on our behalf (see Romans 5:8). We have not earned His love, so why would we expect others to have to earn it? To operate in this mindset is not to abide in His love, but our own twisted idea of love that has been tainted through our human experience. After he establishes this love mandate, John then makes an interesting statement: "No one has ever seen God." Notice how the translation implements a semicolon here, indicating that the translators understood this statement to be intrinsically connected to the following statement. However, at a glance, this statement would not seem to fit the context of the rest of the passage. Did John jump off on a momentary rabbit trail? Not quite. John established earlier that God is love. However, here, he establishes that no one has ever seen God. If God is love and no one has seen God, then that implies that they are not able to properly perceive His love. It does not mean His love is not for them, for as we said, He loved us in our sins. However, their tainted perception has hindered their ability to properly perceive His love. How, then, do they perceive and experience His love? John answers this question for us. He says, "If we love one another, God abides in us and his love is perfected in us." In essence, what the Apostle John is saying is, the only way people who don't know God experience His abounding love is through our lives. Thereby, if we fail to love them, we fail to demonstrate God to them.

The Apostle John then ends his discussion on love with this emphatic statement: "If anyone says, 'I love God,' and hates his brother, he is a liar; for he who does not love his brother whom he has seen cannot love God whom he has not seen. And this commandment we have from him: whoever loves God must also love his brother" (v.20-21). John makes another very interesting statement here: "For he who does not love his brother whom he has seen cannot love God whom he has not seen." He is implying that it ought to be easier to love our neighbors because we have a greater awareness of them due to them abiding in the same realm of being as us. However, God does not abide in the same realm of being. God is Spirit (see John 4:24) and cannot be seen in the natural unless He manifests Himself. Therefore, if we are unable to love those we are more aware of, there is no way we could love one we have less awareness of. John closes with a statement that leaves no room for misunderstanding: "Whoever loves God must also love his brother." This statement is both a command and a declaration. We are commanded to love our neighbors as ourselves, however, it is likewise a declaration because if we truly love Him then love for our neighbors will naturally flow from that.

To summarize simply why it is important to abide by this command: if we fail to love our neighbors as ourselves then we will quickly fall out of right relationship with Jesus. Allow me to word it another way, if we fail to love our neighbors as ourselves that means we have never been in right relationship with Him. When we truly love Him, loving others will be a natural byproduct of that love.

The question that follows understanding the importance is, what does this love look like? The Bible is replete with beautiful examples of love. One of my personal favorites is contained in the Book of Ruth. It has always been one of my favorite books, and I thoroughly enjoy the looks of confusion when people ask me what my favorite book of the Bible is, and that is my answer. I have found that there are many who either had no idea there was a book of the Bible called Ruth, or know it exists but have no knowledge as to what it is about. Regardless of its lack of publicity within Christendom, I believe the Book of Ruth is one of the greatest displays of God's love, kindness, mercy, and grace. We could easily go through and dissect it and extract various qualities and attributes of love that are found within it. However, we will not do so because Paul already did so for us.

Paul writes in Corinthians:

"If I speak in the tongues of men and of angels, but

have not love, I am a noisy gong or a clanging cymbal. And if I have prophetic powers, and understand all mysteries and all knowledge, and if I have all faith, so as to remove mountains, but have not love, I am nothing. If I give away all I have, and if I deliver up my body to be burned, but have not love, I gain nothing. Love is patient and kind; love does not envy or boast; it is not arrogant or rude. It does not insist on its own way; it is not irritable or resentful; it does not rejoice at wrongdoing, but rejoices with the truth. Love bears all things, believes all things, hopes all things, endures all things."
-I Corinthians 13:1-7

In the preceding chapter, Paul instructs the Church of Corinth regarding the Gifts of the Spirit and the importance of abiding together in unity as one Body. I Corinthians 12 concludes with, "But earnestly desire the higher gifts. And I will show you a still more excellent way" (v.31). I Corinthians 13 then immediately dives into what has been dubbed by many, "The Way of Love."

Paul begins his lesson on love by painting a picture of a hypothetical individual who is powerful in the Gifts of the Spirit. Paul alludes to Tongues and Interpretation of Tongues, the Gift of Prophecy, the Word of Knowledge, and the Gift of Faith. One may observe another operating in one or all of these Gifts of the Spirit and think they are a mighty Christian. However, Paul is quick to demonstrate that it is not so much the operation of the Gift that is great, but the motivation behind it. He states that without love at the center, Tongues and Interpretation of Tongues is nothing more than an annoyance, and the Gift of Prophecy, Word of Knowledge, and Gift of Faith result in absolutely nothing.

Further, Paul does not relegate this teaching only to those operating in the Gifts of the Spirit but also points to one who lives a life of great sacrifice. In essence, he paints the picture of a seemingly good Christian. However, if love does not exist at the center of that life of sacrifice, it profits nothing.

Love gives what we do righteous meaning and purpose.

Apart from love, what we do is of no benefit to God or man. We may think that by keeping "busy" for His Kingdom that we are being of benefit. However, if love is not the driving force behind our business, then we are not aligned with Him, for He is love. Further, if we are not aligned with Him and His love, then our "business" is not actually benefiting His Kingdom at all. We are all called to make disciples, as we mentioned in Christians Abide with Christ, but if love is not at the heart of our discipleship, we will never make a disciple. How do I know that? Because He is love, and if we are not operating out of love in our "discipleship" then we are not showing Him to those we are "discipling." If we are not showing Him, then they are not following Him.

After establishing the need for love at the center of all that we do, Paul then dives into defining what love is. First, it is important to understand what Paul is referring to when he speaks on love. The word for "love" used by Paul is "agapē" which is the highest form of love in the Greek language that, in the Bible, is always used to refer to the love of God. Therefore, Paul is not seeking to define man's idea of love, but Jesus'.

The first attribute of love identified by Paul is patience. "Patient" here is "makrothumeō" which carries with it several various definitions all pertaining to the idea of patience, however, two definitions of this word that stand out to me are: "to be long-suffering; to wait with patient expectation." The first definition bears intrigue due to the mere idea of "long-suffering." It is easy to be "patient" when things are going well and there is little to no chaos in your life. The true test of patience is when there is suffering (which can encompass many things). Are you able to endure while suffering? Are you able to "suffer long?" The second definition is likewise extremely interesting because it indicates to us that patience is not merely waiting, it is expecting. Expectation is an interesting concept, for to expect a thing means you truly believe to witness or partake of that thing. Expectation is not optimism, it is a firm belief that exists without wavering. The question then becomes, what are we expecting? If our patience is aligned with His love, then our expectation lies in the fulfillment of His perfect will. Therefore, for love to be patient means it is willing to endure suffering while waiting on Him who turns all things for the good.

The second attribute of love is that of kindness. "Kind" is "chrēsteuomai" which can refer to the typical manifestations of kindness, however, it can also mean, "to show one's self useful." Thereby, another way in which we could understand kindness is to be reliable. To be someone who everyone can count on. This does not mean you become a doormat for everyone to walk over, it simply means you present yourself gently and meekly, faithfully performing the tasks that have been asked of you. Thus proving yourself to be someone that others can count on. When those above you know that they can trust you with a little, they will begin to trust you with a lot (see Luke 16:10). Therefore, for love to be kind refers to being someone others can rely upon and count on to be there for them in their time of need.

After establishing that love is patient and kind, Paul then transitions to demonstrating what love is not. His first on the list of "nots" is envy. Love does not envy. Envy is an interesting concept. Many possess the misunderstanding that envy and jealousy are synonymous when, in fact, they are quite different. To define it simply, jealousy refers to wanting something that another person has. For example, if two little kids are playing with one another and one has a toy that the other wants, the one who wants the toy that he does not have is jealous. However, envy is not concerned with having what someone else has. Envy is birthed out of hatred. Envy looks at what another has and, out of hatred, seeks to take that thing from them. Not because they want it for themselves, they merely don't want the other person to have it. Love and hate cannot coexist. Therefore, if one entertains envy in their heart, they do not abide in the love of Jesus.

Paul continues his list of "nots" by saying that love does not boast. "Boast" is "perpereuomai" which refers to placing one's self upon a pedestal. To boast about one's self is to make self the center of attention and to excessively draw attention to one's own accomplishments. Tied to this practice of boasting is exaggeration, or to put it plainly, lying. Those who boast embellish the truth to make themselves look better in the eyes of those around them. Boasting is completely self-centered and self-focused with little to no regard for anyone else. This is quite the opposite of the love that we are called to abide in. His love is other-focused, thereby, ours ought to be as well. Therefore, to keep the focus on the self is to abide in a place contrary to His love.

Further, Paul states that love is not arrogant. "Arrogant" in Greek is "phusioō," which, very simply, means "to inflate." The imagery this word creates is one of a balloon that is inflated to the point where it pops from the pressure within. One who is arrogant is only concerned about being filled and has no concern with filling others. The concept of arrogance is similar to boasting in regard to it being self-focused and not other-focused. However, "arrogant" draws more attention to the end result of such an attitude. That is, becoming so high on one's self to the point where you explode from the inside out due to the ever-increasing pressure of an egotistical spirit. In the end, the one who inflates themselves will be left with nothing.

Next, love is defined as not being rude. "Rude" is "aschēmoneō" which means, "to behave in an unbecoming manner." Further, "unbecoming," according to Webster's Dictionary, means, "improper for the person or character." In essence, Paul is saying that love abides in proper character. What we need to remember is that Paul is defining the highest level of love, or God's love, that manifests in us and through us. Thereby, when we speak on behavior that is improper for the person or character, that person or character is Jesus. Therefore, to abide in His love is to abide by His character. We could readily define His character as the Fruit of the Spirit laid out in Galatians 5. We will come back to such in a subsequent chapter.

Continuing, we learn that love does not insist on its own way. This phrase is made up of three Greek words: "zēteō ou heautou." One way this phrase could be translated is, "absolutely does not strive after itself." This type of mindset not only keeps self at the center of focus but also neglects all other pursuits. This attitude strives only after what is appealing to self with an utter disregard for everyone else and their thoughts and desires. Such a mindset and attitude abides in direct contradiction to love, for love considers others and endeavors to include them in what it strives for. Love is willing to lay itself aside for a time for the sake of another.

Paul then says that love is not irritable. "Irritable" is "paroxunō" which means, "to stir up; to easily provoke; to irritate; to arouse to anger." In essence, this refers to one who is quick to respond in anger. One way this could be understood is being the opposite of patience. Patience, as discussed, is to endure suffering. While to be irritable is to lash out at the first sign of just the possibility of opposition or suffering. To be irritable is to respond irrationally, without first taking into consideration, one, what is actually happening, and two, others whom your irrational outburst would impact.

Furthermore, love is not resentful. It is interesting that the ESV translates this portion of Scripture as "resentful" because it is actually three Greek words, "logizomai ou kakos." The KJV translates this phrase, "thinketh no evil." This translation more accurately captures the meaning behind the Greek words used here. Another way we could understand it would be, "to take inventory of no wickedness." In essence, this would refer to storing up sin or wickedness within you. What we store up within us will determine what flows out of us (see Luke 6:45), so if we take inventory of (store up) wickedness within us, wickedness will soon flow out of us.

Finally, love does not rejoice at wrongdoing, but with the truth. "Rejoice" is "chairō" which simply means "to find joy in," and "wrongdoing" is "adikia" which means "deceitfulness." The only truth is His truth, and to rejoice in anything contrary to His truth is to rejoice in wrongdoing. Love rejoices at His Word and when His Word is made evident in the lives of others. To rejoice in deceitfulness is to encourage the habit of giving place to deceit. If we rejoice in the deceitfulness in the lives of others, we encourage them to abide contrary to His truth. Jesus warns us that for the one who causes another to stumble, it would be better for him to have a heavy weight tied around his neck and then to be cast into the sea (see Matthew 18:6).

Paul ends his discussion on love with a summarizing statement as to what love concisely is. He says that loves bears ("stegō" which is "to patiently endure"), love believes ("pisteuō" which is "to be fully persuaded"), love hopes ("elpizō" which is "to have expectation"), and love endures ("hypomenō" which is "to persevere"). To concisely define love based on these summarizing statements from Paul: love faithfully gives time, attention, and strength to those around it with no partiality; love diligently pursues after what is right and true, not according to their own standard, but according to His standard.

There is a vitally important note we need to add regarding this discussion to stifle any misconception surrounding love. There is a very well-known story by Shel Silverstein called "The Giving Tree." This story is structured to be geared toward young children, which is quite unfortunate because young children are immensely impressionable and this story could easily birth a tainted view of love in their minds. If their perception of love is not set straight while they are still young, it will become increasingly difficult to reframe their idea of love as an adult. As the saying goes, "You can't teach an old dog new tricks." While you can, in fact, teach an old dog new tricks, it is increasingly difficult compared to teaching a puppy a new trick. A puppy is not yet set in its ways but is considerably impressionable. However, with an older dog, before you can teach it a new trick you must first break it of an old habit or mindset that would stand in contradiction to the new trick. Therefore, it requires twice the amount of time and effort. This is quite similar to the way humans work. As I mentioned above, a child is so impressionable. As we grow, we become set in our ways regarding certain mindsets and behaviors. Breaking these mindsets and behaviors as an adult is no easy feat.

Returning to "The Giving Tree," the story is centered around a large apple tree and a young boy. The story begins with the young boy playing with the tree, climbing the tree, eating its apples, and so on. The boy partakes of all that the tree has to offer, and then it says, "And the tree was happy." The story follows the boy as he ages, and at each point of his life, he desires something different. First, it is money, so the tree gives him its apples to sell. Then, it is a house, so the tree lets him cut off all its branches to build with. The house does not satisfy, now he wants a boat. Therefore, the tree gives him its whole trunk to cut down so that he can build a boat. Lastly, the boy comes back a tired old man and simply wants a place to rest. The tree, having nothing left but a stump, invites him to sit on it and rest. After each of these interactions between the boy and the tree it says, "And the tree was happy."

The moral of this story is meant to be that the tree loved the boy so much that it willingly gave everything it had to the boy. However, what this story teaches is not love, but self-negligence and self-deprecation. The tree found no happiness apart from acting out of self-deprecation on behalf of the boy. Do not misunderstand, love is indeed sacrificial and considers others. However, love is not and will never be self-neglecting or self-deprecating.

Some may say, "Does not God give just as the Giving Tree?" Many would likely quote John 3:16 in conveying this argument. Yes, He is the God of love and, as C.S. Lewis states, He largely operates in "gift-love." However, there is a key difference between God in His love and the Giving Tree's "love." That is, yes God gives, but He also expects something from us. He gives to us far more than we could ever earn or deserve, but He does expect that we worship Him and give ourselves (our time, energy, devotion, finances, etc) to Him. In The Giving Tree, however, it is never noted that the boy ever gave back to the tree. Rather, he only continuously took and demanded more.

As we pointed out at the start of this chapter, Jesus calls us to love our neighbors as ourselves. This implies that there must be a level of love that we have willingly experienced for ourselves before we can share it with others. The same love that we experience, we demonstrate to our neighbors. If love was truly what The Giving Tree attested it was, then what we would be demonstrating to others would be negligence and deprecation.

We have this idea that to love ourselves is an act of pride, but this is not true. To lust after ourselves would be an act of pride. However, to love ourselves simply means to care for and consider ourselves as well. Paul admonished us with these words: "Or do you not know that your body is a temple of the Holy Spirit within you, whom you have from God? You are not your own, for you were bought with a price. So glorify God in your body" (I Corinthians 6:19-20). Just as the Old Testament temple was greatly cared for and

181

looked after, so too ought we to be with ourselves. For we are now the temple for His Spirit within us. Just as they cared for the temple of old, we ought to care for this temple that we now possess.

Arriving at our final point for this chapter, we must understand just who our neighbor is. It is only when we truly grasp the scope of who our neighbor is that we can properly operate under this commandment to love them as ourselves.

Often our mindset regarding who our neighbors are correlates to those we are close to, such as family, friends, and loved ones. When we think of a neighbor, we tend to think of those whom we enjoy spending time with. Or, even if we don't necessarily enjoy it, we can tolerate it. This is not only the common mindset of today, it was also the common mindset of times past.

Jesus spoke to the Jews of His day and said, "You have heard that it was said, You shall love your neighbor and hate your enemy.' But I say to you, Love your enemies and pray for those who persecute you, so that you may be sons of your Father who is in heaven. For he makes his sun rise on the evil and on the good, and sends rain on the just and on the unjust. For if you love those who love you, what reward do you have? Do not even the tax collectors do the same? And if you greet only your brothers, what more are you doing than others? Do not even the Gentiles do the same? You therefore must be perfect, as your heavenly Father is perfect" (Matthew 5:43-48).

It is immediately obvious how the Jews had created a distinction between who they defined as their neighbors and who they defined as their enemy. They created this distinction which led to them loving the one while hating the other. The word for "hate" used here is "miseō" which is a powerful word. This word can possess a range of meanings spanning from thinking ill about someone else to detesting them to the point of persecuting them. In other words, this word not only encompasses the feeling of hatred but also the act of hatred. Jesus, then, flipped the paradigm. He first admonishes us to love our enemies. We have already extensively defined how we are to love, so we will not do so again. However, an examination of the word "enemies" proves to be of interest. "Echthros" is the Greek word here and it does not strictly refer to someone who actively opposes you. In fact, this word can refer to someone who is the object of your hate, even if they have not done anything against you. Therefore, this could refer to an unjust, unwarranted disdain. Jesus admonishes us that we ought to change our attitude (the issue is likely with us, not them) and instead of hating them, we need to show them love.

When looking at the Greek word for "hate" ("miseō") we conveyed how it can encompass the act of hatred, which is to persecute. It is interesting then that Jesus, in His flipping of the paradigm, says that even if others persecute us (hate us) we are not to retaliate in like fashion, rather, we are to pray for them. To pray on behalf of another is to tap into intercession which is to stand in the gap between them and God. We tap into intercession for others when they don't have the strength or understanding to be able to pray for themselves. In other words, by Jesus' admonishing us to pray for them, He is not saying to offer a cute prayer that lacks sincerity. Rather, He is commanding us to stand in the gap on their behalf, creating a connection between them and God that they are not able to create themselves. It is through such a connection that strength, wisdom, guidance, healing, deliverance, and salvation are manifested in the lives of those we intercede for. Therefore, when people persecute us, our response ought to be striving in prayer to connect them to Jesus. Jesus concludes His admonishment to love our enemies and pray for our persecutors by revealing that when we do so we will become sons of our Father who is in Heaven. Implying that we are never more like Him than we pray for those who seek to do us harm.

After establishing that the scope of who our neighbors are reaches beyond those whom we like, Jesus then says, "For if you love those who love you, what reward do you have? Do not even the tax collectors do the same? And if you greet only your brothers, what more are you doing than others? Do not even the Gentiles do the same?" It is easy to love those who love us, this type of relationship requires little effort. Even those who do not abide in His grace are able to do this. Therefore, for those of us who do abide in His grace, how much more ought we to display love? If we meet only the world's standards regarding love, then our focus is on the wrong thing.

Jesus then ends by saying, "You therefore must be perfect, as your heavenly Father is perfect." The word "perfect" here is not "perfect" as we understand it in Western culture. We see or hear the word "perfect" and automatically think of something without fault or blemish, something that has fully arrived. However, the Greek here is "teleios" which refers to growing in maturity. What is Jesus saying? In essence, failing to love our neighbors, even if they are an "enemy," is a sign of spiritual immaturity and a sign that you are not His child. For those who are children of the King abide in like character with the King.

Before closing out this chapter, I feel it pertinent to draw attention to a parable of Jesus that beautifully demonstrates what it truly means to love your neighbor as yourself. We read in Luke:

> But he, desiring to justify himself, said to Jesus, "And who is my neighbor?" Jesus replied, "A man was going down from Jerusalem to Jericho, and he fell among robbers, who stripped him and beat him and departed, leaving him half dead. Now by chance a priest was going down that road, and when he saw him he passed by on the other side. So likewise a Levite, when he came to the place and saw him, passed by on the other side. But a Samaritan, as he journeyed, came to where he was, and when he saw him, he had compassion. He went to him and bound up his wounds, pouring on oil and wine. Then he set him on his own animal and brought him to an inn and took care of him. And the next day he took out two denarii and gave them to the innkeeper, saying, 'Take care of him, and whatever more you spend, I will repay you when I come back.' Which of these three, do you think, proved to be a neighbor to the man who fell among the robbers?" He said, "The one who showed him mercy." And Jesus said to him, "You go, and do likewise."
> -10:29-37

This is a very well-known parable and we are not going to dissect it here, merely point out a few key points. Perhaps the key point of this parable revolves around the characters Jesus creates. We aren't told exactly who the "man" is, but it is heavily implied that the "man" is to be understood as being a Jew. The story goes that this presumed Jew is robbed and beaten to the point of death, utterly helpless. As he lies helpless, two members of the Jewish elite (a priest and a Levite) walk past him with utter disregard, to the point of crossing to the other side of the road. An argument could be made that these two members of the religious elite were abstaining from helping him due to their religious duties. Due to his beaten state, if they had touched him it would have made them unclean, thus hindering them from their religious duties. However, if we accept this argument that means we value duty over love. Regardless of their duties and what may have transpired had they touched him, they ought to have shown him love and cared for him in his time of need.

The story continues and Jesus adds another character into the fold, that is, a Samaritan. Why is this significant? To properly comprehend the magnitude of what Jesus was saying, we need to understand the significance surrounding the relationship between Jews and Samaritans.

An in-depth study of the relationship between the Jews and Samaritans is beyond the scope of this book, but there are a few key factors we need to understand. It is important to understand that the Jews and Samaritans were related, albeit distant relatives. The Samaritan people were birthed when Jews intermingled with Gentiles, thus creating an "off-breed" Jew. While these people still aimed to live as if they were Jews, the "pure-bred" Jews refused to welcome them into their fold. This separation went so far as the Jews viewing the Samaritans as "dogs" and utterly avoiding even the slightest of interactions with them. One thing of interest to note regarding the whole "off-breed" versus "pure-bred" analogy: Jews themselves were not truly "pure-bred" as they might have liked to think. A careful study of the Old Testament will quickly reveal several non-Jewish spouses that added to the Jewish lineage.

We see various examples of this divide played out in the

Gospels. One is found in John 4, we read Jesus interacting with a Samaritan woman and her utter astonishment that He is doing so. At one point she says to Him, "How is that you, a Jew, ask for a drink from me, a Samaritan woman" (v.9)? Further, to ensure that the audience understood this question, the Apostle John adds, "(For Jews had no dealings with Samaritans)" (v.9). The story continues and His disciples witness Him interacting with her. It says, "Just then his disciples came back. They marveled that he was talking with a woman, but no one said, 'What do you seek?' or, 'Why are you talking with her' (v.27)? They marveled in such a way not because he was interacting with a woman, for there were several women that followed Him, but their marveling was predicated on the fact that they recognized her as a Samaritan.

A second example is found in Luke 9. We read of Jesus seeking to enter into a Samaritan village to minister to them. He aims to first prepare the village by sending messengers ahead of him (v.52). However, the Samaritan village rejected His messengers, thereby rejecting Him (v.53). Being rejected, He turned to head toward Jerusalem. His disciples, James and John, were not so content with just moving on. Their underlying, cultural hatred for the Samaritan people quelled up within them. We read, "And when his disciples James and John saw it, they said, 'Lord, do you want us to tell fire to come down from heaven and consume them?' But he turned and rebuked them" (v.54-55). It is evident that the disciples' responses were birthed from a cultural bias that had been passed down to them from the generations prior. Jesus, who is the God of love, sharply rebukes this response because it is birthed out of hatred.

Thus, returning to the parable, we see how revolutionary this concept presented by Jesus was. The idea of a Samaritan man endeavoring to love and care for a Jewish man never crossed the minds of the people. However, this parable aimed to answer the question, "Who is my neighbor?" By Jesus centering the story around a Jewish man and a Samaritan man, He was stating that who our neighbor is extends beyond what is comfortable, convenient, or the cultural norm. To love our neighbor as ourselves requires a radical adherence to the way of love.

The word choice of "radical" is very intentional. Oxford Languages translates this word, as "(especially of change or action) relating to or affecting the fundamental nature of something; far-reaching or thorough." To love our neighbors as ourselves requires us to break outside not only what is the cultural norm, but what our natural inclinations are. To love our neighbors as ourselves requires radical transformation from the inside out that only comes through abiding in the God who is love.

Focused Reflection

Love is an essential aspect of a Christian's walk. Truly, one cannot claim to be Christian at all if there is no love in their hearts. John said, "Anyone who does not love does not know God, because God is love" (I John 4:8). Therefore, we could say that love is the essential aspect of a Christian's walk. This love that we walk in is not just toward God or just toward man but toward God and man. Further, it is not love as humanity defines it, but as God defines it in His Word.

Regarding loving our neighbors, we must understand that we cannot fully love our neighbors until we first abide in a love-filled relationship with God. When Jesus was asked about the greatest commandment, He first quoted Deuteronomy 6:4, which is to love God with our whole being. He then followed that with Leviticus 19:18, which is to love your neighbor as yourself. God is love, therefore to be able to convey that love to others, we must first have it for ourselves.

1. How would you define "love"? Now read I Corinthians 13:1-8. Does your definition of love align with God's?

2. Would you say that love is not just present in your life, but the major factor behind what you do, what you say, and how you respond?

3. How do you think you could display a more love-filled demeanor that reflects Christ?

No one has ever seen God; if we love one another,
God abides in us and his love is perfected in us.
-I John 4:12

12
Christians Freely Forgive
Christians Love Their Neighbors II

"For if you forgive others their trespasses, your heavenly Father will also forgive you, but if you do not forgive others their trespasses, neither will your Father forgive your trespasses."
~Matthew 6:14-15

Truly, one cannot speak about loving their neighbors without discussing forgiveness. To do so would be to fall short of discussing the topic to an adequate extent. Therefore, we will endeavor to examine this topic thoroughly. Why give such thorough attention to forgiveness though? The answer to that question is answered by our opening text: "For if you forgive others their trespasses, your heavenly Father will also forgive you, but if you do not forgive others their trespasses, neither will your Father forgive your trespasses." We mustn't take this Scripture lightly, for it has eternal ramifications.

There is a Scripture that is very commonly quoted throughout all of Christendom, that is, "Give, and it will be given to you. Good measure, pressed down, shaken together, running over, will be put into your lap. For with the measure you use it will be measured back to you" (Luke 6:38). What is interesting about this Scripture is that when we quote it, we so often take it completely out of context. Many can attest to hearing this Scripture quoted by the man or woman of God when they are receiving the tithe and offerings. Truly, taken at face value by itself, it is easy to understand where this understanding came from that linked this Scripture to financial giving and sacrifice. That is, however, not what this Scripture is pertaining to at all.

To understand the true meaning of this Scripture, we need to take into context the preceding verse: "Judge not, and you will not be judged; condemn not, and you will not be condemned; forgive, and you will be forgiven" (Luke 6:37). Understanding that this verse is the backdrop upon which the proceeding verse is positioned, we come to understand that Jesus is declaring that according to the measure of judgment, condemnation, and forgiveness that we give to others He will, thereby, determine what to give us. In other words, we determine the eternal reward we receive.

The word "measure" in verse 38 is the word "metron." This word specifically refers to a set standard or the thing against which all others are weighed. Truly, I cannot stress this enough. We (and by "we" I mean the totality of humanity) have this incredibly bad habit of being very narrowly focused. We see or hear something that we like, something that is pleasing to us, and we hone in on that thing. In doing so, we exclude everything that is seeming contradictory to it. However, we assume too quickly. Often what we assume to be contradictory is, in actuality, an integral part of the thing we are focused on. Because of our narrow focus, we fail to perceive the vast scope of the thing. We do this all the time with Scripture. We are all guilty of it. I pray that we lay aside our self-righteous attitudes and come with a repentant heart unto Jesus, seeking to come to proper alignment with Him and His Word.

Why do I say all this pertaining to this topic? Because so often we violently grab hold of one Scripture and allow that one Scripture to become the totality of our belief system. God forbid! How often do you hear it quoted, "If we confess our sins, he is faithful and just to forgive us our sins and to cleanse us from all unrighteousness" (I John 1:9)? I am not discounting the truth of this Scripture. I praise and thank Jesus for the truth of this verse. Without it, where would we be? What I am saying is that a Scripture such as this must be taken into context with the rest of what He says about forgiveness. Only when we bring into a cohesive whole all of what Scripture declares regarding a particular topic do we come to the full, proper understanding of it.

To truly begin our discussion here, I feel it necessary to begin by outlining why we, indeed, need forgiveness. From there, we will endeavor to discuss His mercy toward us. Finally, we will then end by examining our participation in forgiveness by bestowing it on others.

Beginning with why we need forgiveness; some of what we will discuss here has been discussed in previous chapters, either in little or abundance. However, we mustn't dismiss it merely because it has been said elsewhere. We must endeavor to garner a cohesive understanding.

Our need for forgiveness begins at the beginning. True to its name, Genesis assuredly serves as the firm foundation for the rest of the Bible. We read how God created all things and then created man in His own image. He created man, forming Him unto His likeness, breathed into him His Spirit (breath of life), and then placed him in the Garden of Eden. Placing man in the Garden, He decrees that man has dominion and authority over all creation, and that the fruit of the Garden would be their sustenance (see Genesis 1:28-30). But, there was an exception. We read, "And the LORD God commanded the man, saying, 'You may surely eat of every tree of the garden, but of the tree of the knowledge of good and evil you shall not eat, for in the day that you eat of it you shall surely die'" (Genesis 2:16-17).

We could go into a long discussion about this Tree of the Knowledge of Good and Evil and why it was placed in the Garden and why Adam and Eve were forbidden from partaking of it if everything He created was "very good." However, such a discussion is beyond the scope of this chapter. What is important to understand is that God presented Adam and Eve with a choice: to love and obey Him, or to love and obey themselves (their carnal desires). God created humanity with the sole intent of having someone to have genuine relationship with. This could not be a forced relationship, for love is a choice. For this relationship to be fulfilling, man had to choose God.

The story goes, as we all likely well know, man failed to choose God and, indeed, chose self. They partook of the Tree of the Knowledge of Good and Evil, thus disobeying God. In doing so, just as He declared, they invited death into their lives.

A common question I have frequently been asked: "Why are the wages of sin death (as stated in Romans 6:23)?" We must understand that He is righteous (see Psalms 145:17), holy (see Leviticus 11:45), perfect (see Deuteronomy 32:4), pure (see I John 3:3), and that He is life itself (see Acts 3:15). It is not merely that He exhibits these attributes, it's that He is these attributes. Or, in other words, apart from Him these attributes are without existence.

He is the source of them all. Further, He cannot contradict Himself (see Numbers 23:19). Thereby, He could never act outside of these attributes. Why is this important to understand? Because, if He is the source of all these things, then where these things are absent, He is absent. Therefore, when Adam and Eve partook of the tree, they forsook righteousness, holiness, perfection, and purity, thereby forsaking life itself. In doing so, they partook of death. That is why, the wages of sin is death.

Unfortunately, by Adam and Eve partaking of death, it opened the door for death to grab hold of each new generation. This is confirmed to us not only through examining Scripture but also very directly by Paul in I Corinthians 15:22 wherein he declares that in Adam all die. Regarding this, there is an important distinction we need to make. It is not that every human is immediately born a sinner. Sin is a choice just as love and obedience are a choice. However, what we are born with is a sinful nature or an inclination toward sin. Thereby, all ultimately sin because we are not strong enough, in and of ourselves, to resist that inclination toward sin. This is confirmed to us by both the Apostle John and the Apostle Paul. John writes, "If we say we have no sin, we deceive ourselves, and the truth is not in us…If we say we have not sinned, we make him a liar, and his word is not in us" (I John 1:8,10). Paul, then, writes, "For all have sinned and fall short of the glory of God" (Romans 3:23). Elsewhere, he states, "As it is written: 'None is righteous, no, not one; no one understands; no one seeks for God. All have turned aside; together they have become worthless; no one does good, not even one. Their throat is an open grave; they use their tongues to deceive. The venom of asps is under their lips. Their mouth is full of curses and bitterness. Their feet are swift to shed blood; in their paths are ruin and misery, and the way of peace they have not known. There is no fear of God before their eyes" (Romans 3:10-18).

Each and every one of us are filthy, rotten sinners because we have all chosen our carnal desires over Him. Each and every one of us is deserving of death because of the choices that we have made. That is the truth of the matter. If God were to righteously judge us according to our works, we would all be sentenced to death. Remember, however, He created us so that He could have a people to abide in relationship with. He wanted a people to love who would, in turn, love Him back. Therefore, because of His great love for us, He chose a different route than that of righteous judgment. God, in His abundant and steadfast love, chose mercy.

We see this act of mercy played out from the very beginning. Looking back to the account revolving around the fall of man. We read, "Then the LORD God said, 'Behold, the man has become like one of us in knowing good and evil. Now, lest he reach out his hand and take also of the tree of life and eat, and live forever—' therefore the LORD God sent him out from the garden of Eden to work the ground from which he was taken. He drove out the man, and at the east of the garden of Eden he placed the cherubim and a flaming sword that turned every way to guard the way to the tree of life" (Genesis 3:22-24).

Some interpret this passage as an act of judgment on God's behalf, but that is the incorrect understanding of what is transpiring here. Man had just partaken of sin, which is death, ultimately separating them from Jesus. If, then, He had allowed them to stay in the Garden and then partake of the Tree of Life, they would have lived forever in this state of separation. To put it quite literally, paradise (Eden) would have become what Christendom defines as "hell." That is, eternal separation from God. If He had allowed them to remain and partake of the tree, that would have been judgment. To live for eternity in their mistake. Rather, because of His desire for love, He cast man out of the Garden of Eden to save them from the possibility of eternal separation. In doing so, He opened the door to the possibility for that relationship to be rekindled, that separation to be mended.

When approaching the subject of God's mercy, we must understand that it is completely undeserved on our end. In truth, we deserve the separation and death that we sought out. Mercy is not something we are owed, but something that is freely given to us. Webster's Dictionary defines "mercy" as, "that benevolence, mildness or tenderness of heart which disposes a person to overlook injuries, or to treat an offender better than he deserves; the disposition that tempers justice, and induces an injured person to forgive trespasses and injuries, and to forbear punishment, or inflict less than law or justice will warrant. In this sense, there is perhaps no word in our language precisely synonymous with mercy. That which comes nearest to it is grace. It implies benevolence, tenderness, mildness, pity or compassion, and clemency, but exercised only towards offenders. Mercy is a distinguishing attribute of the Supreme Being." Therefore, whenever we witness mercy being displayed, it is purely due to the goodness and love of God. Nothing else.

It is of vital importance that we firmly grasp this truth. We've noted previously how humanity is prone to exhibit the mindset and attitude that we are owed things. We are heavily inclined toward pride. God forgive us if we ever operate out of the mindset that we are owed mercy. As stated above, we are owed separation, death, and damnation. No more, no less. It is His goodness that has saved us from those things.

The mercy of God is prevalent all throughout the Old Testament. All one must do is read through the history of Israel and see how frequently they forsook Him for other false gods and idols. Yet, He never forsook them. Did He allow them to experience turmoil? Absolutely, but as a means of drawing them back to Him. C.S. Lewis describes suffering as God's megaphone to a people who are deaf of hearing and dull of seeing. And it worked, but for only a time. The people would feel the weight of the suffering and cry out for Him and He would respond in but a moment. Time and time again we witness this: them forsaking, Him drawing, and then them forsaking again. Yet He never loosed His hold on them.

The Prophet Jeremiah in his Book of Lamentations declared, "The steadfast love of the LORD never ceases; his mercies never come to an end; they are new every morning; great is your faithfulness" (Lamentations 3:22-23). The love of God is forever intertwined with His mercy. For one can be merciful apart from love, but that mercy will last but a season. What causes the mercy of God to be perpetuated is His steadfast love which never ceases. That is why Jeremiah declared, "They are new every morning." "They" is referring to His love and His mercy, for it is His love that causes His mercy to be made new every morning. Then it is proclaimed, "Great is your faithfulness." Paul declared, "If we are faithless, he remains faithful—for he cannot deny himself" (II Timothy 2:13). The truth of the matter is we will be faithless, for we are imperfect and flawed. It is because of His great love and mercy that He remains ever faithful to us even in our wandering.

Taking a step back for a moment, we noted how His mercy has been on display since the beginning. How His expulsion of Adam and Eve from the Garden of Eden was, indeed, an act of mercy and not judgment. We likewise see another act of mercy demonstrated by Him in the Garden. The sin that Adam and Eve partook of produced shame within them. This shame caused them to feel the need to cover themselves. They felt naked (even though they had been, by definition, naked the whole time). God, then, took the life of one or more of His creations for the express purpose of covering them and their shame. If He sought to judge them at this moment, He would've forced them to remain in their shame. However, because of His love, He took life to cover shame.

This act foreshadowed what was to come. For not only do we see animal sacrifices in the very next chapter, but later we read of how God implemented animal sacrifices as the means of pushing back the sins of the people. We all know this and take for granted this knowledge, but truly think on that truth for a moment. God allowed man to kill and slaughter other creatures within His creation so that they could benefit from their life. He so loved humanity which was created in His image that He allowed lesser aspects of His creation to suffer on their behalf.

This, as we know, was ultimately insufficient, for humanity was created in His image, and the various animals and creatures that were slain were not. The creatures slain could not truly cover the sin of humanity because they were unequal. The author of Hebrews said it well wherein he wrote, "For it is impossible for the blood of bulls and goats to take away sins. Consequently, when Christ came into the world, he said, 'Sacrifices and offerings you have not desired, but a body have you prepared for me; in burnt offerings and sin offerings you have taken no pleasure. Then I said, 'Behold, I have come to do your will, O God, as it is written of me in the scroll of the book'" (Hebrews 10:4-7). The latter portion of this passage speaks of His greatest act of mercy ever.

The blood of the various creatures did not fully suffice but left a void still. That, therefore, meant that the separation between God and man had not been mended. Man still dwelt in death. For man to be renewed in life, one equal to humanity would have to die in their place. This, however, could not be just any human, but the perfect sacrifice, without spot or blemish. The issue was, man could never do this themselves. As we have discussed, man is born with this inclination toward sin and we all ultimately give into that inclination. Man could never suffice as the perfect sacrifice, for all that we have to offer is death.

God, in His abundant wisdom and knowledge, was not ignorant of this truth. In fact, He knew the path man would follow before He called forth anything into being. We are told in Revelation 13:8 that He is the Lamb slain from the foundation of the world. What is a foundation? A foundation is a baseline, it is the support, it is what gives strength and security to all that stands atop it. Therefore, the fact that He was the Lamb slain from the foundation of the world indicates that His sacrifice was what all creation was built upon. Meaning, God brought all things into existence on the back of His plan to become the perfect sacrifice. The fall of man did not catch God off guard, rather, He knew it before He ever said, "Let there be…"

The incarnation was the ultimate act of mercy ever performed. The Apostle Paul writes to us and says, "But God shows his love for us in that while we were still sinners, Christ died for us" (Romans 5:8). Jesus Himself echoes this truth in the well-known passage that declares, "For God so loved the world, that he gave his only Son, that whoever believes in him should not perish but have eternal life. For God did not send his Son into the world to condemn the world, but in order that the world might be saved through him" (John 3:16-17). No longer did He merely allow humanity to take advantage of the blood of animals, now He offered His own life and blood on behalf of humanity. Acts 20:28 very directly declares that He purchased the Church through His own blood. Because of His sinless nature, His blood was perfect and full of life. Thereby, when it was shed, it conquered the sting of death that had tormented humanity for generations.

Not only did His act of great mercy bring about redemption

from sin and life evermore, but it also gave Him a new perspective. What do I mean? The author of Hebrews tells us, "For we do not have a high priest who is unable to sympathize with our weaknesses, but one who in every respect has been tempted as we are, yet without sin. Let us then with confidence draw near to the throne of grace, that we may receive mercy and find grace to help in time of need" (Hebrews 4:15-16). He was already a God of great mercy before the Incarnation (as we discussed), but being manifest in the flesh and being tormented with the same struggles that we are birthed within Him a deeper understanding as to what we experience. His experiencing our weaknesses created a greater level of sympathy within Him to where now He affords even more mercy.

But why it is important to understand our sinfulness and His mercifulness? When we understand who we were and are and who He is toward us, it cultivates within us a greater level of gratitude and love. When we understand how much mercy we are bestowed day after day, it creates a spirit of thanksgiving within us. A truly thankful heart does not hoard everything to itself but longs for others to experience what has made them so thankful. Therefore, when we understand our depravity and His abundant mercy, we will become more willing to share that same mercy we have experienced with others.

We opened up this chapter by discussing the utter necessity surrounding forgiving others if we truly desire to be forgiven. It is a truth rarely talked about, but it is vital nonetheless. Therefore, not only ought we to display forgiveness through the overflow of thankfulness within us, but also because it is in alignment with His character of love. If we refuse to forgive, not only do we forsake forgiveness ourselves, but we also forsake His abiding presence in our lives.

There is a passage from the Gospel of Matthew that further speaks on this truth. The passage begins with an interaction between Peter and Jesus. We read, "Then Peter came to Him and said, 'Lord, how often shall my brother sin against me, and I forgive him? Up to seven times?' Jesus said to him, 'I do not say to you, up to seven times, but up to seventy times seven'" (Matthew 18:21-22 NKJV). The first thing of importance to notice is that Peter is not asking in reference to forgiveness for a whole day but for one individual. He was not saying, "Should I give forgiveness up to seven times in one day?" Rather, he had the understanding (at least in part) that forgiveness ought to be prominent in his life. In Peter's mind, forgiving a single person seven times in a single day sounded like a lot. And, indeed, it would be. I honestly cannot recall a time I had to forgive one person in one day even close to seven times. However, it is not outside the realm of possibility. Therefore, Jesus countered by taking that number and multiplying it significantly. Many translations (such as the ESV, BSB, NIV, and so on) translate Jesus' response as "seventy-seven times." The KJV and NKJV, however, translate it as "seventy times seven." I chose the NKJV for this passage because it more accurately conveys what Jesus was trying to get across. In truth, Jesus was not implementing an exact number of times we are able to forgive one person in one day, rather, the Greek word for "seventy times" is "hebdomēkontakis" which more accurately refers to "countless times." Meaning, Jesus was saying that there ought to be no limit to how many times we are willing to forgive one individual in a single day. But, just for good measure, He also added seven more times on top of the countless times, lest we misunderstood.

Let's stop and think about that for a minute. Imagine a brother or sister continually sinning against you, over and over again. In our human nature, we struggle to forgive just once. Imagine if we had to forgive over and over again for the same offense by the same person on the same day. The very idea of that annoys us, but it's Bible. We may ask, "Why would Jesus ask such a thing of us?" My answer would be to point us back to our previous discussion. How many times in a single day do we sin against Him? There are many times wherein we sin against Him and are unaware of it. Despite our ignorance, we still need forgiveness. That is how it will often be regarding our forgiveness toward others. They may be ignorant of the need for forgiveness. They may be completely unaware of how they have offended us. And it is not always necessary for us to point it out to them either. There are times when there needs to be healthy confrontation, but most times we simply need to forgive and let go.

So often we have this twisted mindset that if we withhold

forgiveness that it will hurt that person. How much further from the character of Christ could this be? Lord purge us if we ever operate out of this mindset. One, our aim should never be how to get back at others. If judgment is required then He is the One to pass it. Time and time again we are told throughout Scripture that vengeance belongs to Him (see Deuteronomy 32:35; Leviticus 19:18; Proverbs 20:22; Romans 12:17-19; Hebrews 10:30). Why? Because He is righteous and holy, without fault or sinful nature. Our judgment is tainted by our inclination toward sin. His judgment is perfect. Two, this idea that withholding forgiveness somehow hurts the other has no basis in Scripture. In truth, the only one we are hurting is ourselves, as we have discussed. Forgiveness is freeing and healing to all involved.

Returning to our passage; after Jesus restructures Peter's way of thinking, He then tells a parable illustrating the importance of forgiving others. The passage reads:

"Therefore the kingdom of heaven may be compared to a king who wished to settle accounts with his servants. When he began to settle, one was brought to him who owed him ten thousand talents. And since he could not pay, his master ordered him to be sold, with his wife and children and all that he had, and payment to be made. So the servant fell on his knees, imploring him, 'Have patience with me, and I will pay you everything.' And out of pity for him, the master of that servant released him and forgave him the debt. But when that same servant went out, he found one of his fellow servants who owed him a hundred denarii, and seizing him, he began to choke him, saying, 'Pay what you owe.' So his fellow servant fell down and pleaded with him, 'Have patience with me, and I will pay you.' He refused and went and put him in prison until he should pay the debt. When his fellow servants saw what had taken place, they were greatly distressed, and they went and reported to their master all that had taken place. Then his master summoned him and

said to him, 'You wicked servant! I forgave you all that debt because you pleaded with me. And should not you have had mercy on your fellow servant, as I had mercy on you?' And in anger his master delivered him to the jailers, until he should pay all his debt. So also my heavenly Father will do to every one of you, if you do not forgive your brother from your heart."
-Matthew 18:23-25

The parable told by Jesus is centered around a servant who owed a king a great debt. The time came for the debt to be settled and the servant could not pay. The servant begged for mercy from the king and promised to repay him. However, the king likely knew the servant would never be able to repay the debt, for it says that the servant owed him "ten thousand talents." By presenting the amount of "ten thousand talents" Jesus was signifying an absurd amount, for this was more money than the servant would have likely seen throughout his whole life. Therefore, the king chose mercy and cleared the insurmountable debt. How, then, did the recently forgiven servant respond? In thankfulness and gratitude? In love and appreciation? No, unfortunately, he chose greed and selfishness. He chose the mindset of, "How greatly can I profit?" Therefore, he went to a fellow servant who owed him a mere "hundred denarii." In essence, this amount equaled around a hundred days' worth of wages. Not a small amount, but not impossible to pay back like the first servant's debt was. When the second servant begged for mercy, the first refused to give it.

The story goes that the king caught wind of what the forgiven servant had been doing and ordered him to appear before him again. Because of the servant's lack of thankfulness, gratefulness, appreciation, and love, the debt he was released from was now placed upon him once again. Let's think about that for a minute but concerning our own lives. The parable begins with the servant being forgiven. Forgiveness had been granted. However, due to him not abiding in the spirit of forgiveness, what he had been forgiven of was placed back on him. What sin, weight, and debt could possibly be placed back on us if we forsake the spirit of forgiveness? It is a chilling question. We all have a testimony regarding where He brought us from. We all could tell stories that would make jaw drops. We praise and thank Jesus for His mercy and grace. What then would happen if we refused to offer the same?

Jesus makes a critical statement at the close of His parable that we cannot overlook or ignore. Forgiveness cannot be a half-hearted, in-genuine, and in-sincere thing we do. Forgiveness is not merely uttering "I forgive you," those are just words. What is the heart behind what is being said? That is exactly what Jesus conveys, that forgiveness must be birthed from the heart. The word "forgive" from verse 35 is "aphiēmi" which can be translated in a plethora of different ways, but each possible translation ultimately refers to a releasing, a freeing, or a letting go. This freeing must take place within our "heart." "Heart" here is "kardia" which refers to the inward man (the emotions, thoughts, and will of an individual). There must be a release that transpires within us that is then capsulated with the utterance of that release: "I forgive you." Only after the declaration has been made inwardly can it mean anything outwardly.

As I stated at the start of this chapter, you cannot speak about loving others without speaking about forgiveness. We all experience the incomprehensible love of the Father through Jesus' astounding display of mercy. Having been so loved, and having been so forgiven, it is not too much to ask that we do the same. For, in truth, we are merely inviting others to experience what we have been so gracious to experience ourselves.

If we truly claim to abide in the love of Jesus and claim to have experienced His mercy, the natural by-product of those things will our bestowing them upon others. The best way for Christians to live is with open hands stretched out in front of them, palms facing toward Heaven. In living this way, we are able to both freely receive and freely give.

Live with open hands before God and others.

Kristopher David Grepke

Focused Reflection

One cannot speak on love without discussing the topic of forgiveness. Forgiveness cannot truly be apart from love, likewise, love is not truly present if there is not also forgiveness. Forgiveness is a major point of teaching primarily in the New Testament, but it is also present in the Old Testament. Jesus made it a major focal point in many of His teachings and parables. At several different points, He went so far as to say that if we refuse to forgive, then He will likewise not forgive us (see Matthew 6:14-15).

People often think that by withholding forgiveness they are, somehow, hurting the individual seeking forgiveness. One, that statement alone should reveal the lack of love in the heart of such an individual. Love never seeks to cause unnecessary suffering. Furthermore, while you may hurt the feelings of the one you refuse to forgive, you are actually hurting yourself more. It is like holding a rose bush twig and poking the person with it. Being poked may be slightly irritating, but the twig you are holding is covered in thorns.

1. Can you think of a scenario recently where you were in the position to give or withhold forgiveness? How did you respond?

2. What was the heart behind the decision you made?

3. Have you ever withheld forgiveness? How did it make you feel?

And forgive us our debts, as we also have forgiven
our debtors.
-Matthew 6:12

13
Christians Are a Light

"You are the light of the world. A city set on a hill
cannot be hidden. Nor do people light a lamp and put
it under a basket, but on a stand, and it gives light to
all in the house. In the same way, let your light shine
before others, so that they may see your good works
and give glory to your Father who is in heaven."
~Matthew 5:14-16

In the previous two chapters, we have discussed in-depth
loving our neighbors (which extends to our "enemies") and, thereby,
freely giving forgiveness just as we have been forgiven. While I am
not treating this chapter as a direct tie-in to the previous two, the
discussion on being a light is predicated upon what was discussed
in the previous two chapters. In truth, no one will ever receive you
as a light until you love as He loves and forgive as He forgives. The
words of Theodore Roosevelt have forever become engrained in the
pages of history: "People don't care how much you know until they
know how much you care." Those profound words have been uttered
more times since their original conception than one could number.
While that exact wording is not found in the Bible, the Bible does,
however, present the same truth to us through example.

We could easily look to our Example, the One and Only,
Jesus Christ Himself. Jesus was YAHWEH incarnate, and the
purpose for His incarnation was to draw unto Him a people that
would love Him and enter into His Kingdom with Him. Jesus came
preaching and teaching the truths pertaining to His soon-coming
Kingdom. However, this was not all He did. While His Words were
powerful, life-changing, and full of wisdom and grace, and many
were astounded at how He spoke, the majority of the people were not
drawn by His Word, but first they were drawn by His compassion.

To give an example of this we could quote Matthew's
presentation of the beginning of His ministry:

And he went throughout all Galilee, teaching in their synagogues and proclaiming the gospel of the kingdom and healing every disease and every affliction among the people. So his fame spread throughout all Syria, and they brought him all the sick, those afflicted with various diseases and pains, those oppressed by demons, those having seizures, and paralytics, and he healed them. And great crowds followed him from Galilee and the Decapolis, and from Jerusalem and Judea, and from beyond the Jordan.
-Matthew 4:23-25

Notice how it does not say that His fame spread due to His Word, but it was His compassion that was displayed through power over sickness and oppression that caused the crowds to flock unto Him. Don't misunderstand, I am not saying His Words were unimportant or of no effect. His Word is the most powerful thing in all creation. It was His Word that ushered all things into being and it is by His Word that all things are sustained. His Word has the complete power to change, transform, renew, and restore. However, it was His loving-kindness that drew the people unto Him. Once they were then drawn unto Him, that is when they then stayed to receive His Word.

We again see this demonstrated in the same reference from Matthew. Chapter 4 of Matthew ends with the crowds flocking to Him due to His compassion and power. After pouring out into the lives of the people His power, He then begins to pour into them His Word. Chapters 5 through 7 of Matthew contain what is known as "The Sermon on the Mount," possibly some of the most profound teaching in history. Therefore, they came for His love but stayed for His Word.

All of this has been said simply to demonstrate emphatically the truth that being a light is predicated upon love and showing that love to others. What does it then mean to be a light? To rightly understand this I feel it pertinent to demonstrate how He is the Light.

The discussion of His Light begins at the beginning. We read,

205

"In the beginning, God created the heavens and the earth. The earth was without form and void, and darkness was over the face of the deep. And the Spirit of God was hovering over the face of the waters. And God said, 'Let there be light,' and there was light" (Genesis 1:1-3). There are a lot of profound truths contained within these first three verses of the Bible. We could spend a great deal of time diving into and dissecting these seemingly simple verses. However, such is beyond the scope of this book. If you are interested in a rudimentary look into these things, I host a podcast with Pastor Brent Fisher called Grounded in The Word, and in the second episode (Episode 1: The Foundation) we spend an hour looking into these specific verses. Our focus here will pertain simply to the light that we see mentioned.

What is so interesting about the light mentioned here that it bears examination? Notice, if you will, the source of the light. Or, I should say, the absence of a source. Nowhere in these first verses is it indicated to us that there was a natural source for the light present. In fact, natural light was not brought forth until day four. We read, "And God said, 'Let there be lights in the expanse of the heavens to separate the day from the night. And let them be for signs and for seasons, and for days and years, and let them be lights in the expanse of the heavens to give light upon the earth.' And it was so. And God made the two great lights—the greater light to rule the day and the lesser light to rule the night—and the stars. And God set them in the expanse of the heavens to give light on the earth, to rule over the day and over the night, and to separate the light from the darkness. And God saw that it was good" (Genesis 1:14-18). What, then, was this light at the beginning?

Most scholars will assert, and I wholeheartedly agree, that this light was the glory of God Himself. However, while I hold this to be true, I believe merely leaving it at His glory is to fall short of the full revelation. To truly understand just what this light was, we need to jump to the very end. John, under the inspiration of His Spirit, writes, "And night will be no more. They will need no light of lamp or sun, for the Lord God will be their light, and they will reign forever and ever" (Revelation 22:5). What is the impact of this verse? How does it pertain to our discussion? We must understand that Jesus does not work as we do. We are stuck in the flow of time. We are slaves to its rule. Jesus, however, is the Creator of time itself (see passages from Genesis 1:14-18), thereby, He is not ruled by time as we are. Rather, He exercises dominion over the constraints of time. While we are stuck in the flow of time that moves from beginning to end, He stands at the end declaring the beginning. This truth is demonstrated to us by the Prophet Isaiah, he writes, "Remember this and stand firm, recall it to mind, you transgressors, remember the former things of old; for I am God, and there is no other; I am God, and there is none like me, declaring the end from the beginning and from ancient times things not yet done, saying, 'My counsel shall stand, and I will accomplish all my purpose'" (Isaiah 46:8-10). Notice here how it states that He declares "the end from the beginning and from ancient times things not yet done." Isaiah is emphatically revealing to us the nature of God. As the Creator of all He stands at the end of all things and declares how they ought to be.

Taking this truth back to Revelation 22:5 in relation to Genesis 1:3, we see Jesus standing at the end of all things, looking backward, and shining forth His Light into creation. However, what is the significance of His shining Light?

The Apostle John, author of the Gospel of John, began his Gospel account in the most profound way. Contrary to the way his fellow Gospel writers began their accounts (beginning with either the birth of Jesus in the flesh or with His ministry), John instead endeavors to take his readers back to the very beginning. He begins by asserting that the same One who became incarnate was the very One that brought all things into being. He writes, "In the beginning was the Word, and the Word was with God, and the Word was God. He was in the beginning with God. All things were made through him, and without him was not any thing made that was made" (John 1:1-3). This beginning statement lines up well with Genesis 1:1-2. John then continues with, "In him was life, and the life was the light of men. The light shines in the darkness, and the darkness has not overcome it" (John 1:4-5). This aligns well with Genesis 1:3-4. The main point of focus here is found in verses 4 and 5 of John. John establishes a profound correlation: life is equal to light. Or, to put it another way, where there is light, there is life.

Jesus further emphasizes this profound truth later in the Gospel of John. We read, "Again Jesus spoke to them, saying, 'I am the light of the world. Whoever follows me will not walk in darkness, but will have the light of life'" (John 8:12). Wherever Jesus is His Light is shining forth, and when His Light is shining forth, life is being made manifest. This is a powerful truth. Jesus being the Light meant His Light was always shining forth. If His Light was always shining forth that meant that life was always being offered unto those who would receive it. Jesus was a walking beacon of life.

Understanding these things, we must now take them and focus on ourselves. Jesus said, "You are the light of the world. A city set on a hill cannot be hidden. Nor do people light a lamp and put it under a basket, but on a stand, and it gives light to all in the house. In the same way, let your light shine before others, so that they may see your good works and give glory to your Father who is in heaven" (Matthew 5:14-16). Here we are presented with an interesting truth. We have demonstrated that Jesus is the Light and that His Light is life itself. However, now He is conveying that we are the light. How can this be and what does it mean?

An important foundational element pertaining to this that is imperative to understand: the light that Jesus is talking about here is not generated by our own merit. As we have said, light is equal to life. Further, as we have also demonstrated previously, we are born with a nature that is inclined toward sin which is death. Pastor Fisher, in our podcast Grounded in The Word, recently worded it beautifully when he said, "When Adam and Eve sinned by partaking of the Tree, it flipped the order of submission. Previously, the flesh was submitted to the spirit. Now, the spirit became submitted to the flesh." What does this mean? Simply that we have no life to offer. If we could offer life to others, then we would have had no need for a Savior. That fact that we needed Jesus our Savior indicates that we needed life and couldn't give it to ourselves. Therefore, this light that shines forth from us is not from ourselves. Where, then, does this light come from? To keep it plain: it comes from Him.

There is a purpose as to why this book has been structured in the manner in which it has been. It would have been of no effect for me to position this chapter on being a light at the forefront of the discussion. Why? Because it would have no foundation and thereby produce no understanding that can be manifested. Understanding that we are a light for Him unto this world begins by understanding how He dwells in you and how you walk in relationship with Him and with others. As we demonstrated in the chapter, Christians Love Their Neighbors, and how Pastor Fisher stated, once again, in our podcast, "Our love for Him is demonstrated by how we love others." Only after establishing the foundation elements of a walk with Him, how to abide in that relationship, and how to abide in love with others, can we then understand how to be a light.

Understanding that His Light is manifested through us by our abiding with Him and in love for others, we return to our passage from Matthew 5:14-16. Jesus, in this passage, presents to us an interesting truth: we have the distinct choice as to whether or not we will allow His Light to manifest through us. Some may think that His Light shining forth from us is automatic when one claims to be in relationship with Him. In revealing this key truth, Jesus begins by demonstrating the absurdity of trying to hide a light. He first gives an illustration of a city that is positioned atop a hill. Due to where the city stands, it is evident to all who would come into its vicinity. Yet, in Jesus' analogy, it is implied that some would try and hide this city. For He says that this city, "cannot be hidden." Meaning, some have tried but failed. He follows that analogy with a second, "Nor do people light a lamp and put it under a basket, but on a stand, and it gives light to all in the house." What is the point of these sayings by Jesus? The entire point of a light is, one, to be seen, and two, to illuminate. Therefore, to try and hide or diminish the light would be to refute the very purpose of the light. Thereby, if one aims to walk in relationship with Him but at the same time aims to diminish His Light, they contradict one of the main purposes for abiding in relationship with Him.

We walk in relationship with Jesus for ourselves, yes. Paul said, "Therefore, my beloved, as you have always obeyed, so now, not only as in my presence but much more in my absence, work out your own salvation with fear and trembling" (Philippians 2:12). However, our relationship with Jesus was never meant to be for our own salvation alone. All throughout the Gospels and epistles we read about the truth that we are called to bring others along with us. A prime example of this is Matthew 28:19 where we are admonished to make disciples of every nation. Therefore, if we negate this foundational principle of abiding with Him, we forsake one of the main purposes for our relationship with Him. We discussed this in the chapter, Christians Abide with Christ, how in the passage from John 15 we are admonished to bear good fruit. One of the examples of good fruit that we demonstrated is that of discipleship.

We already, albeit briefly, touched on discipleship in the above-mentioned chapter, so I will not repeat myself here. However, I believe it is important to note that there is a difference between being a light and making disciples. Just because you allowed His Light to shine forth from you into the life of another does not mean that individual became your disciple in that moment. Jesus was the Light, as we have demonstrated, therefore His Light was always shining onto all people. Yet, not all chose to follow Him. Discipleship is a conscious choice made by the individual to follow after you as you follow after Jesus. Thereby, being a light in someone's life may lead to discipleship, but it is not discipleship.

Returning once again to Matthew 5:14-16; Jesus ends this passage by declaring, "Let your light shine before others, so that they may see your good works and give glory to your Father who is in heaven." We mentioned earlier how allowing His Light to shine forth from us is a choice we have to make. That truth is made evident in this portion of Jesus' statement. We are to "let," or allow, the light to shine before others. This is an interesting idea. Normally when one thinks of being a shining light they think of attention being focused on them. However, while they look at us, evident by the statement, "so that they may see your good works," the attention is meant to be diverted to Him, evident by, "and give glory to your Father who is in heaven." Our lives (how we act, speak, and carry ourselves) are supposed to be a living representation of Him so that our lives point to Him. If people cannot see Him when they look at us, then there is something wrong and we need to allow His Spirit to show us where we are wrong and give us the grace to change (see John 16:8; II Corinthians 12:9).

The question we need to ask is, "In what manner are we

to allow His Light to be made manifest in our lives?" In truth, there are a plethora of directions we could take in this discussion. Unfortunately, to fully engage in the full scope of such a discussion is beyond the reach of this book. Truly, entire books could be written on the subject of being a light. Due to the plethora of directions this discussion could be taken, we will hone in on one specific vein.

I believe the most evident way we can allow His Light to be made manifest in our lives is by allowing His character to be made evident in us. What does this look like? Paul spoke on this very thing, but he referred to it as the Fruit of the Spirit. We mentioned the Fruit of the Spirit in brief in the same chapter mentioned above, Christians Abide with Christ. Here we will endeavor to take a deeper look into this vital topic.

Paul lays out the Fruit of the Spirit in Galatians 5:22-23. He writes, "But the fruit of the Spirit is love, joy, peace, patience, kindness, goodness, faithfulness, gentleness, self-control; against such things there is no law." I mentioned this in the aforementioned chapter, but it bears repeating: many believe that this passage ought to be translated as "But the fruit of the Spirit is love. Love is joy, peace, patience, kindness, goodness, faithfulness, gentleness, self-control." The premise behind this way of thinking is that love is the catalyst and there is validity to this, for we read how the core of who God is, is love (see I John 4:8,16). Further, all throughout the Old Testament and New Testament God often identifies Himself in some manner pertaining to love. Additionally, Paul informs us that without love at the center of all things, whatever we do is in vain (see I Corinthians 13:1-3). Love is the foundation for all that we do that gives all that we do meaning. We have already extensively written on love in both the chapters, Christians Abide with Christ, and, Christians Love Their Neighbors, so I will not endeavor to do so again. However, the essentiality of love cannot be overstated. Love gives life meaning. Some might say, "Doesn't God give life meaning?" Yes, but in case you've forgotten, "God is love."

Paul continues by listing joy as the second Fruit of the Spirit. Before we dive into defining love, I feel it vital that we take a moment to address the idea of happiness. The words "happiness" and "joy" are often used interchangeably in our current culture.

However, we need to understand that happiness and joy are not the same thing. We could easily rabbit trail off onto a discussion about happiness, but I will keep my thoughts focused. To define it simply, "happiness" is purely based on what is happening. What do I mean? Happiness cannot transcend circumstance. Happiness is slave to circumstance. If the events that are happening are favorable, happiness abounds. On the flip side of this, if the events that are happening are unfavorable, happiness is absent. Therefore, one who is ruled by a desire for happiness is an unstable individual, for the constant rising and falling of life will take them on a roller coaster ride of happiness to sorrow, over and over again.

The truth of the matter is life is chaotic. This is made evident from the very beginning. Genesis 1:2 reads, "The earth was without form and void, and darkness was over the face of the deep. And the Spirit of God was hovering over the face of the waters." "Deep" here is "tehôm" which refers to a state of water that is chaotic and unable to sustain life. However, we see God take dominion over the chaos (made evident by how God resided over the deep, indicating a place of authority or dominion) and bring about order (made evident by the word "waters" which is "mayim" which refers to life-giving waters). What is the point in me saying all this? Simply this: the endless pursuit of happiness is equal to chaos, but God took dominion over chaos and brought about order, this is equivalent to joy. To walk in joy is to exercise dominion over the chaos of life.

Sin has distorted the perfect world of order that God created and has allowed chaos to be prevalent once again. However, despite the present reality of chaos around us, it remains true that God is a God of order. Therefore, to abide in chaos is to abide in a state contrary to God. It is then imperative that we step out of the chaos around us and step into the order in which He desires us to dwell in. Joy is the means by which we do so. How do we abide in joy amid chaos? We must understand that joy is eternally intertwined with biblical hope. We will define hope in the following chapter, Christians Walk in Childlike Faith, but I will give a quick precursor here: Hope is more than a mere optimistic viewpoint, it more readily refers to expectation. Thereby, joy operates through expectation. What does this mean? I will attempt to make it as plain as I can; to abide in joy is to live with one's eyes firmly fixed on Jesus, fully expecting Him to bring order amid chaos. When we keep our eyes on Him, the chaos of this life has no hold on us. It is only when we take our eyes off Him that the chaos consumes us. This truth is made evident by the account of Jesus calling Peter to walk on the water (see Matthew 14:28-31).

The third Fruit of the Spirit listed by Paul is that peace. "Peace" in Greek is "eirēnē" which refers to the typical ideas associated with peace, that is, tranquility, rest, unity, and such the like. However, it is important to understand that Paul, as a Jew, would have approached the concept of peace through a Jewish lens. What is the significance of this? The Hebrew word for "peace" is "shâlôm" which transcends mere tranquility and more so refers to a state of completeness, or wholeness. An analogy we could use to demonstrate this word is that of a brick wall; for the wall to abide in "shâlôm" would mean there was not a single brick out of place. Therefore, again understanding that Paul would have written through a Jewish lens, peace here less refers to having rest and more so to being complete.

Understanding that peace more so refers to completeness or wholeness, we come to realize that, like joy, peace is intertwined with another biblical concept. That is, biblical contentment. Paul wrote, concerning contentment, "Not that I am speaking of being in need, for I have learned in whatever situation I am to be content. I know how to be brought low, and I know how to abound. In any and every circumstance, I have learned the secret of facing plenty and hunger, abundance and need. I can do all things through him who strengthens me" (Philippians 4:11-13). Webster's Dictionary defines "content" as, "having a mind at peace." Taking this understanding to the words of Paul, we receive a much greater understanding as to what he was saying. Whether brought low or abounding, in hunger and plenty, and in need and abundance, Paul's mind was at peace.

We quickly come to understand that our definition of peace does not align with God's definition thereof. Often, we define peace as the absence of chaos, yet, Paul experienced chaos but still had peace. How was Paul able to abide in peace amidst seemingly tumultuous circumstances? The answer comes from the final verse of our above-quoted passage: "I can do all things through him who strengthens me." The key to understanding this verse is by examining what Paul declares just a few verses earlier. He writes, "Rejoice in the Lord always; again I will say, rejoice. Let your reasonableness be known to everyone. The Lord is at hand; do not be anxious about anything, but in everything by prayer and supplication with thanksgiving let your requests be made known to God. And the peace of God, which surpasses all understanding, will guard your hearts and your minds in Christ Jesus. Finally, brothers, whatever is true, whatever is honorable, whatever is just, whatever is pure, whatever is lovely, whatever is commendable, if there is any excellence, if there is anything worthy of praise, think about these things. What you have learned and received and heard and seen in me—practice these things, and the God of peace will be with you" (Philippians 4:4-9). There is much we could say about the truth set forth by Paul here, we will endeavor to keep it simple.

The peace of God (which surpasses all our carnal understanding) guards our hearts and minds when we align ourselves with Him in prayer. We bring our worries, cares, and anxieties unto Him, place them in His hands, and then let them go, trusting that He will take care of them. Operating in God's peace means taking your hands off your situation and allowing Him to place His hands on it. When we take our hands off and let go, we are then to reorient our way of thinking to be melded around things that revolve around Him (truth, honor, justice, purity, love, commending, excellent, and praiseworthy). An important note to make: it is not just our bad situations that we are to bring to Him, but also our good. Paul said that he was content in the good and the bad. Meaning, he had taken the good and the bad to Him. In doing so, in every situation he walked in His peace.

The fourth Fruit of the Spirit is patience. Patience is a highly admirable trait that many in our world fawn after. Often we witness an individual display seemingly great levels of patience and we cannot help but display admiration toward them. It is important to understand that patience is not something one is born with, rather it is something that must be cultivated or brought forth. Further, while someone without His Spirit may be able to display a level of patience, their level of patience pales in comparison to the patience that comes by His Spirit. Cultivating patience, however, is not an easy task. Why do I say that? Because patience is birthed amid trying circumstances.

We see this truth demonstrated to us by the Apostle James. He writes, "Count it all joy, my brothers, when you meet trials of various kinds, for you know that the testing of your faith produces steadfastness. And let steadfastness have its full effect, that you may be perfect and complete, lacking in nothing" (James 1:2-4). "Steadfastness" here is "hypomonē" which can also be translated as, "patience." Trial and testing are the birthing grounds for patience. However, if we allow patience to be birthed in this season of testing it will turn for our good, for patience being present in one's life leads to being "perfect and complete, lacking in nothing."

Earlier we stated that joy is intertwined with biblical hope (expectation). I believe that patience is also eternally intertwined with biblical hope. Joy interlocks with hope by looking beyond the present circumstance, the present chaos, and looks unto Him who is above the chaos. Patience, then, interlocking with hope, stands firm and strong in the midst of circumstances, expecting Him to bring all things into order.

In our day and age, patience is becoming less of a virtue and more of a liability. What do I mean? It seems with each passing day things become faster, or are expected to be faster. With each passing day, there is less and less tolerance for a thing that takes more time than what the individual is willing to give. In the podcast I host with Pastor Fisher, I commented that the further away from the Garden of Eden (and consequently the further away from God) we have gotten the more complex we have become. When God created all things in the Garden they were utterly simple. It was sin entering creation that brought about complexity. Unfortunately, that complexity has continued to grow and as it grows things are expected to function more perfectly which, in turn, means they are expected to function more quickly. We must understand that God cannot be rushed. He does not operate on our timing, we operate on His. Therefore, when seeking God and His will, one must abide in His patience and wait on Him and His timing. He will answer.

Paul continues by listing kindness as the next Fruit of the

Spirit. The Greek word here, "chrēstotēs," is interesting, for it can refer to things that we would typically associate with the concept of kindness (moral goodness; integrity), however, it can also mean, "to show one's self useful." Therefore, we have two different veins we could follow in discussing kindness. We will endeavor to discuss both concisely.

First, I want to explore this idea of integrity. Oxford Languages defines "integrity" as, "the quality of being honest and having strong moral principles." A keyword from this definition is "moral" which Oxford Languages defines as, "concerned with the principles of right and wrong behavior and the goodness or badness of human character." Therefore, this first aspect of kindness points to walking in honesty and moral rightness.

We must understand that honesty transcends that which proceeds forth from our lips. Usually, when we think of honesty we think of speaking the truth. This is an important aspect of honesty. Jesus taught us that His Spirit is the Spirit of Truth and that He would lead us into all truth (see John 16:13). Further, Jesus demonstrated that to abide in falsehood is to be the offspring of Satan himself (see John 8:44). However, there is a critical point we need to understand in conjunction with this aspect of truth. Often, and this is particularly true regarding young children, we separate truth from kindness. What do I mean? Little kids are some of the most honest-speaking people you'll ever meet; they will say anything with little to no regard for the individual's feelings. While, as I said, this is most prevalent in young children, it does manifest itself in older generations as well. While we may be speaking "the truth" what benefit is it? For while being "truthful" we are completely destroying the individual's healthy state of mind and emotions. That is why it is important to keep in context the words of Paul: we are to speak the truth in love (see Ephesians 4:15).

As I stated just a few lines earlier, honesty transcends merely what proceeds forth from our lips. Honesty is not only a way of speaking but a way of living. We read in Proverbs 16:11, "Honest scales and balances are from the LORD; all the weights in the bag are His concern" (BSB). Therefore, to be honest in our way of living is to be free from stealing, envy, greed, covetousness, gluttony, and lust. In truth, to be honest in our way of living directly connects to the second definition of kindness, that is, "to show one's self useful." What does it mean to be useful? A few moral behaviors that immediately come to mind are responsibility, reliability, trustworthiness, and honesty. To show yourself useful is to demonstrate to others that you can be trusted. We demonstrate this by living in alignment with Proverbs 16:11. How do honest scales and balances correlate to being useful? We prove ourselves useful by judging all things according to His Word, Spirit, will, and character.

Following kindness, we come to goodness. "Goodness" here is "agathōsynē" which can mean, uprightness of heart and life, virtue, or beneficence. I believe defining uprightness, virtue, and beneficence individually will aid us in understanding biblical goodness.

First, "uprightness" according to Oxford Languages means, "the condition or quality of being honorable or honest." Second, they define "virtue" as, "behavior showing high moral standards." Finally, "beneficence," according to Webster's Dictionary, means, "the practice of doing good; active goodness, kindness, or charity." What is immediately evident when we examine these three definitions pertaining to goodness, is that someone who abides in the character of goodness exhibits consistency. What do I mean? So often individuals are concerned only with appearing good when around certain individuals. Allow me to speak directly to those of you who consistently attend church: being honest with yourselves, do you try to appear better when around your pastor or another spiritual authority than normal? If your answer is yes then I'm sorry to say that you are a hypocrite. When we attempt to appear one way around a certain group of individuals but have no desire to maintain that standard, that means that we are being fake, or that there are different masks that we wear. To abide in His character aspect of goodness is to be free from hypocrisy.

Allow me to take a moment here and briefly speak on hypocrisy. Jesus had a lot to say regarding being a hypocrite and what He had to say is extremely relevant to us too because, unfortunately, we are more prone to hypocrisy than we might realize.

There are a plethora of topics throughout the Gospels that speak on the topic of hypocrisy, too many for us to examine here. Therefore, focusing on one passage, we read in Luke 12:1-3: "In the meantime, when so many thousands of the people had gathered together that they were trampling one another, he began to say to his disciples first, 'Beware of the leaven of the Pharisees, which is hypocrisy. Nothing is covered up that will not be revealed, or hidden that will not be known. Therefore whatever you have said in the dark shall be heard in the light, and what you have whispered in private rooms shall be proclaimed on the housetops.'"

It should not be overlooked that Jesus compared hypocrisy to leaven. Leaven is a product, such as yeast, often used in baking. Leaven, in whatever form it takes, is used for the primary purpose of causing the dough to rise. Thereby, it gives that which it was put into the appearance of being full rather than flat. To put it succinctly, leaven alters the appearance of a thing but does not change the makeup of that thing. Therefore, leaven being compared to hypocrisy, we come to learn that hypocrisy may change the outward appearance, but the heart remains the same. Hypocrisy, then, may fool man but it will never fool God. God declared that while man looks on the outward, He looks at the inward (see I Samuel 16:7). That is why Jesus proceeds to say that every hidden and secret thing that has been kept in the dark will be fully revealed. Jesus, the One who sees past our hypocrisy and sees the true state of our heart, will reveal the true state of our heart if we choose to remain in hypocrisy.

Therefore, to abide in goodness is to allow Him to mold you into a consistent individual who abides in goodness no matter who you are around.

We then come to the character of faithfulness. Something interesting is seen regarding this word when we examine the original Greek. That is, the word used here for "faithfulness" is the same word translated simply as "faith," that is, "pistis." I am not going to dive into faith here for the subsequent chapter is devoted to this very topic. For your sake, I do not want to sound like a broken record. However, I do what to briefly address how this one word, "pistis," is translated as both "faith" and "faithfulness." What is the significance of this? From this, we come to understand that faith is not merely something we hold or possess for a moment when needed. We all have heard the expression, "A leap of faith," referring to a specific moment in time where great levels of faith are necessary to move forward. However, from this, we come to understand that faith transcends momentary use and is to be present in our lives at all times. Rarely would we ever think of needing great levels of faith on a daily basis, but, as we will examine in the following chapter, faith is the very foundation upon which our relationship with God is built. Therefore, if we forsake to consistently walk in faith that means that we are forsaking a consistent relationship with God. If we hold faith to only be of momentary use, then our relationship with God is but momentary, possessing no substantiality. His Spirit empowers us to have a daily, consistent relationship with Him.

The second to last Fruit of the Spirit is that of gentleness. The Greek word for "gentleness" is "praotēs" which can also be translated as, "meekness." There is a very simple way in which we can define "meekness," that is, "submission" (both Oxford Languages and Webster's Dictionary attest to this). There is a common idea pertaining to meekness that to be meek is to be weak. This could not be further from the truth and it is quite unfortunate that this false idea exists. Jordan Peterson, who is a world-renowned clinical psychologist, formulated a definition of meekness that I quite love. He states, "I was looking up the multiple translations of the word 'meek', and meek is actually derived from a Greek word… and that word didn't exactly mean meek, it meant something like, those who have weapons and have the ability to use them, but determined to keep them sheathed… And that means people who are capable of force, let's say, but decide not to use it, are in the proper moral position." To put it simply: meekness is power under control. However, I feel that we need to expound upon that. The one in control is not us, for we lack the proper judgment on when and how to use power. Rather, meekness refers to possessing great power but willingly yielding that power to the control of another. As we stated, meekness can be defined as "submission."

Again, like meekness, there exists a false idea regarding the nature of submission. Often we think that to submit is to forfeit any degree of power we may have, but the opposite is actually true pertaining to God's divine order. In His Kingdom, power comes through submission. One example we see of this truth is found in James 4:7, "Submit yourselves therefore to God. Resist the devil, and he will flee from you." Notice the flow of thought presented to us here. First, there is the admonition to submit. Once we have obeyed and submitted ourselves unto God, we then are given power to resist the devil. We have spoken previously about how, due to what transpired in the Garden of Eden, we are all born with a nature inclined toward sin. Meaning, on our own we have no power over the devil. If we relied on our own false idea of power we would never overcome sin and temptation. This is the sad reason why addict recovery programs simply do not offer permanent fixes. No man-made program can overpower our inclination toward sin. It is purely by the grace of God that we are given power over Satan and his devices.

Paul wrote to us about an interaction he had with Jesus in prayer. We read, "So to keep me from becoming conceited because of the surpassing greatness of the revelations, a thorn was given me in the flesh, a messenger of Satan to harass me, to keep me from becoming conceited. Three times I pleaded with the Lord about this, that it should leave me. But he said to me, 'My grace is sufficient for you, for my power is made perfect in weakness.' Therefore I will boast all the more gladly of my weaknesses, so that the power of Christ may rest upon me" (II Corinthians 12:7-9). How does this correlate to submission? There are a couple of different Greek words that are used throughout the New Testament that correlate to submission. One of these is found in Hebrews 13:17. The Greek word here is "hypeikō," and one way in which we could define this word is, "to become weak." Paul submitted to Jesus by bearing his weakness before Him. In doing so, Jesus' power was made perfect in Paul's weakness, thus giving Paul power over the thorn that so tormented him.

When we walk in submission to Jesus, becoming weak before Him, His power is made perfect in us. Therefore, meekness does not equal weakness, meekness equals power.

The final Fruit of the Spirit listed by Paul is that of self-control. Oxford Languages defines "self-control" as, "the ability to control oneself, in particular one's emotions and desires or the expression of them in one's behavior, especially in difficult situations." This definition could potentially cause confusion, for it would seem that we have the ability to assert mastery over ourselves. This is simply not the case. If we possessed the ability to assert mastery over ourselves then we would have been able to save ourselves. If we would have been able to save ourselves then we would have no need for a Savior. However, we know all this to not be true. We possess no mastery over ourselves nor can we save ourselves.

Paul writes to us in the letter to the Galatians:

"Yet we know that a person is not justified by works of the law but through faith in Jesus Christ, so we also have believed in Christ Jesus, in order to be justified by faith in Christ and not by works of the law, because by works of the law no one will be justified...For all who rely on works of the law are under a curse; for it is written, 'Cursed be everyone who does not abide by all things written in the Book of the Law, and do them.' Now it is evident that no one is justified before God by the law, for 'The righteous shall live by faith.'"
-Galatians 2:16; 3:10-11

To assert that we are able to exhibit mastery over ourselves is to negate the truth that we are saved by grace through faith. He did the works we could not and died the death we had ought so that, by His grace, we too can walk in the works of righteousness and live the life that He purchased for us.

When speaking on gentleness we also, albeit briefly, dived into the topic of His grace. It is interesting how gentleness (submission) is the means by which His grace is made manifest in our lives, and how "self-control" is the fruit of His grace in our lives. It is almost as if Paul is creating a flow of understanding of how one creates an atmosphere where His grace can abound and the results of that proper atmosphere.

Creating an atmosphere in our lives wherein His grace can

abound is truly essential. If His grace is absent from our lives then we become slaves to the way of the world. What is the way of the world? John declared, "For all that is in the world—the lust of the flesh, the lust of the eyes, and the pride of life—is not of the Father but is of the world" (I John 2:16 NKJV). We have here three primary ways in which the way of the world manifests itself in our lives: the lust of the flesh, the lust of the eyes, and the pride of life. We could easily spend a great deal of time defining these three categories of sin, but we will keep it simple. One who abides in the lust of the flesh is one who passionately pursues that which our carnal man impurely desires. The lust of the eyes is one who passionately pursues that which is appealing to the carnal man. These two sound similar, and they are, but there is also a distinct difference. We could define it as the lust of the flesh pertains more to material things, whereas the lust of the eyes refers to the immaterial. Finally, we have the pride of life. This refers to one who possesses the belief that they can provide for themselves everything that they need and more. This is one who puts all their trust in their own livelihood, trusting in the world's systems to provide for them.

The grace of God gives us power over these worldly ways and empowers us to walk in purity and humility before Him.

Some may wonder how the Fruit of the Spirit being made manifest in our lives correlates to being a light. We discussed this before in, Christians Abide with Christ, when we first mentioned the Fruit of the Spirit, but it bears repeating here; the Fruit of the Spirit is not something that can be cultivated in us by our own merit or our own goodness. Paul, in his discourse on this topic, specifically stated that the Fruit of the Spirit is a product of living and walking in the Spirit. Meaning, the Fruit of the Spirit cannot be exhibited by one unless His Spirit abides in them. The Fruit of the Spirit is not merely a list of qualities that a "good person" will display, but a concise list of His characteristics that will be made evident in the lives of those who abide with Him.

Understanding this truth, we come to understand that the exhibition of the Fruit of the Spirit is not a commonality in our world, unfortunately. Understanding that the Fruit of the Spirit is only present in the life of one who is filled with His Spirit, we come to the realization that many in our world have never witnessed or experienced the Fruit of the Spirit. Therefore, when the Fruit of the Spirit is made manifest in their midst they recognize it as something different because it is something new. Again, it is more than just them recognizing that the one exhibiting them is a good person, they realize that that individual possesses something different than they've ever known. This witnessing of something new and unknown draws people because they want to know what you have that they, and most others, do not. Thereby, allowing the Fruit of the Spirit to be cultivated in us is a light unto those who would witness that Fruit. That light draws them because they recognize that you have something and it is unlike anything they've ever experienced and they want it.

You may say, "Well, Kristopher, I've never had anyone be so drawn to me in that way." To that, I would say two things. First, if you've never had anyone drawn to you then you need to examine yourself and determine if you are allowing His Light, the Fruit of the His Spirit, to be made evident in your life. As I said, being a light is a choice we make. Are you allowing His Light to be made evident in your life? Or are you putting it under a basket? Second, if you determine that you are allowing His Light to shine forth from you, then it is likely that others are being drawn to you. You may ask, "Why do I not see it then?" To keep it plain, it is likely that you're not paying attention. Being a light and making disciples is not something that happens unconsciously. It requires intentionality on our part. Are you aware of those around you? Are you aware of how you are impacting their lives? Are you aware of how they are responding to you and being drawn to you? Because if you are allowing your light to shine, then I promise that people are being drawn to you. The question then becomes, what are you doing about it?

Being a light is what sets the stage and opens the door for you to have a real impact on someone's life, but it is not going to happen unawares. We must understand that we must walk with intentionality and purposefulness. As long as we go through our days, simply drudging through the routine of life, we will never be a light and never make a difference. It is of the utmost importance that we break free of the chains of slothfulness and tap into a spirit of zeal.

Let your light shine.

Focused Reflection

Theodore Roosevelt uttered the now timeless words, "People don't care how much you know until they know how much you care." The Bible talks a lot about being a light, about being a living witness unto those around us who don't know Him as we do. However, we often fail to understand that being a light is predicated upon displaying His love and mercy.

Further, we are not lights in and of ourselves. Rather, He is the Light. We only become a light when we are in the Light. Additionally, we only truly become a light when we are reflecting His Light. We are a light only when it is His love, His mercy, His truth, and His character that is being displayed through us.

Finally, His Light shining forth from us is not something that occurs by accident. We only become a light through intentionality. One does not live for God by accident, and neither does one walk as a disciple apart from intentional pursuit. Each day we must make it our directive to live with intentionality toward the One who has saved us. If we do that, then we will become a light.

1. Being a light is predicated upon love and forgiveness; do you feel like His love and forgiveness are actively present in your daily life?

2. Intentionality is key. How would you define the level of intentionality toward God with which you live?

3. Paul said, "Imitate me, as I imitate Christ" (I Corinthians 11:1). Take an honest look at your life. Do you feel that it is worthy of imitation? If not, what keeps it from being worthy of such? Finally, what is keeping you from making those necessary changes to make it so?

Let your light shine before others, so that they may see your good works and give glory to your Father who is in heaven.
-Matthew 5:16

14
Christians Walk in Childlike Faith

At that time the disciples came to Jesus, saying, "Who is the greatest in the kingdom of heaven?" And calling to him a child, he put him in the midst of them and said, "Truly, I say to you, unless you turn and become like children, you will never enter the kingdom of heaven. Whoever humbles himself like this child is the greatest in the kingdom of heaven." ~Matthew 18:1-4

What is the first thing that comes to mind when you hear, "child-like"? For many, I imagine our minds gravitate toward something along the lines of immaturity. Immaturity refers to a lack of social and economic intelligence mainly due to a lack of experience in those areas. That is one definite way that we could define "child-like," but I do not believe that was Jesus' intent when He admonished us to become as children. At several points throughout the Gospels, Jesus issues the command that we are to mature. We looked at this Scripture in an earlier chapter, but Jesus says, "You therefore must be perfect, as your heavenly Father is perfect" (Matthew 5:48). The word "perfect" does not refer to perfection as we understand it in our culture (without fault or blemish), but rather refers to growth, or the process of maturity.

What are other things that come to mind when we think of "child-like"? Possibly that to be "child-like" is to be pure, or innocent. This would align more perfectly with what Jesus was attempting to demonstrate. Oxford Languages offers three definitions for "pure": "1. Not mixed or adulterated with any other substance or material; 2. Without any extraneous and unnecessary elements; 3. Free of any contamination." Further, the definition they offer for "innocent" is, "a pure, guileless, or naive person." It is not uncommon for people to comment on the purity and innocence of young children.

There is another aspect to this purity and innocence of children that I believe plays into Jesus' admonition to become like children. That is, children have the most wonderful imagination. They believe almost anything you tell them. This, in part, goes back to the innocence of children which often manifests through naïveté. However, they are able to believe almost anything you tell them because they are able to imagine almost anything you tell them. It is truly incredible. Even if a child has no true concept regarding a particular thing, if you tell them about it they will create a concept of their own purely from within.

It is a sad truth that many of the children from the more recent generations do not possess the same level of imagination that former generations possessed. This is due, in large part, to the explosion of easily accessible entertainment in our homes. It is not uncommon to see a toddler, or even younger, walking around on their parent's phone or tablet. Many would consider me to still be relatively young, but if you would have handed me an iPad when I was six, I would have had no idea what to do with it. I digress, the focus of this chapter is not to point out how different children are today compared to even just twenty years ago. Regardless of the day and age in which we live, it is still true that children possess incredible imaginations that allow them to believe just about anything.

When I was growing up, we did not really have television or video games. Later on in my childhood, my parents expanded more into DVD movies and tv shows, but our library was still limited. Even when these things became more prevalent within our home, it still was not a common thing for us to engage in. I recall the majority of my childhood years spent outside, creating imaginary worlds either by myself or with my friends. It was nothing for us to fully immerse ourselves in this make-believe world. Further, it did not matter what props we had, or how closely they resembled what they represented in our worlds, as long as they did the job on a rudimentary level they sufficed. If I was not outside, then I was inside either playing with my action figures (not dolls), legos, or drawing. Again, all of these were mere avenues for my imagination to unfold.

Growing up there was one consistent source of entertainment if you will in our home. It was a Christian radio show geared toward children called, Adventures in Odyssey. I loved listening to that show, and once again, it allowed me to use my imagination. All the show presented to us was the voices of the people in the show. This left it up to us to determine what they looked like, where they were, what their town looked like, and so on. Just as children nowadays sit around the television and watch shows, we would sit around the stereo and just listen, allowing our imaginations to soar.

As adults, we often reminisce over how we were as children. We chuckle to ourselves, thinking that we were so cute and naive. We laugh at the things we used to believe, knowing now, as sophisticated adults, how absurd many of our childish ideas were. What we fail to realize, through all our sophistication, is that we have lost something truly spectacular.

The creation story is something that we all know well. Whether you are one who was raised going to Sunday School or not, we all know the Scripture, "In the beginning God created the heavens and the earth." Due to the familiarity with this biblical account, it is something that we have come to take for granted. We all know that God created all things, yes, yes, move on. Our failure is that we too often view God so impersonally. We recognize how personal we each are, yet fail to remember that we were created in His image (see Genesis 1:26-27). Just as we are personal beings that have a uniqueness of character, so too does the One that brought us forth. We approach creation, as I said, so impersonally. We merely recognize that He is the Creator and we move on. Have you ever stopped to think about what was going through His mind before He began to create? That's an interesting thought.

When we set out to create something, we first must imagine it in our minds. This imaginative thought creates the baseline, the starting point. From that image, we then begin to put the pieces together in an endeavor to bring into being what we formed in our mind's eye. Being created in His image, why would it be any different with Him? It is not outside the realm of possibility to suggest that before He first said, "Let there be," there was first an imagination. It is not far-fetched to suggest that He formed the world based on a thought that was first formed in His mind.

In fact, the Bible tells us that this is exactly what He did. We read in John 1:1 and 14, "In the beginning was the Word, and the Word was with God, and the Word was God...And the Word became flesh and dwelt among us, and we have seen his glory, glory as of the only Son from the Father, full of grace and truth." We looked at the Greek word for "word" in the chapter, Christians Abide with Christ. We demonstrated how the word "logos" can refer to a thought that is conceptualized in the mind, and then the utterance of that same thought into existence. Therefore, God created all things through the Word which was first a thought, then an utterance. John goes on to reveal how the Word became flesh, an obvious reference to Jesus. Thereby, the thought that formed the basis for all creation was the Incarnation of YAHWEH in the flesh of Jesus Christ.

This truth is further conveyed to us by the Apostle Peter wherein he says, "He was foreknown before the foundation of the world but was made manifest in the last times for the sake of you who through him are believers in God, who raised him from the dead and gave him glory, so that your faith and hope are in God." (I Peter 1:20-21). The word "foreknown" is "proginōskō" which means, "to know beforehand." Meaning, that before the foundation of the world, God had a thought and a plan which was the basis for all things. This truth is further confirmed in Revelation 13:8.

Returning to an earlier point; as we traverse into adulthood, we lose sight of this imaginative nature. Often we relate this to merely being a part of growing up. We hold this belief that imagination is for immature little kids with nothing better to do, and that being an adult demands that you grow up and focus on the "real world." This determined shift in focus leads to the suffocation of every ounce of imagination within us until all that is left is logic and reason. Don't misunderstand, logic and reason are not all bad. Jesus Himself is logical and reasonable, but that is not all that He is. He is also imaginative and creative. By suffocating that imaginative aspect of us, we utterly stamp out a vital part of God's nature that He placed within us. In doing so, we become less like Him.

Taking all of this into consideration, we return to our focus passage. It reads, "At that time the disciples came to Jesus, saying, 'Who is the greatest in the kingdom of heaven?' And calling to him a child, he put him in the midst of them and said, 'Truly, I say to you, unless you turn and become like children, you will never enter the kingdom of heaven. Whoever humbles himself like this child is the greatest in the kingdom of heaven.'"

Notice the level of importance that Jesus placed on becoming child-like. He said that if we do not become like children, we have no home in heaven. Such a thought ought to set a fire ablaze within us. Truly let that statement sink into the core of your being: "Unless you turn and become like children, you will never enter the kingdom of heaven." While some may have scoffed at our seemingly unimportant discussion of imagination, it is, in truth, a matter of the utmost importance. Some may ask, "If imagination is so integral to our salvation, why is it never preached about?" My rebuttal would be to say that it is often preached about, but a different word is usually used in place of imagination. That is, faith.

It is an interesting concept, comparing faith to imagination. Many would never think to make such a correlation. However, the definition of faith that we are presented with in the New Testament aligns with a proper understanding of imagination.

In one place, we are told, "For we walk by faith, not by sight" (II Corinthians 5:7). This is a well-known, often-quoted passage. But what does it mean? That is an interesting habit we often have as humans, we reference out of familiarity, not understanding. First, the word "walk" is "peripateō" which refers to the conduct of one's life. Therefore, the admonition to follow impacts our whole life. It ought to manifest itself in all that we do and how we do it. We are admonished to conduct our lives through faith, not by sight. What does this latter portion mean? We will come back to what faith is momentarily. Before we do so, the word "sight" provides key insight that is beneficial to our walk with Him. "Sight" is the word "eidos" which overall carries a few different meanings, but each meaning of the word points to something that is externally evident. Something that is immediately obvious.

Something I point out often in various discussions that I have with others or various classes that I teach is how focused we are on what is immediately evident. Who can blame us? It's hard not to focus on what is immediately evident for the simple fact that it is immediately evident. The natural man cannot perceive the spiritual realm as he can the natural realm. Due to this truth, the natural man has to valiantly pursue and press beyond what is immediately evident and allow God to transport him into the spiritual. While focusing on what is immediately evident is not always necessarily a bad thing, it does not make it beneficial for us. Paul strictly encourages us to, "Set your minds on things that are above, not on things that are on earth" (Colossians 3:2). To live with our focus on what is externally evident shifts our direction off of God. Your focus determines your direction. This is why Paul admonishes us to not conduct our lives based on what is immediately obvious (see II Corinthians 5:7) and to not focus on externally evident things.

Again, the natural man cannot immediately perceive the things of the Spirit. Once again quoting Paul: "The natural person does not accept the things of the Spirit of God, for they are folly to him, and he is not able to understand them because they are spiritually discerned" (I Corinthians 2:14). Therefore, since we are unable to perceive the spiritual through the natural, we must endeavor to see beyond what is immediately obvious. The only way in which we can do such is by faith.

We return to this question, "What is faith?" The author of Hebrews provides us with the most concise definition. We read, "Now faith is the assurance of things hoped for, the conviction of things not seen" (Hebrews 11:1). There are several keywords from this passage that bear examination. We will begin by examining the words used by the author to define faith, and then examining the Greek word for faith itself.

First, we have the word "assurance." The Greek word used here is "hypostasis" which more directly refers to the supporting structure of a thing, or the foundation. "Hypostasis" refers to that which gives shape and substance to another. Connected to this word "hypostasis" we have the statement, "of things hoped for." Hope is an interesting concept. In present-day culture, hope is little more than an optimistic point of view. When someone says they hope for a thing, they are more accurately referring to merely wishing for a thing but not necessarily expecting it. The original meaning of hope was quite different. "Elpizō" is the Greek word here and it truly means, "to expect." Therefore, bringing this first definitive statement into a whole, the author of Hebrews tells us that faith is founded upon firm expectation. Faith is not merely a weak belief, but a strong expectation for what is to come.

The author of Hebrews plays upon this truth with his next statement. He declares that faith is, "the conviction of things not seen." Interesting word choice by the author here. First, the word "conviction" is "elenchos" which precisely refers to evidence presented in court that determines a person's guilt or innocence. Thereby, another way we could translate "elenchos" would be "solid evidence." This word holds the implication that it is something that fully persuades the mind and the heart. The second key word in this second phrase is "seen" which is "blepō" which contains a plethora of meanings, all of which point to the ability to physically discern a thing. Therefore, according to the author, to have faith is to be absolutely persuaded that a thing is true, even if it is not immediately evident.

Taking these two definitions into a concise whole; faith is built upon genuine expectation, and that expectation so grips us that we become absolutely persuaded, even if there is no outward evidence of it yet. Arriving at the Greek word for "faith," "pistis," we see that it aligns with this understanding. For it means, "to be fully persuaded."

Many have often translated faith to simply refer to belief. This, however, is a gross misunderstanding. To define faith as mere belief is to strip away all power the word contains. "Belief" is a vague and indescriptive word. Anyone can claim to believe in anything, but that does not mean they have faith in it. One could claim to believe that the grass is actually purple, but do they have faith in that statement? How do you prove if they do or don't? By putting their belief to the test. If they do not stand firm on their belief in the midst of testing, they have no faith. Faith is comparable to a great anchor that is able to hold firm even the greatest of ships, whereas mere belief is a poorly constructed raft amid a great storm.

Why is faith so important to possess? The author of Hebrews demonstrates the importance for us just a few verses later. He writes, "And without faith it is impossible to please him, for whoever would draw near to God must believe that he exists and that he rewards those who seek him" (Hebrews 11:6). The importance of faith that the author stresses ought to be obvious. Apart from faith being manifested in our lives, we can by no means live lives that are pleasing in His sight. Why is faith so crucial concerning our relationship with Him? We are told at different places throughout Scripture that no one has seen God (see John 1:18 as one example). This is true because God is Spirit (see John 4:24). Understanding this truth, we return to II Corinthians 5:7 wherein Paul admonishes us to not walk by sight but by faith. In truth, we can't walk by sight in relation to our walk with God because He cannot be seen. Therefore, if we pursued relationship with Him based on what was immediately evident, there would be no relationship. Relationship with God requires faith. The author expounds upon this truth that "belief" (which is the same word translated as "faith") is essential in simply acknowledging His existence. That is where it begins. We must have faith in His being. If we have no faith in His being then there will be no subsequent relationship. However, it is not merely about faith in His being, but also faith in His character. As the author states, "Whoever would draw near to God must believe...that he rewards those who seek him."

Taking a brief moment here to peer back through the pages of history; Christianity was brought forth during a time when Israel was engulfed in the Roman Empire. Israel was surrounded on all sides not only by Roman ideology but also by Greek ideology. The Roman and Grecian people had a starkly different perspective regarding "the gods" interaction with creation. In their way of thinking, "the gods" had no personal part in the human story. To them, "the gods" merely set creation in order and then stepped back from that creation. There was no personal aspect, there was no intimate relationship. There was only this chasm that separated the people from their gods. In other words, their view of a god was "an unmoved mover," as Aristotle defined divinity. Returning, then, to our passage from Hebrews; the Christians held a much different view of God that confounded the pagan world. The Romans and Grecians thought the Jews and Christians as absurd for thinking they could have personal interaction with God. One way we could understand this would be that the pagan world viewed "the gods" as mysterious, while Christianity views Him as miraculous.

In the podcast I host with Pastor Fisher, Grounded in The Word, we discussed, in brief, this concept of mysterious versus miraculous. Spring-boarding this topic, Pastor Fisher referenced Paul's interaction with those in Athens which is recorded in Acts 17. It reads as follows:

> The God who made the world and everything in it, being Lord of heaven and earth, does not live in temples made by man, nor is he served by human hands, as though he needed anything, since he himself gives to all mankind life and breath and everything. And he made from one man every nation of mankind to live on all the face of the earth, having determined allotted periods and the boundaries of their dwelling place, that they should seek God, and perhaps feel their way toward him and find him. Yet he is actually not far from each one of us, for "In him we live and move and have our being"; as even some of your own poets have said, "For we are indeed his offspring."
> -Acts 17:24-28

It is interesting because if we go back just one verse prior to this discourse, we find that Paul was speaking to them about One whom they named, "The Unknown God." Paul, therefore, took what they deemed as "unknown" and revealed how easy He is to know. Paul states, "Yet he is actually not far from each one of us." Paul enunciates this truth by declaring, "In him we live and move and have our being."

A phrase commonly used all throughout Christendom is "God works in mysterious ways," but this phrase is not biblical. You can look it up right now if you'd like, I promise you that you won't find that saying in the Bible. Some may say, "Well, it's not exactly said, but it's implied." Show me where. I am genuinely curious. There are passages that talk about the hidden things of God, but not hidden in the sense that they are mysterious, but hidden in the sense that He plans to reveal them at a future time. In Daniel 2:22

we read, "He reveals deep and hidden things; he knows what is in the darkness, and the light dwells with him." Jumping to the New Testament epistles; we often read of Paul referencing a mystery of God, but then how God revealed or made known that mystery. A few examples of this are Ephesians 1:9, Colossians 1:26, and I Timothy 3:16.

The simple truth is that God is not mysterious and has never desired to be mysterious. From the very beginning, we see that He desired to have intimate relationship with His creation. After the fall of man in Genesis 3 we read how God entered the Garden of Eden in the cool of the day (v.8). It is heavily implied in the text that this was a common occurrence because when He showed up and His creation was not there, He asked, "Where are you" (v.9)? That is truly a profound question. The God of the universe, the One who created all things, is asking His creation, "Where are you?" We see, therefore, that the divide between God and man was not instituted by God, but was a consequence of an act of man. We become frustrated because it is not effortless to have a relationship with Him, yet we are the ones to blame for such a truth.

Genuine faith is the means by which we trample underfoot the ideology of a mysterious God and understand that He is indeed miraculous but He is also intimate. To abide outside of genuine faith is to remain in the frame of mind that He is "The Unknown God" as the Athenian people described Him. Faith makes Him knowable. Faith makes Him real. Though we do not see Him we love Him and serve Him. Why? Because we are fully persuaded (faith) that He is true.

Faith, however, goes beyond the foundation upon which our relationship with Him is built. Abiding in faith in Him and His power allows us to tap into that same power. We will dive more into this in the following chapter, but is beneficial to note here at least in part. Jesus, speaking to His disciples, said, "Truly, I say to you, if you have faith and do not doubt, you will not only do what has been done to the fig tree, but even if you say to this mountain, Be taken up and thrown into the sea,' it will happen. And whatever you ask in prayer, you will receive, if you have faith" (Matthew 21:21-22). Notice here the determining factor that sets the precipice for the remainder of Jesus' statement: "If you have faith and do not doubt." We have defined faith as being fully persuaded, standing in stark contradiction to faith is this word "doubt." "Doubt" here is "diakrinō" which could aptly be defined as all the things that faith is not. If faith is to be fully persuaded, then doubt is to lack persuasion. If faith is to be firmly rooted and grounded, then doubt is to be as one standing on ever-shifting sand. Jesus here is presenting two contradictory ideas that cannot coexist. You cannot claim to be fully persuaded and yet lack persuasion.

There remains, however, an interesting and vital aspect that correlates to this faith versus doubt truth. It is often misunderstood that in order to be right before God we must have perfect faith. Such a truth is never presented to us in the Bible. In fact, Jesus said, "For assuredly, I say to you, if you have faith as a mustard seed, you will say to this mountain, 'Move from here to there,' and it will move; and nothing will be impossible for you" (Matthew 17:20). It should not be overlooked how Jesus correlated faith to a mustard seed. "Mustard seed" here in this text is "sinapi" which refers to a specific seed that is very small when first planted, however, the seed does not remain small. The mustard plant that grows from that small seed can reach up to ten feet. Therefore, while our faith may begin as something seemingly insignificant, when planted in the right soil and atmosphere it will grow exponentially.

Thereby, perfect faith is not a biblical concept, maturing faith, however, is. It is likewise important to understand that the road to maturing faith is not always going to be seamless. There will be hiccups along the way. We thank God for His mercy and grace that sees us in our time of lack and meets us where we are at. We see this demonstrated in an interaction between Jesus and a father whose son was demon-possessed. The father said unto Him, "If you can do anything…"(see Mark 9:22), to which Jesus answered, "'If you can'! All things are possible for one who believes.' Immediately the father of the child cried out and said, 'I believe; help my unbelief'" (Mark 9:23-24)! What we see is that the man had a level of faith in Jesus, which is why he brought him to Him. There was a level of persuasion. However, there was also a war within him trying to keep him from that path of maturity. Internally there was a war between his level of faith and his level of faithlessness. It ought to be obvious to us that his level of faith was greater, for he brought his son to Jesus, but that did not mean he was not struggling. The father, presenting himself vulnerably unto Jesus, declared that he had faith in Him, yet there was a part of him that struggled to step into the realm of faith. How did Jesus respond to this? Did He send him away? No, rather, we see Jesus respond to the father's vulnerability by freeing his son.

Whenever we discuss abiding in relationship with Jesus, it is essential to lay out the understanding that it will not always be perfect. This truth is often of great discouragement to some. It is unfortunate but many have had it impressed upon them that they must be perfect or else He will not love them. That is not love, and it is definitely not His love. We read, "For the righteous falls seven times and rises again, but the wicked stumble in times of calamity" (Proverbs 24:16). The idea of a righteous man is in reference to one who abides with Christ. For man has no righteousness in and of himself. Our righteousness is a result of His righteousness (see II Corinthians 5:21). Thereby, the fact that the righteous man rises again time after time is not a testament to his own strength, but to the grace of God at work in his life.

Living the life of faith is not always easy, and there will be times wherein your faith is tested. No one enjoys being tested, yet James admonishes us to count it as joy when we are tested. Why? Because the testing of our faith, when responded to properly, produces steadfastness, which then produces one who is perfect and complete, lacking in nothing (see James 1:2-4).

Faith ushers us into a place of completion in Him.

Focused Reflection

Faith is essential to the Christian walk.

The author of Hebrews said, "And without faith it is impossible to please him, for whoever would draw near to God must believe that he exists and that he rewards those who seek him" (Hebrews 11:6).

Despite its essentiality, faith seems to be at an all-time low among those who profess to be Christian. We say we believe one thing, but our actions prove another. We fail to realize that faith is not merely a mental assent or something spoken but not acted. This could not be further from the truth. In truth, faith is not present unless demonstrated by one's works.

James put it succinctly: "So also faith by itself, if it does not have works, is dead" (James 2:17).

To mature in our Christian walk, we have to allow what we claim to believe to escape the confines of our inward man and become evident in outward manifestation. For faith to truly become evident, we must truly trust in Him.

1. The old saying goes, "Actions speak louder than words," and that is abundantly true regarding faith. Would you say that your actions align with what you claim to believe?

2. If there is a disconnect between what you claim to believe and how you act, how you would remedy that? What would you need to do to align your actions with your belief?

3. If God were to ask you right now, "Do you trust Me?" How would you respond?

> Trust in the LORD with all your heart, and do not lean on your own understanding. In all your ways acknowledge him, and he will make straight your paths.
> -Proverbs 3:5-6

15
Christians Operate in the Miraculous
Christians Walk in Childlike Faith II

"Truly, truly, I say to you, whoever believes in me will also do the works that I do; and greater works than these will he do, because I am going to the Father. Whatever you ask in my name, this I will do, that the Father may be glorified in the Son. If you ask me anything in my name, I will do it."
~John 14:12-14

In the previous chapter, we briefly mentioned the topic of the mysterious versus the miraculous. It is a sad truth that, for many, the concept of the miraculous has become mysterious, spooky, or goofy. In our present society, many hold a very realistic mindset regarding the world around us. We believe what is immediately evident and what can easily be proven true, but anything beyond that we disregard as fairytales and children's stories. It is a very unfortunate truth. However, the miraculous is neither mysterious, spooky, or goofy. The miraculous is biblical.

This book has aimed to usher in a reorientation regarding being Christ-like or Christian. If we are serious in this endeavor, which I pray we all are, then we cannot take some of His teachings and examples while disregarding others. We either take the whole truth or we take none of the truth. Understanding this, in approaching the idea of Christ-like, we need to realize that Jesus performed many miracles in His day. Further, as our focus text demonstrates and as we will discuss, He calls us to do the same works that He did, but not only the same works, but even greater works. If we endeavor to truly be Christian then we must understand that He operated in the miraculous and that He calls us to do the same by His grace. As C.S. Lewis so rightly said, "The mind which asks for a non-miraculous

Christianity is a mind in process of relapsing from Christianity into mere 'religion.'"

Before discussing how the different ways in which the miraculous can be manifested in our lives, I feel it pertinent to discuss the purpose of the miraculous. The devil is always seeking to undermine all that God does. He endeavors to present twisted representations of what God has set in order to deter people away from the things of God. For example, speaking on the miraculous, two ways in which the enemy has attempted to twist this gift from God is with magic and sorcery. We aren't going to dive deep into these various veins, our focus is on the work of Jesus, not Satan. However, it is important to note that these two veins are twisted and evil. Even seemingly harmless magic tricks. While there may not be any immediately obvious repercussions, the root of what is being demonstrated is demonic.

Magic shows have commercialized the "miraculous," turning it all into a sideshow and party tricks. Sorcery is much darker and much more serious. Sorcery occurs when one intentionally seeks demonic power to be manifested in their lives. While sorcery is, at face value, more serious, it is as I said, both are rooted in evil. Magic seeks to turn the miraculous into a joke, while sorcery seeks to twist it for evil gain.

There, however, is a distinct purpose for the miraculous being manifest in our lives. The Gospel of Mark ends with the statement, "And they went out and preached everywhere, and the Lord worked through them, confirming His word by the signs that accompanied it" (Mark 16:20 BSB). The word "signs" here is "sēmeion" which can also be translated as, "a wonder; a remarkable event; extraordinary phenomenon; miraculous operation; miracle." What was the purpose for such to be made evident? For the purpose of "confirming His word." The word "confirming" is "bebaioō" which means, "to confirm or establish; to render constant and unwavering." In essence, the miraculous is made evident for the express purpose of demonstrating that His Word is true.

Jesus Himself said this when speaking with the religious leaders of His day. During a discussion wherein they were questioning Him on His identity He said, "But the testimony that I have is greater than that of John. For the works that the Father has given me to accomplish, the very works that I am doing, bear witness about me that the Father has sent me" (John 5:36). The works that He is referring to here are the miracles that He had been performing. His miracles testify that His Word is true.

A prime example we see pertaining to this in the ministry of Jesus is His interaction with the lame man whom his friends brought before Jesus. We read, "And behold, some people brought to him a paralytic, lying on a bed. And when Jesus saw their faith, he said to the paralytic, 'Take heart, my son; your sins are forgiven.' And behold, some of the scribes said to themselves, 'This man is blaspheming.' But Jesus, knowing their thoughts, said, 'Why do you think evil in your hearts? For which is easier, to say, 'Your sins are forgiven,' or to say, 'Rise and walk'? But that you may know that the Son of Man has authority on earth to forgive sins'—he then said to the paralytic—'Rise, pick up your bed and go home.' And he rose and went home. When the crowds saw it, they were afraid, and they glorified God, who had given such authority to men" (Matthew 9:2-8). Jesus first declared that the man's sins were forgiven. The people, mainly the religious leaders, then began to doubt within themselves and judge Him over His words. Therefore, as a testimony that He was able to forgive sins, He healed the man. His works confirmed His Word.

Relating to the concept of miracles confirming His Word, but also slightly different, is that miracles help to prepare the way for the receiving of the Word by building faith. We read in Luke 10:1, "After this the Lord appointed seventy-two others and sent them on ahead of him, two by two, into every town and place where he himself was about to go." After their mission had been completed and they returned to Him, they immediately made mention of the miracles that were manifested through them and He confirmed the same (see Luke 10:17-19). He prepared the hearts of the people by sending His disciples ahead of Him to perform miracles in His name. The miraculous caused faith in the hearts of the people which then enabled them to receive His Word.

This truth is further confirmed in Acts 1:8. The text reads, "But you will receive power when the Holy Spirit has come upon you, and you will be my witnesses in Jerusalem and in all Judea and Samaria, and to the end of the earth." Notice the sequence of events that are laid out in this declaration by Jesus. First, He declared that we would receive power. The word "power" here is "dynamis" which, as the text demonstrates, refers to power or strength. This is clearly a reference to the infilling of the Holy Spirit that initially transpired in the very next chapter. The disciples, and all who are born of the Spirit, receive the power of the Spirit. However, the word "dynamis" can also mean, "miraculous power." This clues us into the power that the Spirit affords us, that is, miracle-working power. After receiving the power of the Spirit, Jesus then declared that they would be witnesses. While the text does not outright say, "You will receive power to be witnesses," it does, however, imply that the power we receive will aid us in being witnesses. Again, declaring that miracles aid us in sharing His Word by building faith.

It is declared and demonstrated time and time again throughout the Gospels that He has given us miracle-working power. A very straightforward example of this is found at the conclusion of Mark's Gospel account. Jesus declared, "And these signs will accompany those who believe: in my name they will cast out demons; they will speak in new tongues; they will pick up serpents with their hands; and if they drink any deadly poison, it will not hurt them; they will lay their hands on the sick, and they will recover" (Mark 16:17-18). One important side note regarding this passage: Jesus is by no means advocating for snake handling or poison drinking. The Bible clearly states that we are not to test God (see Deuteronomy 6:16; Matthew 4:5-7; Luke 4:9-12). Therefore, if Jesus were advocating for snake handling and poison drinking, it would be in direct opposition with the rest of His Word. Rather, the common interpretation held regarding this passage is that His miracle power in us will protect us if we unintentionally pick up snakes or drink something poisonous. Miraculous protection.

Returning to our point, Jesus clearly states that those who abide in faith will walk in power over demons, speak by the power of the Spirit, be afforded miraculous protection, and operate in miracles of healing. However, this truth needs to be kept in alignment with what was said above; the miraculous is made evident to confirm His

Word and prepare the hearts of people by building faith. Miracles are never for the purpose of show. The miraculous just does not occur merely because we think it would be cool. God works the miraculous through us for a distinct purpose: ushering people into a salvation experience.

Some may ask, "What about when the miraculous occurs in the life of one already saved?" To that, I would say that the miracle God performed was not meant to be kept to themselves but meant to be shared as a testimony. This, then, would fall under the above-mentioned purpose: to build faith in the hearts of people who are in need of salvation. Or, we could also say that maybe that individual that received a miracle was lacking faith and doubt was creeping in. Therefore, God manifested Himself through the miraculous as to remind them that He is near, that He cares, and that they ought not to lose sight of their faith in Him. Even if the reason is more so aligned with the second example given, I would still say that the event ought to be shared by the individual to build faith in the lives of others.

We may not immediately realize it, but the miraculous transpires in our daily lives more often than we think. We may not see demons cast out or cancerous tumors shrivel up on a daily basis, but the miraculous also works in less demonstrative ways. There are likely several reading this right now that are strongly doubting that they see the miraculous on a daily basis. Surely you would know, right? In truth, we ought to recognize when He is working miraculously through us, but we are not always so in tune with Him as we ought to be. The doldrums of this life often get the better of us. It is my sincere prayer that we become a people more in tune with Him and His Spirit. He is the same God today that He was thousands of years ago. The same God that parted the Red Sea for Israel is the same God living in those who are born of His Spirit. Some may, "Why, then, does He not make known the miraculous to the same degree?" The issue is not with God, it is with us. Our level of faith has drastically waned because of the advancements we have achieved in our day and age. We no longer "need" God as they did in the past. God forbid. This mindset is so dangerous. Unfortunately, it is prevalent. We put more faith in man and man's accomplishments than we do in the Creator of all who holds power over all. If we would correct our way of thinking and bring ourselves back into alignment with Him, we would begin to see demonstrative miracles once again.

Returning to the discussion that the miraculous is more prevalent in our lives than we realize: Paul identified nine ways in which the miraculous is made known in our lives. These nine manifestations of the miraculous have come to be known as the Gifts of the Spirit. Paul began his discourse on the Gifts of the Spirit by saying, "Now concerning spiritual gifts, brethren, I do not want you to be ignorant: You know that you were Gentiles, carried away to these dumb idols, however you were led. Therefore I make known to you that no one speaking by the Spirit of God calls Jesus accursed, and no one can say that Jesus is Lord except by the Holy Spirit" (I Corinthians 12:1-3). I feel it necessary to begin here because what Paul has to say is still relevant to us today. How so? Paul was concerned that the Church at Corinth would twist the miraculous work that God desired to do in their midst and turn it into something other than a move of God. How often do we do this very thing?

The idea of "luck" has become a cornerstone in our society. We commonly say, "I wish you luck," or, "That was lucky!" Luck is rooted in paganism and superstition. Luck is contrary to God. God does not work in luck, He works in the intentional miraculous. By participating in this false ideology of luck we twist the miraculous work of God and steal the glory from Him that he deserves. Any discussion revolving around the Gifts of the Spirit and His miracle-working power must begin by conveying His Lordship and authority over all things by His Spirit.

Further, throughout Paul's listing of the Gifts of the Spirit, he repeats over and over that it is the same Spirit that is empowering these Gifts. In pagan culture and religion, each of their various gods had power over a particular thing, whether it be the sun, war, love, and such the like. Meaning, pagan religions believed in gods who operated in a limited sphere of influence. Paul, then, emphatically demonstrated that it was God and God alone who exercised and demonstrated total power over all things. There was and is no other god working alongside Him in areas He cannot touch. Paul declared elsewhere that He is above all, through all, and in all (see Ephesians

4:6). While we do not believe in multiple gods as the pagans do, we do, however, often fail to give God the glory He deserves. How so? I'll make it plain with this one example: healing is a miracle whether it is supernatural or through medicine. It is God who gives medicine its ability to heal. Therefore, He is still the One healing. How often do we fail to recognize His hand in it when it is not demonstrative? We ought to be thankful for doctors and physicians, but at the end of it all it ought to be God who gets the glory.

Only after laying this foundational work does Paul then list the nine Gifts of the Spirit. His list is as follows: Word of Wisdom, Word of Knowledge, Gift of Faith, Gifts of Healings, Working of Miracles, Gift of Prophecy, Discerning of Spirits, Gift of Different Tongues, and Interpretation of Tongues (as translated by the NKJV). Some of these nine Gifts seem more miraculous than others, such as Gifts of Healings, Working of Miracles, Gift of Prophecy, Gift of Different Tongues, and the Interpretation of Tongues. However, even the Gifts that do not seem as miraculous are still just that because they are outside of our ability to perform. It is purely by His Spirit working through us that these Gifts are manifested.

There is one final thing of great importance that I feel we need to understand before discussing the various Gifts. This final note comes at the very end of this chapter wherein Paul says, "But earnestly desire the best gifts..." (I Corinthians 12:31). "Best" here is not the best translation of the Greek. Using the word "best" creates the misconception that some Gifts are overall better than others. This is simply not the case. The word translated "best" is "kreittōn" which, more accurately, means, "most useful, serviceable, and advantageous." Meaning, the Gifts of the Spirit are meant to meet specific needs at specific times. Meaning, some Gifts are more advantageous at the moment given the current need. We should diligently, by His grace, seek after the Gift that will aid us in that present moment. Therefore, the Gifts of the Spirit are not Gifts that permanently dwell in someone's life but are manifested in a specific moment for a specific purpose.

Keeping all these things at the forefront of our minds, we can now dive into our brief discussion regarding the various Gifts. Our discussion here will, in fact, be brief. For a more in-depth look into these Gifts, I would recommend Spiritual Gifts by Bro. David Bernard. You could also read the chapter, The Spiritual Gifts, in my book, Kingdom Progression: Insights into Kingdom Operation.

Beginning with the Word of Wisdom, the first word of importance to understand is the word "wisdom" itself. The Greek word here is "sophia" which can refer to practical wisdom, superior knowledge, and enlightenment, divine wisdom, revealed wisdom, as well as interpreting dreams and vision. Further, Webster's Dictionary defines "wisdom" as, "the right use or exercise of knowledge." Taking these varying definitions into consideration, a concise understanding of this Gift that we can surmise is that of divine guidance or direction.

It is likewise important to understand "Word" used here in relation to wisdom. "Word" is "logos" which contains a multiplicity of meanings, however, a simple way we can understand this word is a thought and then the utterance of that thought. Why is it important to understand this word? Because when God works through us in the Gift of the Word of Wisdom it is not the totality of His wisdom, only a word of it. Or, in other words, a portion of it. Truly, we could not contain within ourselves the totality of His wisdom.

Continuing on we come to the Word of Knowledge. The word "Word" here is the same as just previously examined. Therefore, we can assert the same claim that we made regarding the Word of Wisdom, that is, it is but a portion of His knowledge. Again, as was stated regarding His wisdom, we could not contain the totality of His knowledge for His knowledge is beyond measure.

Looking at this word "knowledge," it is "gnōsis" in Greek. "Gnōsis" simply refers to having general understanding or intelligence. Looking once again to Webster's Dictionary, it defines "knowledge" as, "a clear and certain perception of the truth and facts." In essence, the Word of Knowledge can be understood as divinely imparted understanding that was not previously possessed by the individual.

Looking back briefly to the Word of Wisdom, we demonstrated how Webster's Dictionary defines "wisdom" as "the right use or exercise of knowledge." Therefore, we could come to the understanding that the Word of Wisdom and the Word of Knowledge are often connected. It could be that God grants us understanding of a thing and then aids us in knowing what to do with what we now know. This, of course, does not always have to be the case. God can use these Gifts as He so desires because they are at His disposal.

The next Gift is that of Faith. One's immediate response to this Gift may be that of confusion. In the previous chapter, we took an in-depth look into what faith is and its essentiality in our walk with God. Referencing Hebrews 11:6, if we have no faith then we are not even pleasing unto God. Why, then, is faith an apparent Gift? It is important to understand that there is a difference between the faith that is necessary for us to walk in and the faith mentioned here. We will define the everyday faith that is necessary for us to walk in as "fundamental faith." "Fundamental," as defined by Webster's Dictionary, is "serving for the foundation." The Gift of Faith, then, we will define as "exponential faith." Oxford Languages defines "exponential" as, "(of an increase) become more and more rapid."

The Gift of Faith is an increased level of faith beyond the fundamental level that is necessary regarding faith. This Gift of Faith is given as to bring an individual through a particular circumstance that requires great levels of such. An important note is that trust is eternally intertwined with faith. "Trust" is defined by Oxford Languages as, "firm belief in the reliability, truth, ability, or strength of someone or something." Therefore, the Gift of Faith not only increases our faith levels but also increases our trust in God. The Gift of Faith enables us to endure turbulent times that would likely cause others to stumble and fall but because of this miraculous power at work in our lives, we are able to stand strong in Him with our trust in Him abounding above all.

Paul continues by listing the Gifts of Healings. This is immediately interesting for this Gift presents itself in plural form rather than singular. The KJV translates this Gift as the Gifts of Healing, placing the plural only on the Gifts. The NKJV, however, places the plural on both Gifts and Healings. What does this indicate? Gifts being made plural indicates a multiplicity of Gifts within this singular category. Healings being made plural indicates an abundance of such. What can we infer from this? Simply that the Gifts of Healings is not limited to a singular mode of operation, but its reach spans across multiple areas and presents itself in abundance. Understanding this, how might we witness this Gift in operation? We could witness physical healing, emotional healing, mental healing, and spiritual healing. Multiple areas of our being can be affected by various hurts and pains. Likewise, the various parts of our being can become "sick," whether that is literal or metaphoric. The Gifts of Healings reaches to each of these aspects of our being and is able to bring healing in every way.

It is likewise beneficial for us to examine the Greek word for "healings." "Iama" is the word used here that can refer to either healing or cure. Webster's Dictionary provides a powerful definition for "cure" which is, "to subdue, remove, destroy, or put an end to." Therefore, when the Gifts of Healings are in operation in someone's life, it is not merely placing a band-aid on the issue. Rather, the Gifts of Healings are subduing, removing, destroying, and putting an end to the hurt, pain, and sickness that is trying to come against us.

There is one final point that I feel is vital for us to discuss regarding this particular Gift. There will be times when we seek after the demonstration of this Gift either for ourselves or for another and the healing we are seeking after is not made evident. I have been blessed throughout my relationship with God to be able to witness some truly miraculous healings. However, I have also witnessed times wherein someone diligently sought after a particular healing and never saw it. This truth, unfortunately, causes many to fall away from their walk with God. God does not answer their prayer how they so desire or think that He should, so they lose trust in Him and either His ability and/or His love. It is absolutely essential that we approach the operation of this Gift with the understanding that His will is perfect and without fault. We do not see all as He does, nor do we know all. Therefore, our ability to properly discern the best course of action is not only limited but also tainted. If we are not careful it is easy for us to approach a situation through the lens of our carnal man. We discussed this in the chapter, Christians are People of Prayer, so I would recommend revisiting what was discussed there if needed.

The truth is simply this: if God does the work of healing that we are seeking after, then all glory be to Him; likewise, if He does not, then we still need to give all glory to Him. He is perfect and His will is perfect. He has a personal and love-filled plan for each one of our lives. All that He does is for our good, even if we are not able to immediately recognize that truth.

The Gift of the Spirit that follows is the Working of Miracles. This, like the Gifts of Healings, is also presented in the plural form. However, not in the same way as the Gifts of Healings. By Paul stating that it is the Working of Miracles he was implying that this Gift exists in abundance. Miracles should not be viewed as a rarity or a thing of the past. We have endeavored to demonstrate this very truth throughout this chapter. The miraculous is not only for us today, it is for us in abundance if only we have the faith to receive it. Further, it is important that we make a distinction regarding this Gift. We have previously stated how every Gift of the Spirit is a work of the miraculous. Why, then, is there a distinct Gift pertaining to the Working of Miracles? This should be understood as demonstrative miracles. Or, in other words, what we likely think of when miracles are mentioned.

Webster's Dictionary defines "miracle" as, "an event or effects contrary to the established constitution and course of things, or a deviation from the known laws of nature; a supernatural event." It is helpful to examine the Greek word used for "miracles" to garner a more thorough understanding of this Gift. The word here is "dynamis" which can be translated as, "power; strength; miraculous power." Meaning, this Gift is God working through an individual with divine power. This Gift is God working through an individual to accomplish feats far beyond their physical ability.

We can easily imagine what the previous Gifts look like in operation, but how might we picture this Gift in operation? We could likely think of some pretty, seemingly, crazy things when we think of the demonstrative miraculous. But how much should we allow our imagination to soar? Should we temper our thinking? I would say no. When speaking on the Working of Miracles in Kingdom Progression, I referenced the example from Acts 8:39-40. In this brief passage, we read of how Philip was, in some fashion, miraculously transported from one place to another. How did this look exactly? We aren't told, unfortunately. But not being told the details allows our imaginations to truly branch out. Wherever our imaginations take us, this was a truly demonstrative miracle. How great is your faith?

Following the Working of Miracles we come to the Gift of Prophecy. There is an important distinction we need to make in that operating in the Gift of Prophecy does not mean an individual is a Prophet (as Paul listed in the Five-Fold Ministry [see Ephesians 4:11]). Remember what was said at the start: the Gifts of the Spirit are given by God to meet specific needs at specific moments. Therefore, God can use anyone who is Spirit-filled in the Gift of Prophecy if they allow Him to. The office of a Prophet is not a momentary thing, but an anointing the individual consistently walks in. But what is prophecy?

Prophecy is very intricate. Many people usually only associate foretelling with prophecy, which is the prediction of future events. Without question, this is the most commonly witnessed aspect of prophecy which is why it has become the "face" of what prophecy is. However, there exists another vein of the prophetic which is forth-telling, which reveals past or present things. Therefore, a simple way in which we could understand the Gift of Prophecy is revealing through divine revelation.

Allow me to make one point emphatically clear: the Gift of Prophecy is not given as to reveal everyone's problems. The Gift of Prophecy is not of a gossiping spirit. This Gift is given for the betterment of His Kingdom, not the tearing down of it. What, then, is the succinct purpose of the prophetic? To give direction. Whether the prophetic is made known through the Gift of Prophecy or the office of a Prophet the end result is the same: direction or guidance.

We then arrive at the Gift pertaining to the Discerning of Spirits. This is a widely misunderstood Gift of the Spirit. Many misinterpret this Gift as mere discernment. Discernment is defined by Webster's Dictionary as, "the power or faculty of the mind, by which it distinguishes one thing from another, as truth from falsehood, virtue from vice; acuteness of judgment; the power of perceiving differences of things or ideas, and their relations and tendencies." In other words, all people have the power of discernment, for discernment could simply be defined as paying attention. We fall short of the proper understanding of this Gift when we think it to be a mere heightened level of perception.

The aspect that many overlook regarding this Gift is that it specifically refers to the spiritual world. What are the different aspects of the spiritual realm that one could discern? There are three different realms (if that, indeed, is the correct terminology) of the spiritual: God and His angels, Satan and his demons, and the human spirit (or the individual will). Therefore, the Discerning of Spirits is divine insight as to which aspect of the spiritual realm is motivating a current course of action. Is God driving this path forward according to His perfect will? Is Satan attempting to lead one astray into destruction and death? Or is the human spirit at work, seeking that which provides instant gratification?

We could even take this one step further and state that the Discerning of Spirits gives insight into the specific spirits at work. Meaning, just to give a few examples, is it the Spirit of Love, Peace, Unity, or Holiness (which are all aspects of His One Spirit)? Or is it the spirit of lust, greed, envy, gluttony, or strife at work? Many more examples could be listed but this creates for us a general understanding. The Discerning of Spirits gives us divine insight into what is motivating the current events and helps us to understand what is taking place behind the scenes.

Once again, I feel the need to make an emphatic point as I did with the Gift of Prophecy. The Discerning of Spirits is not given as to reveal people's "baggage." Each of the nine Gifts is given for the edification of the Body of Christ. Whether that be for an individual already in His Body or one coming into the Body. The Gifts are given to grow His Church, not hurt it. We must approach the Gifts of the Spirit through the lens of love.

The final two Gifts of the Spirit we will look at together. Truly, these are two separate Gifts. However, they are directly connected to one another. Where one is in operation, the other ought to also be present. These are Different Kinds of Tongues and the Interpretation of Tongues. We will begin with the former.

The first important thing to draw attention to is that this Gift is different than speaking in tongues which was mentioned in the chapters, Christians Abide with Christ and Christians are Baptized in

His Name and Spirit. The speaking in tongues mentioned previously is the initial sign given when someone is filled with His Spirit. In truth, there are three different references in Scripture pertaining to tongues. That is, speaking in tongues as the initial sign of the infilling, praying in tongues (see Romans 8:26; Jude 1:20), and the Gift of Different Kinds of Tongues. As Paul mentioned, each Gift of Spirit is meant as edification for the whole Body (see I Corinthians 12:7). The Gift of Different Kinds of Tongues is God supernaturally speaking a Word to His Body. How do we understand this Word? That is where the Interpretation of Tongues comes into play. We will come back to that Gift momentarily.

Why is the Gift called "Different Kinds of Tongues"? This signifies to us that there is not one specific tongue with which the individual speaks with when operating in this Gift. In I Corinthians 13:1, Paul states that by the Spirit one could speak in the tongue of men (which is plural, indicating it could be any human language) or the tongue of angels (again, plural, indicating there is not just one heavenly language).

The Gift of Different Kinds of Tongues, then, is Jesus supernaturally speaking through an individual a Word that is of benefit to His Body. It could be a Word of correction, reproof, instruction, encouragement, or such the like. Each of these could serve as edification for the Body (to edify refers to the building up of a thing).

However, a supernatural message in tongues is pointless without an interpretation thereof. "Interpretation," according to Webster's Dictionary, can mean, "an explanation of intelligible words in a language that is intelligible," or, "the act of expounding or unfolding what is not understood or not obvious." Paul said that whenever a message in tongues is given that we ought to pray for the interpretation of that message (see I Corinthians 14:12-13). Paul said that simply standing in front of the Church and speaking in tongues is of no benefit to the Body (I Corinthians 14:2, 4, 9). Therefore, in order for the Gift of Different Kinds of Tongues to be beneficial, the Interpretation of Tongues must be in operation.

Due to this essential dependency upon each other, many merge these two Gifts into one and call it something along the lines of "Tongues and Interpretation of Tongues." While this is understandable, it is not the case. These are two distinct Gifts. Just because an individual operates in one does not mean they will operate in the other. I have witnessed this miraculous event many times throughout my life and most times it is one individual giving the message in tongues and another giving the interpretation. Only on a rare occasion have I witnessed the same individual operate in both Gifts.

Before bringing this discussion to a close there is one final thing of importance we need to bring into view. One cannot talk about the Gifts of the Spirit without speaking on the proper operation of them. We alluded to it earlier throughout our examination of various Gifts, but there is a proper mode of operation regarding the miraculous. Earlier we quoted the first part of I Corinthians 12:31 which reads, "But earnestly desire the best gifts..." The second half of the same verse reads, "And yet I show you a more excellent way." There is a more excellent way (or a way that is beyond all measure) to operate in the Gifts. What is this "more excellent way"?

The answer to that question comes from the very next chapter. That is, love. We have already extensively examined love so we will not do so again. In fact, in our examination of love, we used I Corinthians 13 as a focal point. However, it is essential to understand that love is meant to be the bedrock on which the Gifts are operated in. The miraculous apart from love is of no benefit.

It is an unfortunate truth that many reading this book will have come to this second to last chapter and become "turned off" by it and put the book down, never to open it again. Why? Because as I said, to many the miraculous has become goofy, or a thing of the distant past. But I attest to you today that it is neither goofy nor a thing of the past. It is of God and for us today. Operating in the miraculous is just as much a part of being a Christian as being Born Again, and just as much a part of being a Christian as loving our neighbors. If we truly desire to be Christians as He so desires us to be, then we must receive this truth and operate in it.

I mentioned in the previous chapter, Christians Walk in Childlike Faith, that humanity has become driven by logic and reason. How logic and reason, in and of themselves, are not bad but we have allowed these to become the ruling principalities in our lives to the point where all faith has become null and void. We claim faith, yet we do not exercise it. We speak faith in good times, but in times of tribulation, we are found lacking. We have become so consumed with what we define as "reality" that we are no longer able to perceive anything beyond it. What we fail to realize is that what we define as "reality" is actually not the true reality. The spirit realm is the true definition of reality for it is in such that He dwells. We could almost go so far as to say that we no longer believe in the moving of His Spirit, that Christianity has become nothing more than organized religion. God forbid. We have been called to so much more. It is a deception of the enemy that we have believed that tells us that the miraculous is no longer in operation. He knows the power that Jesus has granted us and has convinced us to not use it, effectively stopping the Church in its tracks.

If we are ever going to be the true definition of the Church then the miraculous must be in operation among us. Now, we mustn't become goofy in our pursuit of these things. Many fail to walk that line. Most either completely deny the existence of the miraculous (as we have demonstrated) or they seek it to the point where it is no longer biblical and make it goofy. We must be spiritual people, but spiritual as in accordance with Scripture. Likewise, we must keep in remembrance the purpose of miracles. Earlier in this chapter we listed two distinct purposes for such: to confirm His Word, and to build faith in those who need salvation. I will simplify this with one combined purpose for the miraculous: a tool to be used in furthering the Kingdom message of salvation. Are we able to benefit from the miraculous? Absolutely. However, the end result of every miraculous demonstration is the furthering of His Gospel.

It is my heart's desire that His Church would begin to seek after the Gifts that He has granted us once again. Not attempting to mimic them, but sincerely seeking Him for the manifestation of His power in our midst. It is time for the Church to stop fighting with one hand tied behind its back.

Focused Reflection

It is an unfortunate truth that the terms "miraculous" or "miracle(s)" have become subject to disdain and scorn in our society. Whenever one employs these terms as they relate to certain events, they are often either viewed as "goofy" or over-dramatic. It is especially sad because this has not only become the mindset of the world toward the miraculous but is the often-held mindset of many professing Christians.

Truly, you cannot separate God from the miraculous. God separated from the miraculous is a being no more powerful than a mere human. If that is the case, why worship Him? But thanks be to God that He is still the God of miracles.

Further, as His children, He has given us access to that same power in Him by which He performs the miraculous. Miracles are not "goofy," nor are they a thing of the past. They are real and they are for us today, if only we have the faith.

1. If God were to do a miracle in your life right now, what would it look like?

2. What's stopping you from believing for that miracle you listed above?

3. Assuming you believe that He is still the God of miracles, do you believe that He could do a miracle through your hands?

Truly, truly, I say to you, whoever believes in me will also do the works that I do; and greater works than these will he do, because I am going to the Father. Whatever you ask in my name, this I will do, that the Father may be glorified in the Son. If you ask me anything in my name, I will do it.
-John 14:12-14

16
Christians Who Are Faithful Have a Future Hope

"And there will be signs in sun and moon and stars, and on the earth distress of nations in perplexity because of the roaring of the sea and the waves, people fainting with fear and with foreboding of what is coming on the world. For the powers of the heavens will be shaken. And then they will see the Son of Man coming in a cloud with power and great glory. Now when these things begin to take place, straighten up and raise your heads, because your redemption is drawing near."
~Luke 21:25-28

We now arrive at our final point of discussion in this book. It could be said that this final chapter is meant to serve as the point of convergence, where all the previous topics meet in finality. Why do I say that this is where they meet in finality? The life that we are called to live by Jesus Christ was never meant to be confined to this earthly life only but was meant to point to something greater. Without the hope of that greater thing, what we do in this life does not attain too much. If you do not have the hope of a greater future, then I suppose you must begin by asking yourself what you believe. But we will come back to this discussion regarding our future hope. First, I want to look at the topic of faithfulness.

The title of this chapter, Christians Who are Faithful Have a Future Hope, aims to present the truth that there exists a prerequisite to obtaining the aforementioned future hope. But what does it mean to be faithful? What is the importance of being faithful? Further, in what ways are we to demonstrate that faithfulness? These are important questions that we need to answer.

In truth, the presence of sincerity in an individual's belief does not determine its level of truth. What do I mean? You can be sincere all you would like, but you can be sincerely wrong. A prevalent issue in our day and age today is that many are attempting to abolish the notion of absolute truth. Many say, "You have your truth and I have my truth." Such a statement contradicts the very definition of truth. Oxford Languages defines "truth" as, "that which is true or in accordance with fact or reality." Therefore, truth is not an idea or an opinion but a thing firmly fixed in reality. You cannot deny reality. People who attempt to do so are what we would define as "delusional," which is defined as, "characterized by or holding false beliefs or judgments about external reality that are held despite incontrovertible evidence to the contrary" (Oxford Languages).

Why do I say all this? One, the entire purpose of this book has been to establish truth according to Scripture, which is the final authority on truth. Additionally, I say this because we need to establish the truth of faithfulness according to its true identity, not according to our opinion. You could ask ten different people to define faithfulness for you and you would likely receive a different answer from each one. Why? Because too often we define something based on opinion and not in accordance with what it truly is. This is an epidemic in our current society. Opinion has become the basis for truth and self has become the representation of god. We need to attempt to define truth less and rather seek to find truth. How do we find truth? Jesus said, "I am the Way, the Truth, and the Life" (see John 14:6). He needs to be the basis for how we define truth. Understanding this crucial point, it would behoove us to examine what Jesus had to say about faithfulness. There are a plethora of passages containing Jesus' insights into this vital topic, our focus will be relegated to Matthew 24 and 25.

The Bible as we know it today is broken up into chapters and verses. This is helpful regarding reference and study, but it can also create a barrier. Often these barriers or divisions in the text break up continuous conversation or teaching. Thus, we perceive them to be separate due to the break in the narrative that we are presented with when, in truth, they are meant to be read together. This is true regarding what is presented in Matthew 24 and 25. These two chapters ought to be read as a cohesive whole. In doing so, we are able to garner a more complete understanding of what Jesus is speaking on.

Matthew 24 begins by clearly establishing that Jesus' focus was on the end of all things. Some topics that He discusses throughout the first portion of Matthew 24 are the signs that we ought to look for regarding His return, perilous time or the Abomination of Desolation as it is worded in the Book of Daniel, the return of Jesus and the Rapture of the Church, and the Parable of the Fig Tree which instructs us on the essentiality of being watchful and aware as to what is transpiring around us. Matthew 24 then ends with Jesus speaking on the necessity of being consistently faithful as we wait for Him. We read:

"But concerning that day and hour no one knows, not even the angels of heaven, nor the Son, but the Father only. For as were the days of Noah, so will be the coming of the Son of Man. For as in those days before the flood they were eating and drinking, marrying and giving in marriage, until the day when Noah entered the ark, and they were unaware until the flood came and swept them all away, so will be the coming of the Son of Man. Then two men will be in the field; one will be taken and one left. Two women will be grinding at the mill; one will be taken and one left. Therefore, stay awake, for you do not know on what day your Lord is coming. But know this, that if the master of the house had known in what part of the night the thief was coming, he would have stayed awake and would not have let his house be broken into. Therefore you also must be ready, for the Son of Man is coming at an hour you do not expect."
-Matthew 24:36-44

Jesus here is demonstrating how easy it is to become consumed in this life. He compares the end to the days of Noah. No one, apart from Noah and his family, was faithfully preparing for what was to come. Everyone was living life how they wanted to live it, eating, drinking, and engaging in personal relationships. Their eyes were set only on what was immediately in front of them, not on what was to come. Due to their willful ignorance (I say willful because we are told that Noah preached unto those around him what was to come [see II Peter 2:5]), they all perished because they lacked faithfulness.

Jesus relegates this same truth to us. It is increasingly easy to become consumed in this life. This life screams at us all the time, demanding our attention. Yet, we still have a choice regarding where we place our focus and attention. Where you, indeed, choose to place such will determine what you are faithful toward. Further, what you are faithful toward will determine your direction which, inevitably, determines your destination. Faithfulness determines destination. Jesus admonishes us, "Therefore, stay awake, for you do not know on what day your Lord is coming." He then adds emphasis to this truth by saying that it's not just that we don't know when, but that "the Son of Man is coming at an hour you do not expect."

To emphasize these truths, Jesus then gives us a parable revolving around a faithful servant and an unfaithful servant:

> "Who then is the faithful and wise servant, whom his master has set over his household, to give them their food at the proper time? Blessed is that servant whom his master will find so doing when he comes. Truly, I say to you, he will set him over all his possessions. But if that wicked servant says to himself, 'My master is delayed,' and begins to beat his fellow servants and eats and drinks with drunkards, the master of that servant will come on a day when he does not expect him and at an hour he does not know and will cut him in pieces and put him with the hypocrites. In that place there will be weeping and gnashing of teeth."
> -Matthew 24:45-51

In this parable, we are first introduced to a "faithful and wise servant." This servant is described as one who faithfully performs the duties that have been entrusted to him. This servant is trusted with the responsibility to care for the rest of the master's servants in his absence. This faithful and wise servant is, therefore, expected to act as a direct representation of the master. If this faithful servant was indeed faithful, the other servants would not suffer from the absence of the master but would continue to thrive under the faithful care of the one who was faithful and wise. In return for this servant's faithfulness, the master promised a hope of great blessing.

The parable, unfortunately, does not end there for we are then introduced to a wicked and unfaithful servant. This servant is described as one who negates the responsibility placed upon him, takes advantage of those in his care, and indulges himself in the desires of the carnal man. The motive of this servant was, "Oh, I have time. I'll get my act together whenever the time of his return draws near." But the servant did not know the time of his return. He should have lived each day with the attitude of, "Today might be the day of his return." If he had done so, he might have lived more faithfully. But he chose to walk the path of arrogance, wickedness, and unfaithfulness. Due to this lack of faithfulness, instead of blessing, he was awarded cursing and punishment.

It is essential that we truly grasp the message that Jesus is presenting to us in Matthew 24. Faithfulness is not a thing you walk in only when you feel like it. Faithfulness is not only for when it is convenient for you. Faithfulness ought to be a cornerstone in each day of our lives. Faithfulness ought to permeate our being. Faithfulness ought to be present in us in abundance. Why? Because the faithfulness that we walk in, or the lack thereof, will determine our eternal reward. I cannot stress it enough that faithfulness is absolutely essential if we desire to partake in that future hope.

Some may, then, ask the question, "What does it look like to walk in faithfulness." Jesus answered this question for us in the proceeding chapter, Matthew 25. We will dive into what Jesus had to say momentarily, but I want to point out, very briefly, how Jesus' description of what it looks like to be faithful reflects what we have talked about throughout this book. Of course, Jesus' statement regarding faithfulness is broader while ours has been specific, discussing precise topics and their related topics. But, His broad descriptions of what it looks like to be faithful cover all the various topics we have discussed here. Each point of discussion throughout this book has been an area we ought to be found faithful in. Nothing that has been mentioned is my idea or opinion on what it means to be a faithful Christian, but each point has come directly from Scripture. Further, not only directly from Scripture but directly from Jesus Himself. We ought not to allow our ideas, opinions, or traditions to determine the areas that we are faithful in. Do you hold Scripture and the teachings of Jesus as true? If so, we ought to be faithful in keeping them. We determine the reward (good or bad) that we receive by our level of faithfulness.

Paul put it well wherein he said, "Look carefully then how you walk, not as unwise but as wise, making the best use of the time, because the days are evil" (Ephesians 5:15-16). The word "walk" here is "peripateō" which can refer to how one conducts themselves. Further, Oxford Languages defines "conduct" as, "the manner in which a person behaves." How do we behave wisely? By "making the best use of the time." How do you spend your time? Or, we could put it like this: "Do you waste your time, or do you invest it?" The greatest thing we could ever invest in is the Kingdom of God. Once more, looking to the words of Paul, "Do not be deceived: God is not mocked, for whatever one sows, that will he also reap. For the one who sows to his own flesh will from the flesh reap corruption, but the one who sows to the Spirit will from the Spirit reap eternal life. And let us not grow weary of doing good, for in due season we will reap, if we do not give up" (Galatians 6:7-9).

Returning to Matthew 25; in this chapter, Jesus presents three well-known parables: the Parable of the Ten Virgins, the Parable of the Talents, and the Parable of the Judgement. Commonly, these three parables are not presented as connecting to one another. However, these three parables are directly connected to the teaching on faithfulness from Matthew 24. The parables presented in Matthew 25 are Jesus' way of expounding upon what was stated in Matthew 24.

First, we are presented with the Parable of the Ten Virgins. It reads:

> "Then the kingdom of heaven will be like ten
> virgins who took their lamps and went to meet the

bridegroom. Five of them were foolish, and five were wise. For when the foolish took their lamps, they took no oil with them, but the wise took flasks of oil with their lamps. As the bridegroom was delayed, they all became drowsy and slept. But at midnight there was a cry, 'Here is the bridegroom! Come out to meet him.' Then all those virgins rose and trimmed their lamps. And the foolish said to the wise, 'Give us some of your oil, for our lamps are going out.' But the wise answered, saying, 'Since there will not be enough for us and for you, go rather to the dealers and buy for yourselves.' And while they were going to buy, the bridegroom came, and those who were ready went in with him to the marriage feast, and the door was shut. Afterward the other virgins came also, saying, Lord, lord, open to us.' But he answered, 'Truly, I say to you, I do not know you.' Watch therefore, for you know neither the day nor the hour."
-Matthew 25:1-13

In this parable, we are presented with ten virgins, five wise and five foolish. The five wise and five foolish are, in actuality, very similar to one another. Both groups showed up for the bridal party, brought lamps with oil in them, and both fell asleep while waiting for the party to start. Truly, the only difference between the five wise and the five foolish was that the wise brought extra oil for their lamps. In essence, there was a level of preparedness that the five wise exhibited. Preparation is an essential aspect of faithfulness.

Both groups slept. Then, late in the midnight hour, the call went forth: "Here is the bridegroom! Come out to meet him." Both groups woke up. The five wise had prepared themselves for the coming of the bridegroom, while the five foolish fell short and did not properly prepare themselves for his coming.

Recently, from the time of writing this, I had the pleasure of attending a conference with my wife, pastor and his wife, and two other close friends. At this conference Bro. Doug Klinedinst preached a message he titled, "Be Wiser Than the Wise." The premise of his message surrounded how the five wise had enough for themselves only, no one else. The question he presented in his message was, "What if the five wise had had enough oil for themselves and for the foolish?" The point he was making was that in our pursuit of faithfulness, we ought not only to focus on our own salvation but endeavor to bring along with us all that we are able to. This, however, requires a great level of preparation and intentionality.

Summarizing this first parable in relation to faithfulness: Jesus is presenting us with the truth that the first area of faithfulness that we must walk in is concerning our level of preparation and readiness in our walk with Him. We are to abide in faithfulness and to, thereby, be prepared for His return. In doing so, we bring along with us all that will join in our walk. Faithfulness unto Him is the first vital aspect.

Jesus continues His teaching on faithfulness and presents to us the Parable of the Talents. It reads:

"For it will be like a man going on a journey, who called his servants and entrusted to them his property. To one he gave five talents, to another two, to another one, to each according to his ability. Then he went away. He who had received the five talents went at once and traded with them, and he made five talents more. So also he who had the two talents made two talents more. But he who had received the one talent went and dug in the ground and hid his master's money. Now after a long time the master of those servants came and settled accounts with them. And he who had received the five talents came forward, bringing five talents more, saying, 'Master, you delivered to me five talents; here, I have made five talents more.' His master said to him, 'Well done, good and faithful servant. You have been faithful over a little; I will set you over much. Enter into the joy of your master.' And he also who had the two talents came forward, saying, 'Master, you delivered to me two talents; here, I have made two talents more.' His

master said to him, 'Well done, good and faithful servant. You have been faithful over a little; I will set you over much. Enter into the joy of your master.' He also who had received the one talent came forward, saying, 'Master, I knew you to be a hard man, reaping where you did not sow, and gathering where you scattered no seed, so I was afraid, and I went and hid your talent in the ground. Here, you have what is yours.' But his master answered him, 'You wicked and slothful servant! You knew that I reap where I have not sown and gather where I scattered no seed? Then you ought to have invested my money with the bankers, and at my coming I should have received what was my own with interest. So take the talent from him and give it to him who has the ten talents. For to everyone who has will more be given, and he will have an abundance. But from the one who has not, even what he has will be taken away. And cast the worthless servant into the outer darkness. In that place there will be weeping and gnashing of teeth.'"
-Matthew 25:14-30

We quoted this passage in an earlier chapter and used it to demonstrate and teach on the call to faithful stewardship in our finances. However, this parable is able to speak on matters beyond financial giving. The truth that we are presented with is that three servants were all entrusted with a portion of the master's possessions. Some may ask, "Why was one given five talents, another two, and the last just one?" I believe it points back to one's level of trustworthiness. Can God trust you? This is a vitally important question that needs to be answered. Jesus will not give you more than He can trust you with. To demonstrate this we could look to Genesis 2 wherein we see God declare that it was not good that Adam was alone, and that God desired to make for him a helper suitable for him. However, we then read an apparent shift in the narrative. After declaring that He would make him a companion, we then see God bring to Adam all the creatures of the earth to name them (which refers to imputing upon them an identity). This can be understood as God testing Adam to see if he could be trusted with something as precious as a companion. Only after passing this test do we then see God create Eve and then bring her to Adam in the same way that He did with the animals, to impart identity. We then see Adam declare over Eve who she was, the same way that he did with the animals. God only entrusted Adam with something so precious as Eve after he had been proven trustworthy.

Returning to the parable; we read then of the master's return from his long journey and upon his return he inquired of his servants regarding what they had done with what they had been given. The servants who had been given the five and two talents both returned to the master double what they had been given: ten talents from the one who had five, four from the one who had two. Notice that the master was not concerned with quantity, but purposefulness. If the master was quantity focused, he would have awarded the two servants differently. However, we see that the two are awarded with the same response: "Well done, good and faithful servant. You have been faithful over a little; I will set you over much. Enter into the joy of your master." Then, we come to the final servant who had been afforded one talent. This servant was not purposeful and faithful with what he had been given. This servant took what had been entrusted to him and buried it. Due to his lack of faithfulness regarding what he had been entrusted with, instead of receiving a blessing as the other two were, he received cursing and punishment.

Therefore, we learn that it is not only essential to abide in faithfulness to Him, preparing ourselves for His imminent return, but it is, likewise, essential to abide in faithfulness in what we have been given. This could be finances, as we have previously discussed, however, it could also be the Gifts and anointings that God has placed on our lives. Are we faithfully using what He has entrusted to us?

The final parable, the Parable of the Judgment, then reads as follows:

"When the Son of Man comes in his glory, and all the angels with him, then he will sit on his glorious

throne. Before him will be gathered all the nations, and he will separate people one from another as a shepherd separates the sheep from the goats. And he will place the sheep on his right, but the goats on the left. Then the King will say to those on his right, 'Come, you who are blessed by my Father, inherit the kingdom prepared for you from the foundation of the world. For I was hungry and you gave me food, I was thirsty and you gave me drink, I was a stranger and you welcomed me, I was naked and you clothed me, I was sick and you visited me, I was in prison and you came to me.' Then the righteous will answer him, saying, 'Lord, when did we see you hungry and feed you, or thirsty and give you drink? And when did we see you a stranger and welcome you, or naked and clothe you? And when did we see you sick or in prison and visit you?' And the King will answer them, 'Truly, I say to you, as you did it to one of the least of these my brothers, you did it to me.' Then he will say to those on his left, 'Depart from me, you cursed, into the eternal fire prepared for the devil and his angels. For I was hungry and you gave me no food, I was thirsty and you gave me no drink, I was a stranger and you did not welcome me, naked and you did not clothe me, sick and in prison and you did not visit me.' Then they also will answer, saying, 'Lord, when did we see you hungry or thirsty or a stranger or naked or sick or in prison, and did not minister to you?' Then he will answer them, saying, 'Truly, I say to you, as you did not do it to one of the least of these, you did not do it to me.' And these will go away into eternal punishment, but the righteous into eternal life."
-Matthew 25:31-46

Jesus, in this final parable, presents to us two different groups of people represented by either sheep or goats. This is an interesting comparison, for sheep are naturally herd-minded, unity minded. Further, they are very gentle and obedient. Another interesting point, sheep are able to truly learn the sound of their shepherd's voice and are able to differentiate between it and another voice. Therefore, it is not only a command they follow, but a voice. These people that are represented as sheep are ones who demonstrated love, kindness, compassion, and selflessness to others. In the end, these are rewarded. Jesus said to them, "Truly, I say to you, as you did it to one of the least of these my brothers, you did it to me."

Jesus will then turn to the goats. Goats are quite the opposite of sheep. Goats are stubborn, rebellious, and self-minded. Such people are those who neglected to show love, kindness, compassion, and selflessness. To them, Jesus said, "Truly, I say to you, as you did not do it to one of the least of these, you did not do it to me."

What, then, do we learn from this? Not only are we admonished to abide in faithfulness unto Him. Not only are we instructed to abide in faithfulness with what we have been given. We are likewise commanded to be faithful to those around us. Faithful in our relationship with Him, faithful in what we have been entrusted with, and faithful to others. Not one of these aspects of faithfulness can be isolated as the "main aspect of faithfulness." No, these three form a cohesive whole as to what faithfulness looks like.

You cannot claim to be faithful to God if you are not faithful with what you have been given. Likewise, you cannot claim to be faithful to God if you are not faithful to others. The Apostle John said, "If anyone says, 'I love God,' and hates his brother, he is a liar; for he who does not love his brother whom he has seen cannot love God whom he has not seen" (I John 4:20). You cannot claim to love and abide in faithfulness to God if you do not do the same to your brother and sister. Each aspect of faithfulness described by Jesus is intrinsically interwoven with each other. They cannot be separated. To abide in faithfulness is to be faithful to God, with what we have been given, and in relation to others.

However, it is not merely that we need to display actions of faithfulness. We need to abide in the heart of faithfulness. The heart that we operate with is essential. Jesus said, in I Samuel 16:7, that while man looks outwardly to what is evidently seen,

He looks inwardly on the heart of man. Further, Jesus, quoting the Prophet Isaiah, declared that outward manifestations of faithfulness are useless if the heart is not faithful (see Matthew 15:7-9). It is not a matter of abiding in faithfulness just because we know we need to, but there needs to be a genuine desire there that drives us toward faithfulness unto Him. When our hearts are right and desire faithfulness, our actions will follow suit.

At the beginning of this chapter, we briefly mentioned the blessed hope that we have. Furthermore, throughout our discussion on faithfulness, we have repeatedly seen and stated that faithfulness always results in blessing and reward. Of course, there are immediate manifestations of such blessings and rewards in this life. He can and does bless us financially, physically, spiritually, and so on. However, there waits an even greater blessing and reward at the end.

Before we truly begin diving into our final discussion, I want to express that this is not going to be a deep study of eschatology. If you are interested in such a study, I would recommend a book called, Life, Death, and the End of the World, by Dr. David S. Norris. It is a truly fantastic read and there is much to be gleaned from it. Our discussion here, however, is more so going to center around presenting the truth that we do, indeed, have a future hope. Not only do we have a future hope, but we need to recenter ourselves with it.

The afterlife, as many call it, is a topic of much debate and speculation. We can look back to Judaism of the Bible and see that there was division amongst the religious elite regarding this topic. Some believed in it, others did not. Even among those who did believe in it, their beliefs regarding it were not all the same. It is much of the same today. Many scoff at the idea of a resurrection and an afterlife, others believe in it but have no real idea as to what it will be, and others still, likewise, profess belief in it but do not live as if it is a thing to be attained.

I believe this final mindset is one that plagues the Church the most: we profess belief in a future hope but live as if we have no hope. It is this very mindset that I wish to combat here at the close of this book. We have a hope, and His name is Jesus. The hope that He offers is not for this life only, but for one to come. Jesus is hope.

There are a few teachings by Jesus that are centered around

the topic of our future hope. However, I believe there is one that conveys this truth the clearest. We read:

"Let not your hearts be troubled. Believe in God; believe also in me. In my Father's house are many rooms. If it were not so, would I have told you that I go to prepare a place for you? And if I go and prepare a place for you, I will come again and will take you to myself, that where I am you may be also. And you know the way to where I am going." Thomas said to him, "Lord, we do not know where you are going. How can we know the way?" Jesus said to him, "I am the way, and the truth, and the life. No one comes to the Father except through me. If you had known me, you would have known my Father also. From now on you do know him and have seen him."
-John 14:1-7

First, Jesus says, "Let not your hearts be troubled." This word "troubled" is "tarassō" which overall refers to something being agitated or stirred up. One, more specific, way that this word can be translated is, "anxiety." Therefore, He begins with an admonition to reject the notion of anxiousness within us. How do we do this though? Jesus said: "Believe in God; believe also in me." This is an emphatic statement of His deity for one. Jesus is stating that we are to believe in Him to the same degree that we believe in God. Thereby indicating that He is God. However, this statement also reveals the antidote to anxiety: faith in God. Anxiety is birthed when an individual is focused on the present problems of this present world. Anxiety comes when we are earthly-focused. Therefore, the solution to that is to shift our focus off of this world and its problems and onto the One who created this world and has the answer to every problem.

Jesus does not stop with this statement on faith though. Jesus continues and what we see is that when we have faith in Him it leads to something greater. That is the natural flow we see presented in this passage by Jesus. Immediately following His statement on faith,

He says, "In my Father's house are many rooms. If it were not so, would I have told you that I go to prepare a place for you? And if I go and prepare a place for you, I will come again and will take you to myself, that where I am you may be also. And you know the way to where I am going."

The word "rooms" in this passage is "monē" in Greek which does not specifically refer to a room, but a dwelling place in general. Therefore, we see that the abode of God (His "house") is a place of dwelling. Not only for Him and the angels, but He says, "I go to prepare a place for you." The word "place" is translated from "topos" which refers to a specific spot within a dwelling place. Therefore, we are promised our lot with Him in His heavenly abode.

Jesus also states, regarding this place we are promised, that He has gone to "prepare" it. Does this imply that there has been mass construction all across heaven for the last two thousand years? I don't believe so. Jesus is the Creator of all who spoke all into existence. If it was a matter of reshaping heaven, all He would need to do would be to speak. I believe that this preparation more so has to do with us. What do I mean? To put it succinctly, we need to be prepared to abide in His heavenly abode. Only after this process of preparation has been completed does He say that He will come again and take us to Himself. This word for "take you" in Greek is "paralambanō" which contains a powerful meaning. This word does not merely refer to accepting someone, but, rather, refers to receiving another unto yourself to where you become joined together. Meaning, upon His return, we will truly become engrafted into Him.

Jesus ends this first portion by saying, "And you know the way to where I am going." What an interesting statement. It is clear that He is talking about something supernatural, that ought to be evident. How, then, would we know the way as if Google Maps could direct us? The disciples were likewise confused by this statement. Thomas said to Him, "Lord, we do not know where you are going. How can we know the way?" Thomas seems to me like the guy who was willing to say what everyone was thinking but that no one else was willing to say. His question was valid though and I believe it was important to ask. If someone tells you to meet them somewhere and you don't know how to get there, how will you find your way?

You must ask for directions. This is exactly what Thomas did, he asked for directions. And Jesus gave them directions.

Jesus answers the question posed by Thomas by saying, "I am the way, and the truth, and the life. No one comes to the Father except through me. If you had known me, you would have known my Father also. From now on you do know him and have seen him." Jesus is the roadmap, the compass, the GPS, etc. Jesus is the Way. The word "way" here is "hodos" which means, "road," or implies a journey that is embarked on. Do you want to know the path that you are to walk on? It's Jesus. You aren't sure whether to go left or right? Which way did Jesus go? He is the Way. He is also the Truth. The word for "truth" is "alētheia" which can be translated as, "objective truth." "Objective," according to Oxford Languages, means, "not influenced by personal feelings or opinions in considering and representing facts." Meaning, Jesus is the answer regardless of what we think or feel. He is the total embodiment of truth. Do you want to know what is right? Look to Jesus. Likewise, He is the Life. The word "life" here is "zōē" in Greek which means, "the absolute fullness of life." Elsewhere in Scripture, He is referred to as the Author of Life (see Acts 3:15). In Him is life, and there is no death at all. If you want to live, look to Him. Apart from Him, there is no life because He is Life itself.

What is all of this indicating to us? Simply, if you want to make Heaven your home, follow Jesus. If you want to abide with Him, you must first pursue Him. He is the Way in which we walk, the Truth that we believe, and the Life that we live. This points us directly back to our earlier discussion on faithfulness. Heaven will only be home to those who faithfully followed after Him.

Jesus in this passage emphatically declares to us that if we remain faithful there exists for us a future hope. This life is not all that there is, there is something greater. Further, He longs for us to abide with Him in that greater thing.

Jesus is not the only One who spoke on our future hope. Paul penned what is possibly the most famous words concerning this future hope. He wrote this to the Church of Corinth:

I tell you this, brothers: flesh and blood cannot inherit

the kingdom of God, nor does the perishable inherit the imperishable. Behold! I tell you a mystery. We shall not all sleep, but we shall all be changed, in a moment, in the twinkling of an eye, at the last trumpet. For the trumpet will sound, and the dead will be raised imperishable, and we shall be changed. For this perishable body must put on the imperishable, and this mortal body must put on immortality. When the perishable puts on the imperishable, and the mortal puts on immortality, then shall come to pass the saying that is written: "Death is swallowed up in victory." "O death, where is your victory? O death, where is your sting?" The sting of death is sin, and the power of sin is the law. But thanks be to God, who gives us the victory through our Lord Jesus Christ.
-I Corinthians 15:50-57

Furthermore, he wrote to the Church of Thessalonica:

For this we declare to you by a word from the Lord, that we who are alive, who are left until the coming of the Lord, will not precede those who have fallen asleep. For the Lord himself will descend from heaven with a cry of command, with the voice of an archangel, and with the sound of the trumpet of God. And the dead in Christ will rise first. Then we who are alive, who are left, will be caught up together with them in the clouds to meet the Lord in the air, and so we will always be with the Lord. Therefore encourage one another with these words.
-I Thessalonians 4:15-18

And of course, the Book of Revelation is replete with example after example of this future hope being played out in dramatic fashion. One thing I will say regarding the Book of Revelation: many approach this book in fear. For many, all they receive from it is judgment and condemnation. Allow me to speak plainly; if all you get from the Book of Revelation is fear, judgment, and condemnation, then your heart is not right. Yes, the Book of Revelation does contain passages revolving around judgment and condemnation but only for those who reject Him. For those who embrace Him, the book is full of hope, life, and love. Truly, the Book of Revelation displays in great measure His abounding love for us. So next time you go to read that book, approach it through the proper lens of understanding and allow God to truly speak to you and encourage you through it.

Why do we bring all of these passages to light? Simply to illustrate with emphasis the truth that we have a future hope waiting for us if we remain faithful. Many would assert that they know and believe this to be true. Praise Jesus for that. However, I feel we often fail to live as if this is a truth that we hold to be true.

It is an unfortunate fact that this present life is full of various things that are all vying for our attention. One does not have to think hard in order to bring to mind all the different things in their life that serve as distractions and demand attention. This life is demanding. Due to this fact, it is incredibly easy to become consumed in this life and to focus solely on it. It is, however, crucial that we keep at the forefront of our minds that this life is not what we are called to. We are called to something greater.

Therefore, I simply want to end our discussion here with an encouraging reminder: Jesus has a future hope in store for you, don't lose sight of it. Remain faithful in your walk with Him. Follow after Him as the Way, Truth, and Life. Live with intentionality for Him in all things. Allow Him to be present and a central aspect of every part of your life. He has something greater in store for us, don't let it go. Don't trade your future hope for temporary, instant gratification. Hold fast to your Hope that promises eternal reward.

He is your Hope.

Focused Reflection

It is an inescapable truth that the day and age in which we live is defined by busyness. Constantly we are pulled in what feels like a hundred different directions all at once. Often, to simply get through our days, we have to make lists of everything we need to do just so we can keep track of everything. Finally, at the day's end, we go home and have to devote additional time simply to unwinding and allowing our mind to process everything that transpired throughout our day. It's overwhelming.

Because of the busyness our society demands of us, we often fail to allow our minds to focus on what truly matters. Anyone who has any sort of experience with church has heard it mentioned how we have a future hope of heaven. But how often do we truly dwell on that truth? Because of the busyness of our lives, I fear that blessed truth becomes an afterthought that is relegated to special Sunday services. But we, indeed, have a blessed future hope.

In our humanity, we like to imagine that everyone we love is going to heaven. However, we must understand that heaven is not a place that is reached through casual means. Rather, making heaven your home requires faithful pursuit. He doesn't demand us to be perfect, but He does require us to be faithful.

1. Speaking honestly, how often would you say you truly think of heaven? Additionally, when you do think of it, what does your thought consist of?

2. When you hear the word "faithful," where does your mind go? How would you define faithfulness? Does your definition of faithfulness align with the biblical definition thereof?

3. When you think of the end of all things, what do you feel? Is it fear, dread, terror, anxiety, or something such as these? Or do you feel peace, hope, joy, love, and anticipation? If you feel along the lines of the former list, why do you think that is? Do you think you're ready? If not, what do you need to do to get ready?

There is no fear in love, but perfect love casts out fear. For fear has to do with punishment, and whoever fears has not been perfected in love.
-I John 4:18

Epilogue

I have attempted to structure and order the things discussed here in a manner in which they all flowed together, each building upon the next. We could say that I aimed to mirror the construction of a building.

Before construction can begin, the need for and purpose of the building has to be demonstrated. Without such, you may finish the building project but no one will know its purpose or intent. This we endeavored to do in the chapter, Redefining Christianity.

Once the need and purpose of the building have been demonstrated, only then can you begin the work. The essential first aspect in constructing a new building is the laying of the foundation. Without a solid foundation, the new building will be short-lived and a safety hazard. This we sought to lay in the chapter, Christians are Monotheistic.

After the foundation has been laid the next stage of the building project is to place the frames that will shape the new structure. The frames not only map the shape outwardly but also shape and give form to each individual room within. The frame of the structure is made up of all that we discussed in the chapters, Christians Abide with Christ, Christians are Baptized in His Name and Spirit, and Christians are People of Prayer.

Once the framing is complete, the following stages of the building project are made up of all the intricacies that give the building completeness. From the wiring, to the plumbing, to the insulation, to the drywall, and so on. Each of these sometimes unthought-of aspects are crucial to the functionality of the building. Without even one of them, the building would not be complete and, thereby, be of little use. The intricacies of the structure of Christianity are made up of all that we discussed in the chapters ranging from, Christians are Worshippers, to, Christians are a Light.

Finally, buildings are not constructed merely so there will be a new building to look at. No, whenever a new building project is begun there is always a future hope for that building. Without future hope, all that was built was in vain. This we brought to a conclusion in the final chapter, Christians Who are Faithful Have a Future Hope.

We need to understand the critical work of grace in our lives concerning the things discussed here. In Christians Abide with Christ we quoted from John 15. One of the quoted verses was "Apart from me you can do nothing" (John 15:5), we also drew attention to this later on in Christians are Worshippers. Paul built upon this truth when he wrote, "For it is God who works in you, both to will and to work for his good pleasure" (Philippians 2:13). The various aspects of our walk with God discussed in this study are not things that can be attained by our own merit. That is one reason why I placed discussing being filled with His Spirit at the forefront of the book. His Spirit is His gift of grace that works in our lives to bring us closer to Him. However, some twist this truth to mean that salvation and right relationship with God are only by grace, consisting of no works at all. This line of thinking stands in contradiction to Scripture. For speaking on His saving grace, Paul said, "For by grace you have been saved through faith. And this is not your own doing; it is the gift of God, not a result of works, so that no one may boast. For we are his workmanship, created in Christ Jesus for good works, which God prepared beforehand, that we should walk in them" (Ephesians 2:8-10). His grace in our lives does not do all the work necessary on our behalf. Rather, His grace gives us the ability to do the necessary work. There is work involved, but the ability to accomplish it only comes by His power.

Again looking back to Christians Abide with Christ, we discussed how true love is demonstrated through obedience. Therefore, once again, we cannot expect Jesus to do all the work on our behalf. He fills us with His Spirit, giving us His power, and then says, "Keep My commandments." Apart from His in-dwelling Spirit, we cannot keep His commandments, but by His power, we can. Obedience is both a conscious choice and an active response. The author of Hebrews said, "And being made perfect, he became the source of eternal salvation to all who obey him" (Hebrews 5:9).

I have said all this simply to stress the truth that being filled with His Spirit is the vital first step in walking with Him. Apart from the power of the Spirit, we absolutely cannot walk in right relationship with Him. The children of Israel tried this for hundreds of years and could never get it right. Time and time again they failed. So would we apart from Him. His Spirit gives us the power, but we must make the conscious choice.

Others may examine the content of this book and think it places too many expectations upon would-be Christians. Many, particularly those in Western culture, want easy. We have been spoiled by our culture of abundance and ease to the point where even the thought of minor lack and some struggle is met with utter disdain. Even if difficulty is necessary to accomplish a particular thing, we will still attempt to find some manner of a loophole that cultivates ease.

No one ever said being Christian was easy. I am not sure when that idea was birthed, but it is not found in Scripture. Jesus, the One whom we are called to be like, suffered and died to bring about the Gospel. The first Church in the Book of Acts was persecuted ruthlessly through imprisonment and even death. They were forced to scatter and meet under the cover of darkness. Yet, it says of them, "And when they had called in the apostles, they beat them and charged them not to speak in the name of Jesus, and let them go. Then they left the presence of the council, rejoicing that they were counted worthy to suffer dishonor for the name. And every day, in the temple and from house to house, they did not cease teaching and preaching that the Christ is Jesus" (Acts 5:40-42).

Countless examples could be given to demonstrate how the Bible never states that living for Him is without difficulty. Many look at this truth and baffle at how so many are willing to suffer and endure hardship for His name's sake. In truth, entire books could be written with the intent of discussing that topic in-depth. We do not have the time or space to discuss it to such a degree here. Therefore, I will make it plain: those who are able to willingly endure suffering for His name's sake are able to do so because for them it is not religion, it is a love-filled relationship that has become their life. That is the key. As long as "being Christian" is just something you do, you will never be willing to sacrifice for it. However, when being Christian becomes who you are, no price is too high, no cost too great, and no sacrifice too painful. When being Christian becomes who you are, everything else becomes as dung as the Apostle Paul put it (see Philippians 3:8). When He becomes your life, the measure of difficulty is no longer of concern. All you come to care about is Him and loving Him and abiding in His love for you.

Some may ask, "How do we reach this place with Him?"

I wrote a free-verse poem not long ago that I feel fits the occasion. It is titled, The Magnitude of God:

He describes Himself as the Alpha and the Omega, the Beginning and the End, the First and the Last, the Almighty. Yet, I feel we often fail to comprehend the incomprehensibleness of the One we serve. We are told, and believe, that He is all-powerful. Yet, we are powerless to grasp the magnitude of His power. We understand that He is infinite, while, at the same time, our finite minds struggle with the concept of infinity.

He is the One who merely said, "Let there be…", and there was. His command, so simple, while the result, so complex. The utterance of His Words seemed so vague. Yet, what we perceived as vagueness creation bore in intricacy. However, it is not only creation being brought forth that demonstrated the power of His Word; for we are told, "He upholds all things by the Word of His power."

However, the magnitude of God is not merely relegated to His nature or His act of creation. In truth, the magnitude of our God is found in the depths of His heart. It says, "He is the Lamb slain from the foundation of the world." Therefore, the magnitude of God is realized when it is understood that before He said, "Let there be…", there was a plan. This plan was the bedrock upon which He built. This plan was centered around a people He could love, and who would love Him, and what He was willing to do in order to bring into fulfillment that love.

The magnitude of God becomes understood when

you realize what He was willing to do for you.

The magnitude of God is His love for you.

Some may be saying, "That's a pretty poem, Kristopher, but what does it have to do with anything?" Simply this: when you understand what He was willing to do for you, you become willing to do anything for Him. You won't always get it right. We are all human and we all mess up. But when you fall, when you get caught up in the mundaneness of life, remind yourself of what He willingly did out of His great love for you. When you bring to remembrance these things it will reignite that great flame within you and it will propel you forward into Him.

It is my sincere prayer that what has been written on these pages has impacted you and your walk with Him. Every day I desire to be more like Him. This is not a journey I want to make alone, but I long to bring along with me all who would be willing to join me. I pray that that includes you today.

No matter where you find yourself in this moment, whether it be merely entertaining the thought of Christianity, possessing a rudimentary understanding of Jesus, or one who considers themselves to possess a considerable understanding of Jesus, I speak to all the same: His love for you is greater than you know, and He desires for you to know Him better.

I pray that you feel the loving arms of Jesus wrapped around you, drawing you in closer to His heart. And I pray that you don't fight His embrace, but run into it.

In the name of our loving Jesus,
Kristopher David Grepke